G000113489

Pr
A Personal Chronicle

A personal narrative to celebrate the history of
international privacy activism

Simon Davies

Electronic Privacy Information Center
1718 Connecticut Ave. NW
Suite 200
Washington, DC 20009

Visit the EPIC Bookstore
http://www.epic.org/bookstore/

ISBN: 1-7326139-0-7
ISBN-13: 978-1-7326139-0-4

Dedicated to my dear friends Jamie, Ed, Annie, Jim, Pete, Aaron, Jason, Phil, Karen, Alan, Marc, Judith, Gus, Ingrid and Ian. And to the memory of my friends and colleagues Caspar Bowden, Guy and Bob Ellis Smith.

Acknowledgements

First, a huge thank you to Marc Rotenberg and the Electronic Privacy Information Center (EPIC), for providing the support that has made this book possible.

I would also like to thank all the amazing colleagues who provided input and inspiration for this work throughout their wonderful careers as advocates.

I am extremely grateful to Edward Allnutt and Vickram Crishna for the vast task of editing the book, and to James Cohen for his help in proofreading it.

And a special thank you to people who also provided much needed support in the early days. These include Gus Hosein, William Heath, Simon Moores, Christopher Wolf, Jerry Fishenden, Clive Gringras, Jim Norton, Alex Deane, Stephen McCartney, Tom Ilube, Angela Sasse, Robin Wilton, Peter Cullen, Rob Wirszycz and Kurt Wimmer. They too have helped shape the privacy movement.

Thank you also to Professor Colin Bennett, whose book 'The Privacy Advocates' inspired me to undertake this work.

TABLE OF CONTENTS

Introduction

As I write these words, it has been sixty years – almost to the day – since Vance Packard's ground-breaking book "The Hidden Persuaders" hit the bookshops.[1] In this sobering analysis, Packard laid bare the covert machinations of the marketing industry and – in the process – pioneered a new dimension of consumer and privacy rights.

Readers were scandalised to discover that they were being secretly manipulated by the advertising industry. "Depth approach" and "Motivational Analysis" (the ancestors of Profiling, Big Data and Data Analytics) came to represent a level of intrusion that millions of people found unsavoury and disquieting. An era of consumer activism was forged from the furnace that Packard created.

And yet, despite Packard's efforts, an even greater number of people seemed at least nervously comfortable with deep manipulation, as long as it provided better targeting of products. They were conditionally happy that an entire industry was dedicated to analysing every particle of personal choice and behaviour. The one conditional element – in common between these ends of the opinion spectrum – was that consumers demanded transparency from marketers.

Sound familiar? These days almost everyone is aware that they are being manipulated by social media and the advertising industry. And yet the exact same dynamics exist now as they did in Packard's time. Back then, the issue was mainly about the marketing of products; now it is more about "services" and the infinitely complex digital realm. But more than two generations on, the element that continues to infuriate people is bad practice and secrecy from organisations.

For me – as a youth – Vance Packard triggered a reflection on privacy. Why should we allow huge organisations to control us? What can we do to combat such manipulation? And perhaps most important of all, is it possible to embed a respect for individual rights into the psyche of

---

1   Packard, V. The Hidden Persuaders. (2007) New York. D.McKay Co. (first published April 1st 1957)

governments and corporations?

While returning time and time again over the decades to such reflections, I've run hundreds of campaigns across the world, irritating the most powerful people and entities. I want to tell you the inside story of some of those actions. More importantly, I want to introduce you to the tireless work of colleagues who have changed the world by taking such actions. In the acknowledgements section I mention Colin Bennett's work 'The Privacy Advocates'.[2] That remarkable book, better than this one, sheds light on this broader ambit.

Regardless of how many perceived advances we make in the realm of privacy, it is time for activists – and indeed for anyone who cares – to take a stronger and more aggressive stand on privacy.[3] And we should take stock of the less obvious – though perhaps more technically lawful – tactics that organisations deploy against privacy. We are, after all, moving quickly into an age of infinite connectivity, and the stakes are high. There are lessons to be learned from some of the notable campaigns of previous decades. They demonstrate how victories can be achieved outside the court room.

Is this view really so unreasonable?

The answer, of course, depends on your world view and your personal experiences, but I believe a more stringent and even polemic approach to privacy protection is entirely reasonable. it is clear to me that the need for smart, fearless and effective activism is as great now as ever before, particularly in a field characterised by highly complex technology and regulation.

So, this is a personal account of a notable sliver of the history of the modern privacy movement from the 1980s to more than thirty years on in 2018. From the analogue era, through those early pre-internet days and on to the present moment of mass surveillance and seamless information, it attempts to explain why privacy has real meaning in the real world and what we can learn from the people who stand guard against intrusion. I have intentionally made this a narrative, so I can provide intimate details

---

2   Bennett, C. J. (2008). The Privacy Advocates. Cambridge. MIT Press
3   Davies, Simon. "Spanners in the Works: How the Privacy Movement is Adapting to the Challenge of Big Brother." In *Visions of Privacy: Policy Choices for the Digital Age*, edited by Colin J. Bennett and Rebecca Grant, 244–261. Toronto: University of Toronto Press, 1999.

of how the decisions were made, and what was going through my mind at the time. There have been countless other initiatives run by my colleagues, but in many cases I was only a small contributing factor in those, and they won't feature here, except as milestones flashing by. If they ever find the time, my friends in the privacy realm need to devote energy to recording their experiences in detail!

I should note that I use the phrase "privacy movement" in the way that environmental rights activists might say "environmentalist movement". That is to say, working outside the mainstream. While there is an increased blurring of the edges as time goes by, the movement mainly represents activists and NGO's who independently influence law, public opinion and business practices for the benefit of human rights.

I'm hoping the accounts in this book will help motivate a new generation of privacy advocates – perhaps people, like me, who never achieved grand qualifications in law or technology, but who feel inspired to support the field.

In mapping out the book I came up with a list of more than five hundred issues that I've dealt with, ranging from Neural Prosthesis (medical machinery implanted in the brain) to airport security systems. However there are several recurring topics on which I can offer very early campaign narratives. Those include electronic visual surveillance (CCTV), identity systems (ID cards), national security, financial privacy, corporate accountability, data protection law, international transfers of personal information, social media, search and encryption policy.

The book is set out in two parts. Part One provides a digestible overview of law and technology, together with scattered anecdotes. This section provides context to the entire field. Part Two brings you to the campaigning years. Seasoned privacy advocates and tech and legal specialists may wish to skip straight to the second part.

Within the book – apart from the fun of the narratives – I'll focus throughout on three key questions.

First, what are the psychological triggers that make this issue important to people? Why do they start caring about privacy?

The answer is surprising. I've concluded that there isn't actually a definable thing called "privacy". All the anger and outrage you see expressed about intrusion into our lives is usually about elements like hypocrisy, deception, secrecy and unfairness. These elements are what I later describe as the "four horsemen of the privacy apocalypse".

In an attempt to counter these elements, institutions have reworked their language to manipulate public perception. Our legal process has been hijacked to deny transparency. This makes people rightfully enraged.

Second, I'll provide accounts that explain the troubling nature of the huge entities that control our lives. What is their modus operandi?

To answer this question we will peek into the secret passageways of the greatest power centres around us. Is there really a corporate "mind" or is the commercial process more organic and chaotic? This of course is a rhetorical question. Large organisations are chaotic by nature. and are thus vulnerable to attack by even the smallest of opponents.

Finally, I'll tackle the question of what privacy means to our everyday life. Why does it matter that Google has a seamless privacy policy that links everything you think and do? Why is it important to be alarmed that Facebook is actually just an advertising company largely devoid of an ethical compass that reaches into parts of our brain that even we might not understand?

This is not a simple matter. As I discuss throughout the text, these huge commercial institutions permeate much of our lives, and have become part of our vocabulary and our lifestyle. There is an interdependence that creates powerful dynamics that are often resistant to challenge. While agreeing that some companies pursue unsavoury practices, many people simply accept what they imagine is a reasonable trade-off for "essential" services like search or social media.

The best way to tackle this syndrome is by simply peeling back the layers of deception practised by many governments and corporations. Looking more forensically at the underbelly of these shiny new services can reveal their true nature.

Is there a methodology in this work? Definitely. The first part is highly structured, providing context and discussing legal and technical elements. It is largely analytical. As for the rest, it's mainly a narrative: an analysis of campaigns and a sketch of the privacy advocates who created them. I believe it is important to understand the campaigns – and the campaigners – who helped change the world.

4

Returning to Colin Bennett's work:

> *One of my respondents, whose anonymity I will protect, offered the insight that "privacy advocates are not normal people." Normal people seek secure paying jobs in government, business, or academia. They do not sacrifice income to work in the nonprofit sector fighting powerful state and corporate interests. Many privacy advocates are euphemistically described as "characters." They are highly visible, somewhat egotistical, very smart, generally unconventional, and extremely interesting. With few exceptions, and paradoxically, they do not lead "private lives." They are extremely social, and they network an enormous amount. Many in this community also joke that the privacy advocates are the biggest gossips out there. So I am not studying here the anonymous foot-soldiers that comprise other social movements. Many of these advocates are "out there", actively trying to shape elite and mass opinion.*

In terms on content, chapter one sets the context. What is privacy and why does it matter in our everyday life? How do we reconcile our demand for privacy with the countless arguments for public interest that oppose it? And importantly, how do we as individuals assert our rights in an age of fear of terrorism (or whatever major issue is at stake at the moment of reading)?

Chapter two looks at the definition of privacy. This is a complex and thorny aspect.

In chapters three and four I explore the technical and legal environments. What are the technologies that threaten us, and what are the legal mechanisms that allegedly protect us?

Chapter five is about the mechanisms that provide oversight and protection over privacy. Do they work?

In chapter six I explore the motivation for people's involvement in the privacy movement. Why did they do it? What were the triggers? I reflect on my first privacy campaign at the age of fourteen.

Chapter seven looks at the various identity card campaigns I've founded since 1987 and chapter eight looks at the consequence of those actions: the creation of the international privacy movement.

Chapter nine gives you an insight into some of the early privacy campaigns and the strategy behind them.

Chapter ten tells the inside story of the biggest privacy campaign against the banks. Chapter eleven talks about the fight in the 1990s against CCTV and chapter twelve describes my efforts to expose the US National Security Agency and its worldwide surveillance.

In chapter thirteen I peek behind the curtains of the biggest IT companies in the world and describe my many campaigns against the likes of Google, Facebook and Microsoft.

Finally, in chapter fourteen, I talk of possible solutions. How can we build a better future for privacy?

A (slightly facetious) Glossary of terms and acronyms

AI (Artificial Intelligence). Systems that are programmed to act rationally and to mimic – or augment – human thought processes. Many people can converse with an AI machine for hours, believing it to be the best and smartest friend they ever had.

Big Data. The technique whereby grand assumptions and trends can be made from countless "bits" of largely unrelated data. Big Data systems can be used to figure out how entire populations may vote or whether sweatpants may go out of fashion because of climate change.

Biometrics. The technique of uniquely identifying you through the capture and processing of various bits of your body, from fingerprints, DNA and iris and on to your unique smell. Biometrics can also identify you through behavioural aspects such as the way you walk. One problem is that the outcome frequently doesn't result in unique identification.

CCTV (Closed Circuit Television). Otherwise known as Electronic Visual Surveillance, this quaint acronym refers to devices that connect a lens to a recording device with the intention of monitoring populations. CCTV is now fused with biometrics to recognise faces and gait.

Cloud. The technique of processing your information in data centres located in geographically diverse locations across the world. Many of these vast centres (sometimes called Server Farms) have been built above the Arctic Circle to reduce the need to cool the systems. This is hailed by companies as a tremendous step forward in the challenge of global warming, though no-one has succeeded in proving this curious claim. It certainly cuts air conditioning bills though.

CPO (Chief Privacy Officer). The person responsible for an organisation's privacy compliance and privacy performance. They are more widely known in Europe as Data Protection Officers.

CSR (Corporate Social Responsibility). This is the unenforceable social contract that organisations make with the world around them. They set out the framework for how issues like the environment, human rights and

7

"social good" will be embraced. CSR| has been known on occasions to actually work.

Data Retention. This is the technique of keeping your information (browsing history, communications etc) for a period of time just in case security and law enforcement may want to see it in the future. Many countries now force communications providers to do this – sometimes for two years – thus confirming that entire populations are regarded as suspects.

DP (Data Protection). A term given to a subset of Privacy that establishes a set of rules and principles for the collection and handling of your information.

DPA (Data Protection Agency). This is the common term for an official (often a Commissioner), who is tasked with the role of upholding privacy and data protection law.

ECHR (European Convention on Human Rights). The legal framework in Europe that serves as the foundation for the protection of human rights, and which specifically includes privacy.

EPIC (Electronic Privacy Information Center). A Washington DC based advocacy organisation that campaigns and litigates on a very wide range of privacy issues. EPIC's work – particularly with regard to the excesses of the US government – has shaped the American privacy landscape.

GCHQ (Government Communications Headquarters). The UK's communications security agency that sits at the centre of SIGINT operations (see below). It's difficult to know where GCHQ begins and the NSA ends. The two organisations are inseparable.

GDPR (General Data Protection Regulation). The Europe-wide privacy law that came into effect in 2018. It replaced the Data Protection Directive and aims not just to update that 1995 instrument for the modern age, but also to require all member states to create harmonised national legislation. Unfortunately by the deadline date, the vast majority of EU countries had still not implemented it.

Geolocation. A technical means of precisely locating a person or entity. The technique can create an extremely detailed record of movements and contacts but does have the advantage of showing which coffee shops in your current area are offering discounts.

ID (identity). This is the process of creating a means of establishing who you are (related to authentication, which is the process of proving who you claim to be). There was a time when this task was achieved with identity cards, but these have now become identity systems that can electronically link many areas of your life.

Internet of Things. The realm of interconnectivity between products, devices and systems. Sometimes described as "things talking with things".

Media Pluralism. The principle that democracy is strengthened and underpinned by a diversity of news and media content. Pluralism is being threatened by the emergence of highly targeted news feeds and search portals that filter the full spectrum of information.

Metadata. All our communications comprise "content" (the body of emails or the actual words we speak on the phone), and communications data, or Metadata, which is all the information related to our interactions – our location, time of call, email headers and so on). Metadata reveals a vast amount about us and our activities but often enjoys a much lower standard of legal protection than does content.

Notice and consent. A core pillar of privacy and data protection that requires organisations to tell you what data they collect and how they will use your information, and which provides a requirement that they seek consent from you so they can do this.

NSA (National Security Agency). The world's most powerful security edifice. It is responsible for monitoring much of the world's communications. And, as it turns out, much of America's metadata traffic. The NSA has a working relationship with most countries.

PbD (Privacy by Design). The technique of embedding privacy protection at every level of a product or organisation, from inception to deployment. PbD replaces "Privacy Enhancing Technology (PET)" as a legal expression. Many organisations say they use PbD but in reality, few do so.

PI (Privacy International). Founded in 1990, PI was the first global privacy advocacy organisation. It is based in London where it conducts campaigns across the world and pursues litigation against agencies such as GCHQ.

Policy Convergence. The phenomenon whereby the laws of various countries start to replicate each other. This can be the outcome of "policy laundering", where countries such as the US and the UK convince other countries to replicate their laws.

Privacy. A fundamental human right that has been established in law in more than a hundred countries. It has numerous definitions, but nearly all of them embrace such concepts as autonomy, dignity and "the right to be let alone".

RFID (Radio Frequency Identification). Tiny embedded chips that use parts of the frequency spectrum for stock control, tracking or security.

SIGINT (Signals Intelligence). The national security process of capturing and analysing communications across all points of the spectrum.

Surveillance. The act of tracking and monitoring all aspects of human action, interactions, transactions and behaviour. This may be through Human Intelligence (HUMINT) or electronic surveillance.

SWIFT (Society for Worldwide Interbank Financial Telecommunications). The largest banking conglomerate on earth, comprising almost all finance institutions, and which is responsible for the transfer of almost all the world's money between them.

Technology transfer. In the context of privacy, this is the process whereby predominately Western nations sell surveillance equipment to developing nations or regions that are in conflict. This sector is closely aligned to the arms industry.

Terrorism. Like privacy, this is a complex expression that defies a common definition. A terrorist in the eyes of one person may be a freedom fighter in the eyes of another. A "lone wolf" attacker may be described by government as either a terrorist or merely "deranged".

Wi-Spy. The infamous Google episode, in which vehicles involved in the company's Streetview project were covertly equipped with technology that could sniff people's Wi-Fi, including content and passwords.

PART ONE

CONTEXT AND FOUNDATION

Chapter One: Setting the scene: the context

> *Privacy is a slippery right, as hard to define as it is absolutely vital. Fallacies abound about it and, often, although we say we care about it, we let it go for shiny, new services, or in the (false) belief that it must be sacrificed for security. Are we simply naive? I don't think so. Rather, we are duped by opaque language and the security discourse of the "terrorist age".*

It is a hot summer day in 2002 in the slightly edgy London inner city district of Finchley Road. A congenial silver-haired man called Derek Jones (we'll name him that to preserve his privacy), has unexpectedly discovered a closed circuit television (CCTV) camera scrutinising him from a neighbour's roof. Jones had been relaxing at the time by the side of his backyard pool, guarding his two young daughters as they played in the shallow water. He gazed with growing horror at the device, which in future months he would describe as provoking a sense of "violation, threat, powerlessness".

Meanwhile, his neighbour, Don Cameron (name also changed), watched eagerly as images of the family filled his newly acquired surveillance monitor. A gentle, quietly-spoken family man, he had steadily become convinced that Jones was physically abusing at least one of his children and he was hunting for evidence. He could hear the screams.

Seeing the camera, Jones became agitated and distressed. He summoned his children from the pool and declared the backyard "out of bounds". Convinced that his neighbour was a pervert, he called social services. As it turned out, the department knew about the situation. It was they who had encouraged Cameron to install the camera – not that they admitted this advice at the time.[4]

Enraged at the lack of empathy from social services, Jones embarked on an expedition to the High Street in search of his own surveillance equipment. That night, as Cameron blithely scrutinised his screen in front of an open bedroom window, a CCTV camera located on Jones's roof was silently recording his every mouse-click. The aggrieved pool owner was determined to catch his neighbour surfing for child-porn.

The two men never communicated about these suspicions, but their implementation of technology spiralled onward to military capability.

Infrared, power zoom, digital recording, automatic motion detection: no expense was too great in the quest to record the sins of the other.

As a neighbour, I witnessed these distressing events first hand. Although I had a nodding acquaintance with the two protagonists (and even drank cheap Burgundy once with Jones) there was little I could do to quell this feud. Social Services didn't help. All they wanted were the images.

As I recount later in this book, for the past eight years, I had been in a largely futile fight against this CCTV trend. Such was the extent of public support for the technology, that it had often felt like Canute trying to turn back the tide. However, I rarely focused on how the technology could be used by people themselves, rather than by governments. This was an eye-opener for me.

The Jones and Cameron dispute was just the beginning of the CCTV spiral. At the time of this suburban conflict, the next generation of the technology was just emerging. In the mid 1990's, miniaturisation was to become the next big thing. Tiny hidden cameras secretly deployed in light fittings, alarm clocks and even cigarette boxes. Partner spying on partner; parent spying on child. Neighbour upon neighbour. The Jones/Cameron issue was pale by comparison with many of the family conflicts that we learned about.

A decade later, Colin Bennett observed:

> *More interesting perhaps are the ways in which individuals*
> *become the watchers, either through a subtle process of co-*
> *optation or through clever marketing. Recent empirical*

---

4   Davies, S. 7th September 2002 "Private Virtue", London, The Guardian ,
     https://www.theguardian.com/uk/2002/sep/07/privacy2 (accessed 14th June 2018)

> work suggests that there are a host of *"peer monitoring"* or *"lateral surveillance"* examples from neighborhood watch schemes, to landlord/tenant monitoring, to citizens groups that publicize the vehicle license nos. of those suspected of soliciting prostitutes, to Web cams for the surveillance of children, teenagers, domestic employees, to the locational devices that can be embedded in automobiles to monitor speed, safety procedures, drug/alcohol use, and so on (Wood 2004). Peer-to-peer monitoring was also institutionalized in the United States after 9/11 through Operation TIPS, a program that allows ordinary Americans, such as mail carriers, meter readers, and repair service persons, to act as informants about any suspicious terrorist activity that they might encounter in their professional capacities. Inevitably, somebody then set up a Web site for *"Operation TIPS-TIPS"* through which people could report on the alleged informants. There is nothing new about this kind of peer-to-peer monitoring in the United States. From 1915 to 1917, the American Protective League boasted around a quarter million badge wearing members, who proudly informed the Justice Department about any suspicious activity, especially among those citizens of German origin.[5]

I featured in three television UK documentaries over two months on this subject, one for the BBC1, one for ITV and one for BBC5. We focused on a chain of surveillance retail outlets called the "Spy Shop". Was there a positive outcome? Sadly, no. After the second interview the CEO of the company came downstairs and shook my hand with the message that my advocacy had been the greatest PR boon in the company's history and it would result in the creation of even more retail outlets for them. Even now there is no licensing or control over such equipment. Companies subtly market the use of these devices as an enhancement of human rights.

* * * * *

---

5   Bennett, C J. The Privacy Advocates. P. 14

It was now winter on Finchley Road – in so many ways. With the surveillance infrastructure operating at saturation levels, both men had erected elaborate shields, fences and barricades to thwart the gaze of the other. This provoked further suspicion. The now legendary state of affairs finally spilled onto the street, when police were called to deal with a particularly bloody fist fight between the two.

In the investigation that followed, it turned out that Jones' youngest daughter suffered from a form of attention deficit disorder, and regularly screamed. For all his noble intentions, the neighbour had seized the wrong end of the stick. The case, which was far from unique, raises complex questions about an individual's rights and responsibilities.

Did either Cameron or Jones have a right to take such a course of action? As caring people, as concerned citizens, did they have any other course open to them? In their quest to resolve a troubling suspicion, where should the line have been drawn?

At least part of the answer can be found by invoking the ancient right of privacy. This complex mechanism sets the boundary between the intrusion of state and society, and the right of an individual to say "go away". It is not a "selfish" right. Rather, it is a means of determining the autonomy of the individual, set against intrusive demands of society.

Privacy is perhaps the most unruly and controversial of all human rights. Its definition varies widely according to context and environment to the extent that even after decades of academic interest in the subject, the world's leading experts have been unable to agree on a single definition. One pioneer in the field, Alan Westin, described privacy as, "Part philosophy, some semantics, and much pure passion". On that point, at least, everyone agrees.

Even before the terrorist attacks of September 11, the privacy issue had never been simple. The protection of individual privacy has always been one of the great polemics of public policy. At its heart is an ancient struggle for power. This struggle is played out each day in countless forms. With each security initiative – be it CCTV, email surveillance or workplace monitoring – society is obliged to assess competing claims for the right to either maintain privacy, or to pursue surveillance.

In spite of popular wisdom, privacy is neither a modern nor a western concept. While the idea of privacy as a fundamental human right still raises eyebrows in some developing countries, the concept is familiar to the citizens of those cultures.

At a societal and government level, privacy may be viewed with some suspicion, and yet at a personal level, each person draws a curtain around certain aspects of family and private life. In Thailand, privacy invasion by the state has rarely been an issue, and yet the boundaries of personal space in family and religious life are universally acknowledged and respected.

In some respects, privacy is a little like freedom: the less you have of it, the easier it is to recognise. And, like the concept of freedom, privacy means different things to different cultures. In France, it equates most closely to liberty. In America, it is an inseparable component of individual freedoms – particularly freedom from intrusion by federal government. Many European countries interpret privacy as the protection of personal data. Since the days of the huge campaign against the government's proposed ID card in 1987, most Australians view privacy as a measure of state power, while the government views it as a set of strictly defined legal rights.

Yet while the issue is more complex than ever, it has never been more pressing. There has probably never been a time in history when so much information has been amassed on the population at large.

Even back in 2002, details of the average economically active adult in the developed world were located in around 700 major databases – enough processed data to compile a formidable reference book for each person.[6] Electronic visual surveillance in urban centres is almost ubiquitous. Nearly all forms of electronic communication are now routinely scanned and profiled. These days it would be impossible to estimate the number of systems we are enmeshed in.

These activities have spawned a burgeoning economic sector. In Britain, the surveillance industry in all of its forms – private investigators, credit agencies, security services etc – employs more than a million people.

This population of professional snoopers is explained in part by the emergence of mass surveillance. In the past, surveillance was based on the targeting of specific individuals or groups. Now, systematic surveillance in a growing number of fields pro-actively profiles millions of people at a time. But it is not merely the increased capacity and decreasing cost of information technology that creates threats to privacy. Globalisation removes geographical limitations (and many legal protections) to the flow of data.

Convergence is leading to the elimination of technological barriers between systems. Modern information systems are increasingly interoperable with other systems and can mutually exchange and process different forms of data. Meanwhile, multimedia, which fuses many forms of transmission and expression of data and images, creates vast difficulties for legislators wishing to protect personal privacy.

Traditionally, public reaction to privacy invasion has been contradictory and unpredictable. While opinion polls consistently indicate that people care about privacy, public opposition even to the most blatant privacy invasion is sporadic. Everyone, no matter what the personal circumstances, is concerned about intrusion. For a single parent the threat may arise from constant interference by benefits authorities. For an employee of a company the threat may be subtler, yet no less significant. Intrusion takes many forms, from covert monitoring to outright harassment.

Whether through cause or effect, privacy now occupies an unenviable place in the catalogue of human rights. Throughout the past quarter century, few other fundamental rights in the arena of public policy have generated such turbulence and controversy. And yet, as one writer has observed "privacy is the right from which all other rights derive". It is central to the freedom and autonomy of people, and it is perhaps the key factor that limits the power of the state.

To those with a strong interest in the protection of their rights, privacy protection is one way of drawing the line at how far society can intrude into a person's affairs. In that context, privacy is a question of power – yours, the government's, your family's, your employer's and your neighbour's.

At its most dramatic level, it reins in the processes of law and government. At a more profound level, it can form a buffer of common

---

6   ibid

sense between two good men fighting for their beliefs on a hot summer's day.

Privacy is a question of power

Vance Packard's work is now more relevant than ever. Cliché or not, all of us are economic units of the information age, and all of us are monetised at one level or another for our economic worth. As I mention elsewhere, Google monetises the advertising value of each of its customers at around thirty dollars a year. Facebook, Twitter and countless other sites use a similar formula.

Yet, like sixty years ago, a vast swathe of people responds: "Well, OK, that seems reasonable to me!" And maybe this is indeed the case. But in every element of economics or society, there is a vast gulf between what is "perceived" as reasonable, and what is "actually" fair and right.

As an example, in the nineteenth century (and even today in many environments such as sweatshops, farms and call centres), many employees perceived that the prevailing workplace safety standards were a "reasonable" part of the employment contract, even though many died or were horribly maimed each day. Others felt differently and changed that equation. Similarly, in the early twentieth century, many people perceived that the limited voting rights given to women were a "reasonable" concession by the status quo. Some people felt differently. Such dynamics – which we might call activism – change the world for the better. You needn't be a student of such works as 'An Unreasonable Man' to instinctively know this to be true.

I admit that this is not a simple matrix, though in the realm of privacy it is even more complex. Unlike gas or electric utilities, digital services are often marketed as a free product for which a contractual concession must fairly be made in terms of unveiling personal information. As a result, we are required to make many choices each day to protect our privacy, but there is one undeniable fact: the commercial entities that run the information age almost always attempt to make us responsible for making those choices. And governments use exemptions in law to openly steal our data.

In legal theory however, our rights do not – and should not – rely on such onerous personal choices. There is a persuasive argument that governments and companies must be forced to treat privacy as a right, not a tradable value. Many people believe tech companies need to understand that respect for privacy should be managed in the same way as respect for the environment or workplace safety. Just as employees should not have to "choose" to have safety, consumers should not be required to opt-in to privacy. Packard knew this, as did so many of the pioneers of the privacy realm.

Apart from notable exceptions – often triggered by political transition – powerful institutions are resistant to all but symbolic change. For example, the trend for companies to develop Corporate Social Responsibility policies has shifted markedly toward a public relations exercise[7], while corporate spending on political lobbying in the US has more than trebled, since 1998.[8] Meanwhile, corporate lobbying in Europe remains a largely opaque and unregulated activity.[9]

Lobbying for legal and regulatory change in the favour of large organisations is now a complex industry in its own right. Meanwhile, the institutional consumer protections such as regulators and watchdogs are frequently becoming timider and less effective. Corruption, secrecy, intrusion and denial of rights have become part of the institutional DNA of many countries.[10] Little wonder then that there is need for more effective activism. Many years ago, I held the commonplace view we are – at any point in time and in all facets of human rights – at a crossroads. We might imagine that proceeding in a straight line to the future leads to much the same environment as before. Little changes. However in the arena of privacy, steeped in breath-taking information growth, such a scenario is impossible. Or we can imagine that the path to the right led to

---

7   The arguments against CSR, Corporatewatch,
    http://www.corporatewatch.org/?lid=2688 (accessed July 12th 2018)
8   Centre for Responsive Politics http://www.opensecrets.org/lobby/ (accessed July 12th 2018)
9   Corporate Europe Observatory
    http://www.corporateeurope.org/pressreleases/2011/lobby-millions-missing-transparency-register-alter-eu-campaigners-say (accessed July 12th 2018)
10 Transparency International. Global Corruption Barometer 2010
    http://www.transparency.org/policy_research/surveys_indices/gcb/2010 (accessed July 14th 2018)

a destination of greater safety and protection of our rights. The road to the left led to dystopia.

It turned out that this analogy was simplistic and – well – incorrect. It was useful as a mental meme but was not helpful in any other respect. The situation we face now is infinitely subtler and more complex. There is no utopia or dystopia, only a fusion of the two.

Not even the most hard-core privacy activist would deny that there have been heartening developments in privacy protection. The nightmare scenario twenty years ago of a data free-for-all is not turning out quite as expected. There are now technological protections and legal rights in place across the world. In some cases, corporations and even governments are being held to account. The blunt dystopia has been shaded and softened, as has the utopian view.

Having said that, there is little cause for celebration – not yet anyway. Government security agencies continue their work almost unabated – likewise their private sector counterparts. Data-hungry corporate business models have remained unaffected. Laws are enacted but are often unenforceable. The authorities that are tasked to enforce those laws are often depressingly timid or under-resourced and must rely on pursuing only symbolic regulation.

In some respects, privacy has become the inverse of the famous 'What have the Romans ever done for us' sketch in Monty Python's film 'The Life of Brian'. That is, yes, we have privacy, but it is subject to so many wide-ranging exceptions and exemptions for public interest that in many cases it becomes almost pointless as a claim.

And, of course, there is little joy for anyone who is concerned at being enmeshed in an information matrix so deep and complex that our autonomy – and even humanity – is compromised. This is the more likely "big picture" concern, and it is one that is possibly beyond remedy.

* * * * *

It is intriguing to realise that in such a relatively small space of time –

fifty years – we have moved from an era when we needed to patiently sit around that cold, black, household Bakelite dial telephone in our hallway – waiting and endlessly waiting for the anticipated call – to the actuality of real-time fusion of flesh and technology. And with the developments there have been myriad complications for privacy. That is the Faustian Pact into which we have entered.

We have ended up with a surprisingly complex and fragmented field, and there's a need to "join the dots" on an issue that provokes conflict and confusion for so many people. The environmental movement never really succeeded in achieving that, but maybe we can do so with privacy.

And yes, privacy is most definitely a conflicting topic. The utterances of intrusive corporations and governments do not help. We are told on a daily basis that huge institutions "care deeply" about our privacy, and yet we know these claims are often a confidence trick. Commercial enterprises offer us cool "stuff" (like geolocation) that enriches our ability to network and communicate, to the point where even the most dedicated privacy advocates can be seduced into handing over personal information which, after a microsecond, is largely out of our control. But hey, we get to amplify our message!

On the matter of joining the dots, there are now so many privacy dots to join, that mapping them looks something like an image of the cosmos. In an era of specialisation, it is hard to imagine how anyone these days can grasp the entirety of the privacy domain. Elsewhere, I attempt to explain this complexity by way of an "Elements Table" of surveillance.

* * * * *

Martin Luther King Jr famously said that we see issues such as equality as "self-evident". I fear that in the mind of some people, privacy these days is increasingly less so. For every advance in popular thinking about the need for privacy, there is a tsunami of PR spin about the need for "sharing" of our information. In the realm of equality, King cut across all such subversive spin in his proclamation of self-evidence.

Likewise, in the 1970s, justice campaigners for rape victims – frustrated by an aggressive, male dominated legal regime and a timid judicial system – coined a powerful phrase that cemented a cultural mindset for decades to come: *"No means No."*

Over time, those three words shifted the centre of gravity in public debate. That simple slogan cut through the quagmire of convenient justifications for male sexual aggression. Consent needed to be explicit – and a clear refusal was an unqualified position.

It is clear that privacy urgently needs such battle cries. Consumers and lawmakers alike are increasingly confused by largely phoney justifications for diminished privacy and increased surveillance. The foundation of evidence for intrusive practices by government is as unstable now as it has ever been. The language and imagery used by many corporations has reached the point of outright deception. And some global corporations such as Google have – at least in the realm of data protection (the legal principles of information privacy) – openly defied the rule of law, in Europe and elsewhere.

Hard-line privacy activism is one way to confront the issues of entrenched power. In 2005, for example, I was invited to speak on the opening plenary of the World Summit on the Information Society (WSIS) in Tunisia. This talking shop of more than ten thousand officials, corporations and NGOs was one of a series sponsored by the United Nations and other major international bodies. I then learned that I was to be sandwiched in between the Foreign Minister of China and the President of Egypt – both countries having a lamentable record on human rights. Rather than giving their inevitable hypocrisy tacit endorsement through my involvement, I controversially boycotted the event, calling it a sham and a fake showcase for the worst dictatorships on earth.

Despite some misgivings at the time – and criticism from some colleagues – I was right to take that action. Four years later I was asked to moderate the closing plenary of the Internet Governance Forum in Egypt (IGF was the successor to WSIS and became an even larger event).[11] I felt that maybe there was a chance at making a difference, but I was wrong. On the morning before the plenary I was called into a meeting

---

11 Chairman's summary of the Egypt IGF
   https://www.intgovforum.org/cms/documents/igf-meeting/igf-2009-sharm-el-
   sheikh/165-chairman-summary-2009/file

with the Deputy Secretary General of the United Nations and assorted Minister and officials. I was told in no uncertain terms that I was expected to pursue the goal of "consensus and harmony". The UN then stacked my panel with two co-chairs, both government ministers from African and Middle East countries with an appalling record on free speech and privacy. In hindsight, I should have walked out.

We might imagine that the current media prominence of privacy scandals (say, surveillance by the US National Security Agency), is evidence that matters are improving. In reality, what is happening now is little short of data rape. The rules of consent that were supposed to underpin the information economy are being attacked with breath-taking ferocity, while the core principles of data protection have – in many parts of the world – never been so exposed. These days it seems in many online realms that almost every use of personal data is permissible as long as it is specified in the privacy policy or if notice is given. That's not how data protection was conceived – nor is it a sustainable formula for a new age of limitless data.

The new EU data protection regulation (to provide just one example) once had the potential to establish a trusted Information Age foundation for decades into the future. Instead it became a playground for aggressive companies and governments, who wished to re-negotiate core rights. Using PrySpeak, they tried to turn the privacy coin around almost entirely in their favour. Were it not for the diligence of a few lawmakers and watchdogs, they would have fully succeeded. Now at least there are new requirements placed on big organisations, even though the often corrosive business models of the information age have barely been touched.

The extent of corporate lobbying against privacy can be quite breath-taking. The passage of Europe's new privacy regime (the GDPR) was subject to the most intense corporate lobbying exercise in history, resulting in an astonishing 4,000 proposed amendments to the legislation.

I was unwittingly in the midst of this turmoil. In 2012 the European Parliament appointed me to advise it on the stakeholder issues relating to the new law. I tried – I really did try. But the problem was that the ground was shifting every minute and it seemed there was no hope of salvaging the process. I addressed a joint EU Parliament meeting and informed it that I simply had given up. Either the Parliament enforced its mandate, or my role was a farce.

It was a shameful retreat. I should have continued my work, but thanks to the tireless efforts of Jan Philip Albrecht, MEP, and his chief adviser Ralf Bendrath, the GDPR survived in-tact and has become a step forward in privacy regulation.

Sure, there are many other notable positive developments – particularly the introduction of privacy law in much of South America and Asia – but these laws will fail if the international privacy scene starts to crumble. Those countries constantly face the risk that their regulatory mechanisms will be left unsupported and under-resourced. Independent advocates have an important role to play.

It is true that an innovative and exciting micro industry of privacy engineering has been created – but again, the take-up of the resulting products depends on an integrated global support by regulators and major industry players. Such support has yet to materialise.

There have, however, been wonderful advances in privacy thinking. Privacy by Design – the concept of embedding privacy into the very fabric of an organisation's business model and engineering practices – is one of the more promising of these ideas. However there are few examples of such a practice in mainstream commerce. We hear of great advances in technologies that enable anonymity, yet there is a risk that anonymity will be made the exception rather than the rule.

Still, the world is moving forward in positive ways. As Nikita Khrushchev put it: "Whether you like it or not, history is on our side."

Privacy; yes, you really do need it

The fallacies about privacy are as numerous as they are blatant. I mean, no-one tries to dilute protections for workplace safety by saying, "You can have employment, or you can have safety". But privacy is open-season, for anyone with an interest in compromising it.

One of the most dangerous fallacies is that you can't have good public security as well as strong privacy. This appears to be a moot point these days, now that government agencies are able to infiltrate just about any network, computer or communication that they choose. Still, in many countries, governments argue that one condition is the nemesis of the other.

Any reasonable assessment will show that this simply isn't a valid claim. It's often the case that the worst enemy of security is secrecy, where organisations operate without accountability or scrutiny. The US National Security Agency is one such example. The FBI throughout the 1950s and 1960s is another. Those agencies had all the privacy in the world – and all the secrecy in the world. The result was wholesale abuse of constitutional protections. Privacy safeguards do not prevent responsible use of personal information by law enforcement and national security agencies – but they do quite rightly prevent unaccountable and irresponsible use of that information. A respect for accountability, due process and privacy also engenders public trust in security organisations.

Then there's the fatalistic fallacy. I always become annoyed when I hear people saying, "There's no point in complaining – they know everything anyway." This fallacy was neatly represented many years ago by (then) Sun Microsystems chief Scott McNeally ("You have zero privacy anyway... get over it.").[12] This is a scare tactic promoted by people who want you to give up on privacy. It is also a mind game, such as you might use to unnerve your chess or snooker opponent. However the claim is fake. "They" might know bits of your life, but those bits are usually contained in different silos that few organisations can link together. Over a hundred countries now have data protection laws that create real impediments to the linking of information. This is why the fights against national identity systems are so crucial. The data hyenas naturally condemn the laws that constrain them.

Here's another one you will have heard countless times: "If you have nothing to hide, you have nothing to fear". This is like saying "only people with health problems have something to fear from health service cuts". It's a vacuous argument, promoted by people who should know better. The only hypothetical circumstance when it might possibly be valid is when every aspect of data management by government and private sector is completely transparent and where those organisations enjoy unconditional public trust (this is the Communitarian thesis adopted

---

12 Despite Facebook, privacy is far from dead. (August 16, 2012). CNN.
https://edition.cnn.com/2012/05/25/opinion/etzioni-facebook-privacy/index.html

by Amitai Etzioni and others).[13] In the real world, this is an argument propagated by data hungry industries, or by people who see the need for a knee-jerk response to a privacy issue that they – at that moment – aren't vested in.

Following the same logic, people like me often encounter the complaint that we're just paranoid. I often hear comments like "I don't care about privacy", to which I always respond "Oh yes you do!"

People say such things, but the reality is that they are usually reacting speciously to the latest news reports about a particular privacy scandal that they happen to take sides with (e.g. I don't care about surveillance cameras, because I have nothing to hide). However, in all honesty, I have never met a person who doesn't care about privacy. Almost everyone is fiercely defensive about their home, and everyone resists invasions of privacy against their family. You might not care about big political issues like identity cards or national security, but you sure will get angry if someone sells your child's school records to an ad agency. And if you don't, there's probably something twisted about your parenting skills.

I must warn you that that this is not the only time in this book that I will raise the question of the definition of privacy. This is because there's a view expressed in certain quarters that privacy is not a real right, because it has never been defined. Or, more precisely, it is a therefore nebulous value rather than a "real" right such as freedom from torture (even though, in reality, the definition of torture is quite wide – including forms of mental harassment and oppression – resulting in a very wide grey area).

After over thirty years of analysis, according to Daniel Solove, the concept of privacy is still in disarray: "Privacy seems to be about everything, and therefore it appears to be nothing."[14]

True, there's no single accepted definition of privacy, but the diversity of ideas about it is what makes privacy so powerful and universal. Sure, the law has defined certain elements of privacy, such as data protection, but it is a living and continually changing right. Public perceptions of privacy change and adapt according to the context and nature of threats. It is

---

13 ibid
14 Solove, Daniel. "A Taxonomy of Privacy." University of Pennsylvania Law Review 154, no. 3. (2006): 477–560.

jagged, unpredictable and infinitely inexplicable – and that's what makes it potent. Having said that, while there is no agreed wording, as such, there are several elements that are common among the hundreds of published definitions.

. I discussed earlier in this chapter the view that people don't really care about privacy because they keep giving their information away. This is a red herring. People do give their information away, but they often get very angry if they are deceived about how it's used. Data hyenas will always claim a contradiction, but their assertion is false.

There was a time, for example, when Facebook enjoyed an enormous degree of public trust. People would cheerfully hand over their information in return for a cool service. Now, in the face of continuous deceptive practice, that trust has fallen to an all-time low. Following the Cambridge Analytica data breach of 2018,[15] trust in the company plummeted. One study, by the Ponemon Institute, a think tank, found just 27% of people thought Facebook would protect their privacy, compared with 79% in 2017. Respondents were upset Facebook did not publicly acknowledge the data breach in 2015.[16] The company had only just recovered from a data breach in 2010 that affected one hundred million of its customers, the data being posted openly on Pirate Bay.[17]

People sky-dive or bungee-jump, despite the intuitive knowledge that this is a scary activity. But they do so because they trust that safe equipment and safeguards are in place. The same applies to the disclosure of information.

Last but not least fallacious, is the view that privacy is a middle-class Western concept. This applies principally when non-Western countries start debating privacy issues – and when the US gets involved in such discussions.

Ironically, people who argue this position are middle-class Western data-

15 Facebook's crisis timeline (2018). PR Week.
https://www.prweek.com/article/1460639/facebooks-crisis-timeline (accessed July 11th 2018)
16 Trust in Facebook has spectacularly nosedived after its enormous data; Business Insider, (17th April 2018). Business Insider. https://www.businessinsider.de/facebook-trust-collapses-after-cambridge-analytica-data-scandal-2018-4?r=US&IR=T
17 Facebook security fears after 'private details of 100m users leaked to web'. (28th July 2010). London. The Daily Telegraph.
https://www.telegraph.co.uk/technology/facebook/7915572/Facebook-security-fears-after-private-details-of-100m-users-leaked-to-web.html (accessed June 12th 2018)

mongers, who want you to believe that developing countries don't want or need privacy protection. It's an indecent proposition, because it presents a false portrayal of the scale of privacy concerns universally. Countries outside the G-20 major economies may have a different set of concepts about privacy, but they still have strong privacy beliefs. US corporations, for example, argue that Asia should not have privacy laws because of the 'Indian Train Syndrome', in which total strangers will disclose their lives on a train to other complete strangers.

In fact the Indian Train Syndrome shows exactly why Indians care about privacy. They speak only to strangers who they will never again meet, they speak anonymously – and they often become extremely angry if other people talk about those disclosures. It's all about having control over disclosure – one of the central pillars of information privacy (I discuss the Indian Train Syndrome in more detail elsewhere in the text).

In another context, junk mobile texts became a huge public issue in the Philippines, while illegal wiretapping caused an outcry in several Latin American countries.

So, why do people often give away their information so readily?

People often ask me to explain why privacy seems such an incongruous concept. Why is it that people who proclaim to love privacy will sometimes cheerfully give it away? Why do some people who oppose ID cards because they are instruments of government intrusion, contemporaneously support national security powers, that are an embodiment of government intrusion?

I'll make an attempt to explain – and please forgive me if this starts off a little simply. It's a surprisingly complex question and I want to tread cautiously.

The family is an ideal microcosm to begin exploring the dynamics.

Imagine the family unit as a miniature nation state. The parents have a protective role, and the children – while dependent – assert certain rights and freedoms. The equation between the two is delicate. In most cases, where successful, it triumphs through negotiation. To nurture trust the parent must agree some areas that are "off limits", and the child must have the right to argue for those limits.

And yet the child will happily agree to renegotiate those limits in times of crisis or aberration. A child who insists that the parent should not inspect her room may shift opinion when there is the threat of a rat or a spider. However, the child will exercise judgment about whether the parent is exploiting the exemption. For example, a room inspection *in absentia* during the day might be completely unacceptable, as would an inspection, where there are no grounds for concern. And if the child is misled about the facts, she will almost inevitably become extremely upset, because trust is damaged.

It's equally true in the adult world that some people may agree to disclosure of medical records in times of crisis or agree to increased police surveillance when there is a threat of terrorist attack. However if the medical information is taken without consent, or police powers are initiated without consultation, the reaction may be completely the reverse.

That doesn't mean privacy is any less important to people – as much as the privacy invaders might like to portray it that way. It just means people exercise their instinct and judgment about the many conflicting issues they need to consider from day to day. They use this judgment in highly specific ways but are offended if liberties are taken beyond that context. That is the key point.

Interestingly, there is a uniting factor. As I mention more than once in this text, what binds people in their support of privacy is a distaste for hypocrisy, unfairness, secrecy or deception. No matter how much a person may support a technology of intrusion, those four aspects are a lightning rod for opposition. This tells us a huge amount about the nature of privacy.

This systematic erosion of citizen rights might at some extreme level be intellectually sustainable were it not for the sheer hypocrisy of its many perpetrators. Elected representatives who cheerfully support laws intended to force citizens to yield personal information, often oppose demands for disclosure of their own expenses.[18] UK Police, most of

---

18 One notable instance was the enduring scandal over improper and unlawful MP's expense claims during the time of the Blair Labour government. Not only was the government's response to this highly volatile issue unsatisfactory for much of the

whom support the idea of mandatory DNA testing of the public, refused EN MASSE to be tested because of fears of paternity checks of their own ranks.[19] Senior civil servants are often happy to help erode Data Protection law, but are frequently not prepared to ensure that Freedom of Information laws are properly enforced. Commentators decry privacy while ensuring that their own telephone numbers and home addresses remain ex-directory. Meanwhile, prominent politicians have lobbied for an "extra secure" data system for themselves and for VIPs in the UK national identity card proposals. The double standards continue endlessly.

If claims made by authorities are misleading, if politicians exempt themselves from the level of invasion imposed on the public or if surveillance is conducted covertly or without due process, people are likely to rise up in opposition.

People will almost universally equate privacy with such keywords as "intrusion" and "solitude", and the majority consistently express grave concern over invasion of privacy, but the ubiquity ends there. Although the issue has galvanised public anxiety more than at almost any time in history, it is equally true that the sheer scale of the field has fragmented public perception. This dynamic is heightened by claims of benefits to security. But people are united in their hatred of the four elements above. In short, this means that people are prepared to conditionally trade some of their privacy, as long as those 'four horsemen of the privacy apocalypse' are not present.

This is a very encouraging dynamic. It indicates that people generally want an evidence based argument to justify privacy invasion.

Why am I ruminating on such things? While I was visiting Washington DC a few years back I appeared[20] on the Diane Rehm show on US National Public Radio, together with renowned hacker Kevin Mitnick, and Washington Post technology correspondent Cecilia Kang. While we were discussing these aspects, I said at length that the public displayed an incongruity, and I described this as a sort of "Cognitive Dyspraxia" in

---

public, but when the new Coalition government released its "Programme for Government" in 2010, the matter of disclosure of MP's expenses was conspicuously absent. See "Programme for Government" (2010). UK Cabinet Office.

19   See the background section of the Privacy Surgeon site at www.privacysurgeon.com

20   The Diane Rehm Show (5th December 2012). National Public Radio. https://dianerehm.org/shows/2012-12-05/illusion-online-security/transcript# (accessed July 4th 2018)

which the conscious mind wanted to take one course of action, but instinctively reacted in an entirely different way.[21]

I was wrong. Well, I think I was wrong. People generally don't react to privacy issues so randomly. On reflection I've concluded that they increasingly base their reaction on the tests of fairness and consistency. The more I consider this matter, the more I come around to the belief that there isn't an incongruity in the public mind – there's merely deception and incongruity in the mindset of those responsible for promoting surveillance.

Privacy v. Surveillance?

A controversy has been slipping increasingly into the privacy realm over the past few years. It concerns the question of whether intrusive surveillance can be justified through its results. That's to say, if surveillance can be shown to – even marginally – benefit public safety, should we accept it?

It's the sort of discussion that pervades many areas of advocacy, though usually with a more unequivocal outcome. Prison reformers don't applaud rhetoric; they want measurable improvements. Environmental protection campaigners don't want fancy CSR language; they seek an evidence-based approach that guarantees positive change. The question in my mind is whether privacy advocates can – or should – use such an equation.

To some extent, many of us already do use that equation. I've lost count of the number of times I've attacked surveillance initiatives on the basis that they simply cannot work and are therefore an orchestrated confidence trick. This is a legitimate argument to link self-interest, hypocrisy and deceit with the premeditated denial of rights. But while such a position is admirably suited to, say, carbon emissions, does it work equally well for

---

21 Davies, S. The Privacy Surgeon. December 12th, 2012 People aren't conflicted about privacy – they just appear that way
http://www.privacysurgeon.org/blog/incision/people-arent-conflicted-about-privacy-they-just-appear-that-way/

privacy?

Volkswagen's reputation was utterly annihilated because of a recent emissions scandal in which emissions data was fabricated, but the reputation of Verizon following the Snowden revelations has remained at least vaguely intact. One breach is regarded as non-negotiable while the other is navigable.

Of course not all branches of human rights will tolerate such an argument. The "non-derogable" (absolute) rights certainly don't. Generally speaking, freedom from torture is freedom from torture, regardless of the pragmatics (the grey areas that I mention elsewhere notwithstanding). When, for example, O.J. Simpson defence lawyer Alan Dershowitz advocated warranted torture he was roundly condemned. Equally, the absolute right of freedom from slavery cannot easily be compromised simply through pragmatic or economic arguments.

The right to privacy may rest on a slightly more negotiable foundation, but we nonetheless need to get that foundation secured. Much has been written about transparency and accountability in surveillance. The measurement (measurability) of its value, less so. This gap is understandable. Many privacy advocates are rightly wary of supporting formulae that may undermine the foundations of privacy rights. What, for example, if it could be proved that mass surveillance was useful even to a fraction of the claimed extent? Would this undermine the principle that we should be able to live our lives free from mass surveillance? And who would be empowered to make such judgments? The courts talk up such considerations, but particularly in Europe they largely leave the final decision to the dubious machinations of national governments. My dilemma is whether the long term interest of privacy is served by agreeing that surveillance can be quantifiably justified, or whether that approach makes this fragile right hostage to fortune.

All the same, measurability is crucial. Consider the moment in 2013 when the deputy director of the National Security Agency (NSA), John Inglis, made an important and unsettling admission that – remarkably – received scant media attention. What he uttered in the studios of National Public Radio should have set alarm bells ringing in the heads of politicians and campaigners across the world.

Inglis conceded that – at most – one terrorist attack might possibly have been thwarted by the agency's huge, unlawful and vastly expensive metadata mass surveillance operations. Actually, it wasn't even directly relating to a single attack; it was to do with possible funding for an attack. This rare moment of quantification at last puts some of the present controversy over mass surveillance into perspective.

If Inglis was right, the NSA isn't Cerberus standing at the gates of hell holding back a tide of destructive evil; it's more a short-sighted octopus that – in his words – has become an "insurance policy" for the future for the agency.

This important disclosure moved the public discussion forward by several leagues. There isn't a measurable surveillance process at stake that combats identifiable clear and present dangers (as we were once led to believe). Instead, we're looking at a global spying operation based to some extent on speculative outcomes.

Civil liberties advocates in the United States had every right to feel at least a little jubilant about the (partial) disinfectant of sunshine being applied to officials such as John Inglis. Even beyond the revelations in the Snowden documents, testimony and public statements from those officials is slowly revealing the agency's true value to the world – and it's a value that appears to be narrower than previously imagined.

This realisation applies internationally. For example, in light of the Inglis disclosure, assurances given by the new head of Britain's MI5 agency regarding transparency seem hollow. Andrew Parker said Britain's Government Communications Headquarters (GCHQ) – the NSA's primary operational partner – had played a "vital role" in stopping many terrorist plots in the past decade. He warned intelligence agencies would not be able to sustain current levels of counter-terrorism work without the help of surveillance from GCHQ.[22]

Someone is gilding the lily. Such unequivocal assurances by Britain fly in the face of the more specific detail emerging from the United States. If new forms of spying are as speculative and "hit and miss" as new information suggests, UK authorities should say so. And yet no UK agency has ever admitted such systemic failure.

Intelligence chiefs claim that their work has disrupted 34 terrorist plots in

---

22 Why NSA reformers must target the deception of Britain's powerful spy agencies. The
    Privacy Surgeon. http://www.privacysurgeon.org/blog/incision/why-its-time-for-nsa-
    campaigners-to-target-the-lies-and-deception-of-britains-spy-agencies/

the UK since 2007. If true, this is a laudable outcome, but it is entirely deceptive in terms of assessing the operations of GCHQ or its more than 6,000 staff. Britain is no closer to understanding the value of SIGINT (signals intelligence) operations compared with other forms of investigation and surveillance such as HUMINT (human intelligence). And no-one is prepared to disclose such information.

Learning that the valuation of mass surveillance outcomes is speculative more than scientific is vitally important. It allows observers to assess the credibility of assertions by spy chiefs in the US and elsewhere.

Meanwhile, under a tree behind the White House...

We all accept at least some degree of surveillance in our lives, and I am well aware of an irony – or even a hypocrisy. Here's one example from personal experience.

One of the best kept secrets in Washington DC happens to be located in one of its most public spots. Some readers will know this place. If of an evening you amble down Madison Place by the side of the President's home via the South Lawn, you end up in a quite lovely park – the Ellipse. The White House stands behind you, and the great monuments of Washington are lined up in front. If you're lucky, you may catch the President fluffing his pillows before sleep.

Even by Washington standards, this is an iconic spot. Millions of people know it, evidenced by the hordes that inhabit it each day. But at night the place is deserted. This stands to reason. Everyone knows DC parks are not the sort of places to hang out at night. Well, for most of us anyway.

Still, for twenty-five years (until 2013, when I boycotted travelling to the US because of its appalling and insular policies)), I regularly visited this place in the dead of night. With friends, colleagues, companions, lovers, we would sit under the moonlight with bottles of whisky in the shadow of the White House and take in this most amazing of locations. And we were utterly alone.

Of course, when I say "alone" I'm being facetious. Only a fool would imagine you could sit in the shadow of the White House and be alone. I was fully aware that our every move was being scrutinised. Snipers on the White House roof were watching us. Covert security operations had already relayed our existence. The park was deathly still, but there was a hive of secret activity that paranoically hovered around us.

Did I care? Not really. It was a controlled situation that worked to my advantage. I never encountered thugs, hoodlums or desperadoes. And I knew if any such characters were to appear, the last thing the Administration wanted was a scandal involving violence so close to the White House.

How is it that a provocative privacy advocate of thirty years standing is happy to voluntarily submit to intensive surveillance? The answer, I believe, is simple. I did so because I believed the trade-off worked measurably in my favour. I entered into the situation in full knowledge of the consequences and in full knowledge of the dynamics.

The reason for relating this story is that it goes to the heart of the privacy issue, and yet it remains one of the toughest questions for many people to resolve. There was much heat and little light a while back when I discussed this matter with strangers in an Austrian bar. Many believed there was some sort of newfound public duty to support surveillance, regardless of outcome.

That pub conversation stirred some misgivings in my mind. Is it more important for privacy advocates to contest the "fact" of surveillance, or should we focus on pragmatism? Do we cut a deal (e.g. more transparency), or do we fight surveillance on principle?

Even the most ardent of privacy advocates agree there must be some sort of equation for assessing the public interest of surveillance. The difference between the view of privacy advocates and view of the surveillance hawks is that we – the advocates – believe this equation must be based on accountability, transparency and measurability. Sadly, those elements are rarely present.

Returning to my anecdote, the White House scenario equated to a tacit agreement between the security forces and me. Yes, I agree to them peering at me through telescopic sights in return for my protected iconic experience. No, I do not agree to them covertly placing audio bugs in the park or using facial recognition software. That's a deal breaker. Fortunately, facial recognition equipment doesn't reliably work in the dark at 150 meters. And using covert audio bugging in a public place would quickly become a fourth amendment issue, so I felt fairly confident.

Just about everyone – including privacy campaigners – regularly enter into such arrangements. And if we don't do it for ourselves, we certainly do it on behalf of vulnerable loved ones. Still – for most sensible and sensitive people – the White House equation applies. We need an assurance that surveillance is fit for purpose and that it is confined to agreed-upon limits.

Countries such as the UK have been grappling with this question for some time. In Britain, for example, CCTV has created a surveillance canopy across the entire country, and yet the benefits to public safety are anecdotal at best. This fact has not stopped the expenditure of billions of pounds on the technology. The measurability applied by privacy advocates against the technology is often trumped by the criteria applied by authorities in favour of it (i.e. it makes the public feel safer and "what price a life"?)

This is powerful imagery. TV footage of some poor victim being mugged proves in the public mind the worth of CCTV, even though the mugging was never prevented. And even if it were to be proven to be prevented, that one incident would be fodder for authorities to proclaim the universal need for the technology. The problem is, you can't prove a negative – and many people are driven by fear. Hence the widespread support for surveillance.

In some respects, applying quantification in privacy can be dangerous. Such a calculation is best suited to outcome-based analysis such as with environmental protection, healthcare, public transport reform or health and safety. If we move in that direction do, we end up with some sort of "privacy sustainability", just like discredited sustainable development? That is, a deal that is cut for convenience. Back in 1991 I told a US conference that this syndrome is "pragvocacy" (pragmatic advocacy).[23]

I have argued that security forces and police must be subjected to the

---

23 CFP (1991) transcript http://cpsr.org/prevsite/conferences/cfp91/hoffman2.html/ (accessed June 10th 2018)

same level of accountability and scrutiny that apply to health authorities. Despite some nervousness, I stand by that assertion. Historically, security services survive on the *subjunctive* – the "what if". What if we didn't identify a terrorist plot? What if there were a planned revolution and we didn't see it? What if the Chinese gained an advantage over our country's crude oil bid?

Rare exceptions aside, government departments can't get away with living in the world of the subjunctive, nor should they. They are required to quantify risks and benefits. Public disease control departments gain their budgets in the margin of the measurably possible, not the speculative. They tell parliaments what is plausible, and then identify the spectrum of likely outcomes for the country. They then run prevention and mitigation mapping, that shows how much an increased budget will reduce risk and be cost effective.

Not so for the security agencies. Their subjunctive narrative is limitless, bolstered not just by an *"if you knew what we know"* mantra, but also a beautifully crafted argument that if incidents of terrorism are shown to have declined, agencies can say this trend is the result of more efficient security, and if the trend is to continue budgets need to be increased to keep pace with new technologies. If terrorist incidents rise, then the budgets are increased without question.

I am bolstered in this view by my constantly drunk acquaintance in a local bar in London who says, "if they're so good, why didn't they stop 9/11 or 7/7 or Madrid?" He makes an important point, inebriated though he is. As I recount elsewhere, even the head of GCHQ's claim of stopping 34 attacks has never been backed up with evidence. That number may well have been pulled out of a hat. The fact is that even parliamentarians are seduced by the heads of security services. You can blame "M" in James Bond for that peculiarity.

Regardless of where we end up on the question of principle over pragmatism, the standards of transparency, accountability and honesty must apply.

How PrySpeak obfuscates awareness

Words matter. By way of example, consider the language in any "Privacy Policy". This is the (usually) opaque document located at the bottom of most major websites that tells you how deeply the company cares about your privacy and that it will bludgeon itself with a hammer rather than doing the wrong thing with your information.

Of course these policies also set out the many conditions under which organisations can share, sell, profile, disclose or process your digital self. In many countries, companies are required under law to make such conditions public. After all, these documents are contracts between the user and the organisation.

Over the past few years there has been an unsavoury trend in the writing of these policies. At some point in the recent past, Public Relations (PR) experts formed an alliance with lawyers to massage language to the point where the documents mutated from impenetrable legalise to outright deception.

Consider the conditions that are set out for the disclosure of your information to police, government and commercial entities.

For example, the simple, conditional word "may" now replace the traditional phrase "reserves the right to". The current Apple policy states that the company "may share this personal information," where in the past, it would have stated "reserves the right to disclose this personal information."

"May" is a more neutral, passive word that doesn't infer corporate power over the customer. Of course, almost no contract would ever use the blunt but more honest expression "probably".

Of equal annoyance is the term "share", which hardly existed in contracts until fifteen years ago. "Share" means "disclose", but it's a far warmer word because it indicates a mutual benefit by mutual agreement. Thus, companies "share" personal information with law enforcement agencies, while customers "share" it with companies. On that theme, companies never "comply" with demands to disclose personal information to agencies; they "respond" to them. Thus everyone's happy, apparently.

Softening and neutralising language is important to organisations, particularly in cases where the topic in hand is potentially controversial.

"Retention" and "Preservation" (keeping data in case the authorities might want it in the future), sound more benign than "storing" and "archiving", while "geolocation" was replaced by the warmer and more consumer-focused expression "location based services". And, of course, the (now) almost universally used phrase "enhancing the user experience" is merely a euphemism for increased customer profiling and surveillance.

Meanwhile, "external party" (with whom information is "shared") shifted to "third party". This mutated to "partners", and then to "trusted partners", before finally being replaced by the more familiar and inclusive expression "family."

Organisations can't help re-engineering language. They've done so throughout history, often in an attempt to sidestep negative imagery. Thus "productivity" had to become "performance", "output" turned into "targets" and "micro management" became "team building". And, of course the demonised "consultant" was transformed into an "Advisory Service".

It doesn't take much to inspire a change of language. The agreement that was put in place in 2000 – "Safe Harbour" – to protect the trans-Atlantic data trade was changed to "Privacy Shield" after the original name was referred to by privacy advocates as "Pearl Harbor".

In much the same manner, "export of data for processing" was shortened to "data transfer", which meant that companies no longer "sold" your data in the event of a corporate acquisition; they conducted a "transfer". It's all about making the customers feel they have some protection and control.

The world of security is laden with such language transformation.

There's a pressing need for an honest blunt English version of the plain English revision of the older English genre of privacy policies.

Public awareness about intrusion is handicapped by the unfortunate reality that technological intrusion takes place with stealth. Slick public relations consultants and wordsmiths are employed to "neutralise" the language of privacy invasion. Sometimes this takes the form of branding. In the case of national ID cards, governments often deploy patriotism. So, the Australian national ID card was the "Australia Card" and the New Zealand equivalent plan was the "Kiwi Card". Again in Australia, the Cash Transactions Reporting Agency, responsible for tracking the use of cash, came out sounding evil in opinion polls, and the name quickly changed to AUSTRAC.

In the same vein, there was the unfortunately named vehicle tracking system Scam Scan. It was quickly changed to Safe-T-Cam to avoid any implication – shock & horror! – that it might in the future be used for something other than the detection of speeding truck drivers.[24]

And Smart cards? They became Chip cards. So it goes on.

It is natural to pin blame solely on corporations for these insulting tactics, but government is no better. For example, privacy is under greatest threat whenever government says it wants to "modernise" privacy law.

Perhaps the most entertaining (or disquieting) adjustment of language occurs in the arena of public safety.

While governments have reached accord on the security measures that should be pursued in response to terrorist attacks, they are still divided on the question of when the label "terrorist" should be attached. In the early stages of the 2014 Sydney café siege, police were anxious to push the message that the incident was the work of an insane "lone wolf", and not terrorist-related. The subsequent appearance of an ISIS flag put an end to that line of reasoning.

Conversely, governments have worked collaboratively to promote provocative imagery and rhetoric in the arena of terrorism. This effort involves shifting arcane transitive verbs into popular language. Historically, the exercise usually signals impending fear and hatred.

The most prominent transitive verb is currently "radicalised". In a very short time, the word has become part of the global political and media vocabulary – to such an extent that many people now see it as a self-evident truth.

To be *radicalised* is to have completed a process of *radicalisation*, in the same way that the transitive verb *poisoned* is the outcome of the process of *poisoning*. Think of another transitive verb: "infected".

When governments link nouns with transitive verbs, they set in place a popular perception that society faces a sinister – often invisible – toxic

---

24 Davies, S. (1992). Big Brother: Australia's web of surveillance and the new
    technological order; Simon & Schuster, Sydney.

element, one that creates an equally toxic outcome. So, radicalisation inevitably breeds radicals. And radicals, by inference, are a toxin.

Transitive verbs used in this way are extremely powerful linguistic devices, chiefly because they indicate a perverted outcome that requires emergency intervention. And, of course, radicalisation has been the justification for a wide range of new police and security powers that test the limits of any liberal constitution.

One dangerous outcome of this trend is that it poisons the concept of radicalism, a noble element in all social and political reform. Government is slowly appropriating the idea of radicalism and turning it into something entirely destructive.[25]

The problem with such linguistic trickery is that it gains a life of its own. McCarthyism showed that "communist infiltration" led to the toxin of subversion, which in turn created the demand for a test of loyalty that applied to swathes of the US population. In a similar vein, new UK legislation requires all public sector employees to report any perceived precursor of radicalisation, even among young children. This cannot end well.

Returning to the corporate sector, this language manipulation goes to the heart of privacy protection, and it also says a great deal about the entities that perform it. Responsible organisations thus describe privacy as a "right", while unaware ones talk of it as a "value", and bad players lambaste it as an "interest".

In terms of privacy policies, "restrict" is another interesting expression, much overused these days. It provides the impression of control over what a company does with your data, while actually meaning relatively little at any practical level. And of course while companies can't always lawfully "discriminate" amongst their customer base, they certainly can "customise".

One clause in the 2014 PayPal privacy policy embraces several of these new terms:

Federal and state laws allow you to restrict the sharing of

---

25 Davies, S. Why we shouldn't allow government to poison the concept of radicalism 15th February 2015. The Privacy Surgeon.
http://www.privacysurgeon.org/blog/incision/why-we-shouldnt-allow-government-to-poison-the-concept-of-radicalism/ (accessed 1st July 2018)

> *your personal information in certain instances. However,*
> *these laws also state that you cannot restrict other types of*
> *sharing. Because we have chosen to refrain from certain*
> *types of data sharing, the only type of sharing of your*
> *personal information that you may restrict is as follows...*

Of course some phrases have been invented to present a neutral spin on what could be seen as a hostile process. For example "we will collect and disclose your information to external parties unless you object" simply became "opt-out" before evolving into the above polite wording in the PayPal policy.

So it continues. The advent of "plain language" contracts and policies has been a tremendous step forward in terms of allowing customers to understand the meaning of complex legal terms, but the downside is that they often leave the reader just as uncertain about what's really going on with their information. At the heart of this change, however, is a desire by many organisations to deceive and distract the customer.

Privacy and public interest

A fiercely complex tension has existed for decades at the core of the privacy realm. It involves a constantly changing equation that determines the relationship between public interest and privacy rights. Put simply, it's the line between my right to own or control my information, versus a demand by others to own or see it.

This complexity pervades almost every aspect of privacy and – of course – it involves not one element, but hundreds or even thousands. And as many of us become publishers on social media platforms, this complexity becomes even greater.

There are few areas of private life these days that one sector or another hasn't laid claim to in the "public interest". Epidemiologists want access to a vast swathe of health data. Historians seek biographical information, even on living people. And much of the media and law enforcement want just about everything they can lay their hands on. Then of course corporations of all types massively increase customer surveillance in the name of "improving the user experience" (and, it goes without saying, improving advertising revenue).

There's now such a vast spectrum of legal devices to enable disclosure, that in many cases the logic of public interest was lost years ago in the white noise of the mechanics. Doctors have darkly giggled at the 'All New Hippocratic Oath', which condemns disclosure of patient information "except in such circumstances as required by law, or where there is an overriding public duty to disclose, or where I am compelled to do so to a third party, or where there is a demand from others claiming a right to know the information, or where there is an exemption from the Data Protection Principles, or where there is a purported national security interest, or where the information is owned by the Crown, or where precedent demands disclosure, or in any situation where a regulation, ordinance, by-law, subpoena, or Statutory Instrument requires surrender of personal information, or in whatever circumstance the Government deems disclosure necessary or desirable."[26]

Disclosure even affects the deceased. Of course, in many countries a person's right to privacy ceases at death, though this is by no means a universal situation. In the US for example, some protection of the deceased exists for up to fifty years. Bulgaria and Estonia have similar provisions.

If this seems a rather arcane scenario, consider my friend, who died in the closing days of this book's completion.

My friend, who was approaching seventy years of age, had a secret – a secret that explained his reclusive nature. His mates were often annoyed or frustrated by this reclusive behaviour, but only I knew why he would disappear for days. In the meantime, he lost friends because they simply didn't understand why he acted in such a way. They took it personally.

Now that he is gone, do I tell his friends the facts? Or do I respect his request that I keep the details secret?

In the end I chose to keep the secret. If a contract can survive death, so should a secret. Having said that, there's no absolute rule. Answers on a postcard please – or in a sealed envelope!

---

26 Davies, S. (1994). Big Brother; Britain's Web of Surveillance, London. Pan McMillan.

Privacy advocates and lawmakers constantly anguish over the interplay of rights and public interest. There is rarely a simple formula that can be applied. Disclosure in the public interest is often conditional. Sometimes disclosure is required by law and sometimes it is a matter of discretion and conscience. And over time those conditions may change in line with shifts in law and technology.

Civil liberties up in smoke: a case study in conflict

The subject that follows exemplifies the interplay between cigarette smoking and the "majority" public interest. It is one of many complex and controversial scenarios relating to the right of the individual versus claims for the "common good". This tension goes to the heart of privacy rights and is worth discussing in some detail.

Tobacco prohibition has sparked one of the most notable and shambolic dichotomies between the right to private life, personal autonomy and the need to protect public health. This is a predictable outcome of the global tsunami of smoking restrictions and it provides a striking example of the tension between privacy and the perhaps wider public interest.

For centuries – and certainly since the time of John Stuart Mill – there has been widely explored connection between personal liberty and state restrictions in such matters.[27] This relationship has been articulated throughout the past century and a half in debates relating to regulation of a wide spectrum of behaviours and lifestyle choices, particularly with tobacco and other substances.

On free speech, it's clear that while freedom can be fundamentally asserted by one person, another person can assert that there is a right not to feel hurt, offended or threatened by such expression. A complex legal framework has emerged to cope with such differences of view. Similarly, while it can be asserted that there is a right to smoke, others can argue that they have a right not to be hurt, offended or threatened by such an activity. A sensitive framework was always required to respond to such

---

27   See in particular J.S.Mill's 1859 text *On Liberty*.

conflicts. Sadly, with smoking regulation – in my experience – this is not always the case.

Routine surveillance and control of tobacco smokers is one outcome of the lack of genuine dialogue between interest groups. The almost unrestricted use of drug testing kits for nicotine, tracking smokers by way of pubic camera networks, infiltrating social network profiles, banning images of smoking in films and establishing whistleblower and reporting hotlines against smokers are signs that a foundation is already being established to treat smokers as low grade criminals.[28] And, in consequence, the creation of a society-wide surveillance system.

The smoking debate is often characterised as a clash between the rights of smokers versus the rights on non-smokers. However this is usually a false dichotomy and is no more valid than a debate over police powers being characterised as a clash between criminality and crime prevention. A free society offers the possibility of creating solutions that satisfy civil liberties while also achieving public policy objectives. [29]

Prohibition driven by zealotry will inevitably result in extreme measures. Even back in 2008, surveillance of smokers has reached the point where several UK local authorities were found to be using anti-terrorist powers to covertly enforce smoking bans.[30] In 2010 a Nottingham man who had gone to the trouble of dropping his butt down a drain, had been monitored by CCTV and was given a fine. The penalty was later overturned by magistrates who saw it as having no legal basis.[31] After being tracked by CCTV, a Black Country pensioner in the UK was handed a £75 penalty for merely dropping ash onto the pavement.[32]

---

28 Davies, S. Civil Liberties Up in Smoke. (2011).Report published by Forest UK.
29 The European Convention on Human Rights for example acknowledges that there is a duty on government to provide security, but only where other rights are not unnecessarily compromised. Article 17 provides that no one may use the rights guaranteed by the Convention to seek the abolition or limitation of rights guaranteed in the Convention. This addresses instances where states seek to restrict a human right in the name of another human right, or where individuals rely on a human right to undermine other human rights
30 Councils covert surveillance operations (24th May 2010). London. The Guardian. http://www.guardian.co.uk/uk/2010/may/24/councils-covert-surveillance-operations
31 Man who dropped cigarette butt in drain has fine overturned (2010). This is Nottingham. http://www.thisisnottingham.co.uk/news/Man-dropped-cigarette-end-drain-fine-overturned/article-2206356-detail/article.html
32 Smoker vows to fight over cigarette ash fine. (16th August 2010). Black County. The Express and Star. http://www.expressandstar.com/news/2010/08/16/smoker-vows-to-fight-over-cigarette-ash-fine/#ixzz11PaGqJ00 (accessed July 8th 2018)

There are countless such examples of heavy-handed tactics, but in an era when moral righteousness often drives public debate, it's easy to stigmatise anyone who goes against the grain of public opinion (i.e. "all dissenters must be users"). I learned this in the 1980's while campaigning for drug law reform. Even though I had rarely smoked dope or taken a grain of any illicit substance, I was often characterised in the white heat of the heroin "debate" as a covert drug user. Cannabis law reformers in the 1970s similarly had to deal with such denouncements.

Again in the 1980s – in an episode of utter hypocrisy – I became an evangelist for tobacco control and was roundly accused of being a non-smoker in the polemic that followed. For example I gave testimony to the New Zealand Parliament's Public Health Committee and even wrote most of the New South Wales Attorney General's second reading speech on the pending state prohibition bill.

I naively thought I was doing the right thing. I had figured out the legal theory quite eloquently and it seemed to me that the legislation in both countries was balanced and sensitive. It was only twenty years later that it dawned on me that all those legislative powers I had helped introduce were being roundly abused by employers, public authorities, private companies and even by the general public.

One of the gravest risks to liberty and rights occurs when government signals open season on smokers and permits uncontrolled limitations and intrusion to occur in the name of public health protection. In such instances government will set out a national framework of minimum requirements, but rarely will it create limitations on excessive controls that may be imposed by lower bodies. Such is the case with the Health Act 2006 in the UK.

The UK government endeavoured to set a moral lead in its 2006 tobacco control legislation. The aim of the then health minister was to take a principled position that smoking was not a generally acceptable behaviour and that the state, wherever possible, would not tolerate it.

A Cabinet decision was taken, albeit controversially, to permit as few exemptions as possible. The home was the most obvious of these, as was smoking in an open public street. However most populated environs were subject to the ban, including public buildings, workplaces, transportation, pubs and restaurants and even in some circumstances, private vehicles. One general rule that permeated the restrictions was the limitation of smoking in an enclosed or "substantially enclosed" space.

This "leadership" soon gave *carte blanche* to private entities to establish their own high ground. Smoking was soon banned on open train platforms, parks and open-air sport facilities. Many institutions took it upon themselves to use the new law as a justification for a limitless extension of the ban even to areas where smoking could not possibly affect non-smokers. CCTV is used routinely to enforce these rules, with operators following smokers with the use of multiple cameras.

As the unfairness and lack of proportionality of the new restrictions became apparent, further surveillance was required to enforce the bans. One park warden in Surrey told Privacy International that he had been instructed to fine smokers even if they were alone in a park and were not littering. Worldwide, reasoned arguments by councilors to provide a small smoking zone in a large public space are generally ignored. [33] If littering is a justification for the outright banning of smoking in open areas, then why not ban plastic bottles and newspapers?

One wonders what good can come, for example, of forcing smokers in Nairobi to stand in the middle of a busy road[34] to smoke. Or why airline passengers in Calgary in the freezing midst of winter are required to smoke outside the terminal. If public health is the driving issue, then why was I seeing seventy-year-old disabled women shivering in the ice?

Rail commuters facing long delays on the network have complained to rail companies that the outright ban on smoking on platforms is simply unfair. And yet all train company staff are instructed to monitor passengers and take immediate action against smoking even if the activity is on the far end of the platform a hundred feet from any other passenger. Even the over-regulated legal environment of the Netherlands permits the existence of designated "roken zones" on platforms.

---

33   POL floats smoking zones for city parks (15th October 2010).New York Daily News.
     http://www.nydailynews.com/ny_local/2010/10/15/2010-10-
     15_pol_floats_smoking_zones_for_city_parks.html (accessed May 12th 2018)
34   BBC online news.http://news.bbc.co.uk/1/hi/world/africa/7497614.stm (accessed May
     12th 2018)

This "trickle down" effect from national legislation can best be seen in the workplace. One of the most absurd examples of stupidity and discrimination was reported to Privacy International in 2008 by a long-distance truck driver working the London-Edinburgh run. The man, a contractor, did the return route as a sole driver, twice a week. The company he worked for demanded that he refrain from smoking in the cab. The basis of this demand was that a non-smoker had to check the odometer each week. When the driver pointed out the idiocy of this demand and protested that not a trace of smoke could be detected in the cab (he stopped smoking two hours before the completion of the journey and kept the windows open), his contract was terminated. Self-employed trades people have been fined for smoking in their own vehicles, even when no other person is present.[35] [36]

Did I oppose the UK anti-tobacco legislation "because" I was a smoker? Absolutely not. If I could have predicted decades ago where the 1980's legislation would end up, I never would have supported the idea of "morality based" laws. In that respect, tobacco regulation provides important context to consider how we should treat any prohibition or regulation.

Public interest or public titillation?

It's one thing to theorise about this interplay, and quite another to deal with it at a direct and personal level. I had such an experience in 2014, when one of my former book editors approached me about the possibility of publishing my autobiography.

The publisher's interest was "bringing the privacy issue to life" through a tapestry of personal stories. I certainly have enough of those, from death threats and corruption to political intrigue and board-room skulduggery.

---

35 The Times Online. http://www.timesonline.co.uk/tol/news/uk/crime/article4393248.ece (accessed July 19ʰ 2018)
36 See Hansson, Sven Ole, and Elin Palm, eds. The Ethics of Workplace Privacy. Brussels: Peter   Lang, 2005, for a good overview of multiple elements of workplace

Over the course of a couple of hours, I took her on a thirty-year journey, recounting tales of confrontation with corrupt police forces and security agencies, wars with global corporations and battles with prime ministers. Then there was all the fun stuff in between – meetings with royalty, rock stars and sports heroes.

The contract was in the bag, but try as I might, I couldn't go through with it. It turned out that "bringing the privacy issue to life" would involve spilling the beans on private moments. That meant a direct conflict in most cases between the public interest and what the public is interested in.

For example, just after the funeral of Princess Diana on 1997, I received a request to meet her brother, The Earl Charles Spencer. At the time, Spencer had one of the most recognisable faces in the world and was the most enduring connection to the former princess. His moving eulogy at her recent funeral service had been seen by 2.5 billion people.

The "fact" of the meeting is a matter of record, but the contents were entirely private. Yes, there was – and perhaps still is – a public interest in what we discussed. I, however, could never be at liberty to disclose such things. Spencer was still in mourning at the time, and the discussion would always rightly be personal. It's a matter of humanity over public interest.

This of course does not imply that the contents of every such meeting should be private. For example, in 2006 following a bitter legal feud with the world's biggest banking conglomerate, SWIFT, I had a turbulent meeting with the organisation's CEO, Leonard Schrank (which I describe elsewhere). I decided to reveal what went on at that meeting because the issue at hand was live and it presented a clear and present danger to privacy. There was no indication or presumption of privacy or secrecy from either side. A secret deal stitched up in the Oval Office with the US president involving every bank in the world could not be ignored.

Contrast this situation with a private meeting I had in 2010 with Google's Chairman, Eric Schmidt. Google and I had been engaged in a very bitter public battle for some years over its information practices. The feud had become bloody and notorious. Still – with the exception of a couple of lines that I quote elsewhere – the discussion with Schmidt was entirely

privacy.

private – an attempt to resolve a complex and entrenched problem. Yes, there was still an element of public interest in disclosing its contents, but in my view, this was trumped by the fact that no prior indication was given by either side that it would be made public. Such distinctions are vitally important – and they become critically important for privacy advocates. Generally speaking, the privacy community is tuned into the need for transparency and disclosure – far more than urban myth may suggest. Even so, the equation can be complex. Many believe that a higher test of transparency should apply to individuals holding public office, as opposed to those people who are directly affected by the decisions of such people.

My life has been inundated by such situations, but I never had any doubt where I stood in terms of disclosure. Take for example the 1970's, when I had a brief affair with an artist who was later to become one of the world's most iconic music heroes. I was a very young man then – in my early twenties – and a music critic for a couple of notable magazines. He said "please don't tell anyone" – and I never did.

Interestingly, many decades later, he called me. I still don't know how he found my phone number. We agreed to meet. That was a difficult challenge, given the hordes of adoring fans and his constant appearances in front of stadiums of fifty thousand people, but we found a way to do it. He thanked me for my respect for his privacy – and for understanding that I could have made millions of dollars off that story. I have similar anecdotes of Olympic heroes and film stars (though to be precise – not all of whom I had an affair with!). As Vickram Crishna observes in relation to privacy in India: what happens in Vegas, stays in Vegas.

It is no easier to make such distinctions, even if a person has passed on. Indeed, there's a persuasive argument that the test of disclosure should be tougher because the deceased have no capacity to correct or contradict information.

The acid test in such matters should be whether a claim of public interest is merely a claim of interest "in" a story. There is a world of difference.

Privacy in an "age of terror"

I keep hearing the critics of privacy saying, "you civil liberties people don't understand the real meaning of terrorism – you're living in an ivory tower". I contest the inference that privacy advocates have no personal connection with the atrocities that have laid privacy bare to wholesale surveillance. Here are a few anecdotes.

Like many of my fellow Londoners, I remember, with vivid clarity the morning of 7th July 2005. More than thirteen years have gone by, but I'll never forget that day.

I was living at the time in a rambling old apartment just off Tavistock Square in the city's central Bloomsbury district. That utterly beautiful area is one of the London's most cherished historic precincts, once home to the likes of Charles Dickens, Charles Darwin, John Maynard Keynes and Virginia Woolf. Even my own humble place had once been occupied by the mysterious feminist poet Christina Rossetti. "Tranquil" is the word people often use to describe the area.

Just after 9AM on July 7th, we became aware of an unusually intense level of activity in the area. Emergency vehicles were streaming along the nearby roads, as the cacophony of sirens grew by the minute. Nothing official was being said on media, but we residents knew something big was happening. Like urban metadata, the weird pattern of sirens signalled bad news.

Before long we started hearing unconfirmed reports of explosions on the London Underground, so just after 9.30, I decided to have a snoop around. I took the scenic path southward to nearby Russell Square tube station, which seemed to be the epicentre of the turmoil.

Within a few minutes I heard a frightening and protracted *bang* behind me, in the direction of my house. Of course in the centre of London such noises could mean anything, so I didn't think too much of it – probably just another under-qualified crane operator dropping twenty tons of girders onto the wrong spot. Still, the ground trembled.

By the time I arrived at Russell Square Tube, the area resembled a war zone. No-one was getting anywhere near it, so I headed back along the side path to my house. It seemed everyone was on their mobile phone.

Had I instead taken the main route home – Upper Woburn Place – I

51

would have soon witnessed the source of the loud bang. A terrorist explosion had ripped apart a packed double decker bus not a hundred yards from my apartment. Fourteen people had just died in that carnage.

Returning in ignorance to my house, it soon became clear what had happened. It was not just images of the nearby bus – its top blown clean off – that burned into my mind, but the stark details of three deadly explosions that had detonated across the London Underground. Somewhere, underneath our house, 27 people had just been murdered as they travelled on the Piccadilly Line.

52 people died in those terrible attacks, and more than 700 had their lives changed forever through injury. Gazing out of my window, I noticed my old apartment on Gordon Square where, less than four years earlier, the Washington Post's New York tech correspondent Robert O'Harrow and I had sat together in horror as the events of 9/11 unfurled before us in his home town. Now it was happening to me – again.

Anyone close to such episodes of horror usually experiences a *"there, but for the grace of god, go I"* moment. For me, it was the realisation that had I taken the more familiar route along Gordon Square, rather than along Tavistock Square, I would have been twenty feet from where the bus was annihilated – and at more or less the same instant. And perhaps, would have been killed.

This hadn't been my first such "close call" moment during a terrorist attack. The first was in 1993, during a series of consultations in Belfast.

I had been talking with various factions of Northern Ireland's horrible war to better understand the nature of the conflict and the sort of conditions that it was establishing for civil liberties. It was a fruitless exercise; the British government officials there thought of me as an Irish Nationalist sympathiser, while the Nationalists suspected I was a Unionist plant. Looking back on those days, I was playing with fire.

Northern Ireland was an utter mess, as everyone there – and throughout the UK – well knew at the time. Americans who complain of having to live under the threat of terrorism could learn much from thirty years of "The Troubles" in Britain, during which bomb attacks had become routine in England's major cities. Thousands died in the conflict.

Even so, unlike today, civil liberties in the UK remained vaguely intact – even if the motivation for keeping them intact was to prove to the bombers that the British government wasn't going to let terrorism prevail over rights. Other countries, take note.

I couldn't understand why this region was being torn apart. I had also tried to understand the Yugoslav conflict that was raging at the time – which slaughtered 140,000 people on Europe's doorstep – but that was beyond me too, regardless of how many people I met in the region. Still, I knew enough about history to judge that there's no point in proposing safeguards for rights, unless you understand the drivers for war.

Being a younger and more reckless man, I spent my idle hours exploring some of Belfast's more troubled and dangerous streets. On 23rd October, having just survived the morning ambling around the notorious Catholic controlled Falls Road I chose to then brave the Shankill Road – heartland of the Loyalist paramilitary.

It turned out to be one of the most notorious days in a notorious war. Ten people died and 57 were injured in a horrific IRA attack on a fish & chip shop that I had passed only minutes earlier. I'd looked into that shop, drooling at the thought of a succulent bag of chips, but the place was too crowded for my liking, and so I kept on walking.

I barely heard the blast above the noise of the street a minute later, but I experienced a phenomenon that friends in similar moments in time had known – an eerie polarisation of human traffic. There's a rush away from the incident – people running, kids on bikes yelling, cars racing. And then there's an equally frantic rush toward the incident – again, people running, kids on bikes yelling, cars racing. Twelve long years later, I experienced the same effect in London.

Of course that episode was (for me) just one of those fortunate coincidences, but sometimes such brushes can be far more intimate.

Six years later, in April 1999, I was walking with friends along Old Compton Street, the centre of London's Gay Village. Being a Friday, the place was packed.

It was one of those impossible dilemmas: which trashy, sweaty, noisy, overcrowded and overpriced dive do you choose?

We stood for a while outside a pub called the *Admiral Duncan*, which I had experienced from past visits. It was rammed, but I told my friends that I knew a little corner bolthole at the back of the makeshift dance floor, where you could usually elbow some space. At least we'd then have somewhere to lay our drinks.

It was a knife-edge decision, but in the end, we opted to move on elsewhere. That choice was clinched through the simple agreement that we despised the Admiral Duncan's policy of never offering any drinks specials. We frothed with indignation over the rip-off mentality of gay pubs, and then settled into a surprisingly quiet wine bar off Leicester Square.

Ten minutes later a nail bomb went off in the Admiral Duncan at the exact spot where I had planned our gathering, killing three people and horribly injuring 79 others, several of whom lost limbs. The perpetrator, deranged neo-Nazi David Copeland, was subsequently given six concurrent life sentences. This was Copeland's third and final attack on a public place, in each of which he had planted an explosive bag packed with four inch nails. In this case, the device had been placed less than twelve feet from where I had planned our drinking position. I knew three of the people who had suffered horrible injuries from that blast.

* * * * *

Back to the events in London of 7th July 2005, and there was much worse news to come. My accountant, Richard Gray, disappeared on that day. His family had reported that he left for work, as always, to catch the underground train to his office in Pall Mall.

It took authorities more than a week to identify Richard. Apparently, he had been standing next to the Aldgate Station bomber.

Richard had helped me through some very difficult times over the years. A caring and gentle man, he never thought twice about going that extra mile for people.

Such terrible instances are what might be termed "first degree" experiences. You can smell the death and the smoke, hear screams, fear for someone lost. Then there are the second degree events, like when my colleagues and I at Privacy International watched speechless as TV reports showed our recently vacated hotel in Islamabad flattened by a massive truck bomb. At times like that you might think "My god... I've been there – I could have been there".

Having experienced both levels, my position on human rights and privacy has not changed. And, again, in my view, it matters little which of those levels of terrorism you experience. The truth is that the fight against unwarranted surveillance, the fight for privacy and the defence of liberty are completely compatible with the aim of creating good security.

Why? Because the more you care about security, the more you should care about the values that civil liberties advocates support. You should care about transparency and accountability; about integrity and honesty. You should demand that agencies which claim to keep society safe are actually doing their job and not lying. Sadly, far too many agencies in security and law enforcement are getting away with institutional deception. That's not just dangerous; it's also a betrayal of public trust.

This has been said a million times before, but the exposure makes it no less poignant: you cannot defend society by speciously removing its freedoms. As a claimed threat to security rises, so too should the expectation of an open and accountable security sector. Our right to privacy is indivisible from our right to expect genuine safety.

Like many of my colleagues in the privacy realm, I've had to deal with accusations by police and security agencies of living in a "fantasy" world of legal theory and safe middle class principles. All of us should be fearless in condemning such attacks as ignorant and self-serving.

Chapter Two: How do we define Privacy?

> *Two case studies from either side of the pond further our*
> *quest for the definition of privacy. Katherine Albrecht had*
> *long been leading the campaign against RFID tags in the*
> *US before, in 2006, furious UK residents began tearing*
> *chips from council-owned bins. What factors motivated the*
> *hitherto uninterested Brits to take action? I argue that not*
> *"privacy", but government hypocrisy, secrecy, deception,*
> *and unfairness, were the catalysts. I end the chapter with*
> *definitions of privacy from history, and from fellow*
> *campaigners.*

The "BinGate" microchip scandal

Winterbourne Monkton is the sort of quaint place that personifies idyllic rural England. With ancient stone walls, rambling lane ways and a sense of unqualified peace, this Wiltshire village and its 160 happy inhabitants represents all that is congenial and harmonious. I went there once, and it was like visiting the set of the "Truman Show".

The village motto could well be "Just Leave us Alone". This retiring – and retired – population minds its own business without much of a care about the outside world.

This attitude was prevalent for most of the town's past two centuries, until 26th August 2006, when the popular Mail on Sunday national newspaper ran a sensational story, titled, 'Germans plant bugs in our wheelie bins'. (For non-UK readers who are unfamiliar with the term, a wheelie bin is a large plastic rubbish container on wheels.) Almost every house in Britain has one.

The impact of this story – and the subsequent firestorm across England – is more than noteworthy.

The article was a xenophobic – though largely accurate – piece of reporting that detailed how local government had been covertly equipping these mobile rubbish bins with tiny RFID (Radio Frequency Identification) chips to monitor household waste.

The chips, which were about the size of a one-cent piece, digitally linked an individual bin to the relevant household. They provided data on the weight of rubbish being left for collection. Local Councils futilely argued that European law forced them to install the devices in order to improve recycling rates. Perhaps this was true, but it certainly didn't mandate secrecy.

It's not that RFID tags are novel. Indeed they've been around for decades. There are billions of them in use today for stock management, payment cards, animal tagging, passports and a hundred other purposes. Britain imports most of its chips from other countries.

For the average Briton, neither RFID nor its Germanic ancestry were controversial subjects. The issue at stake for most people was that councils had made a spectacular blunder by failing to consult or even notify residents. Even the Mail newspaper could not hold EU law responsible for such an oversight.

As reactionary stories go, this one was the Perfect Storm: secretive and unaccountable local government acting under the cover of non-British laws to bloat the coffers of foreign companies at the expense of everyone's privacy.

Anger at local government had been building for some years, fuelled by a decline in the quality of service, continuing increases in tax and a widespread perception of government arrogance. The detonator for public protest was primed. It just needed a rallying cry.

The good people of Winterbourne Monkton – like those of countless other towns across England – bubbled with indignation over the intrusion. They demanded an explanation from local authorities, accusing them of deception and treachery.

Blatant xenophobia was probably not even essential to these sentiments. The main triggers were snooping and non-accountability.

A crusading politician offered all the right words to inflame the moral outrage that was to follow. Conservative MP Andrew Pelling fumed: 'This is nothing more than a spy in the bin and I don't think even the old Soviet Union made such an intrusion into people's personal lives. It is Big Brother gone mad. I think a more British way of doing things is to seek to persuade people rather than spy on them."

Setting aside for one moment Pelling's rather charitable view of Soviet history, the MP got the quote perfect. That is to say, the Mail on Sunday journalist who primed the quote got it perfect.

The technology soon became widely known as 'Bin Bugs' and as the issue spread like a monsoon from region to region across Britain, local residents took up arms against the receptacle menace.[37]

Within two weeks media were reporting, "A huge revolt against wheelie-bin spy bugs is sweeping Britain, with thousands of defiant households removing the electronic devices and either dumping them or posting them back to their local town hall." [38]

"The protesters are ignoring threats of prosecution for criminal damage in their anger at having their rubbish secretly monitored by council chiefs".

Officials confirmed that the defiance was measurable. In the seaside town of Bournemouth, councillors estimated that 25,000 bugs – one-third of the total – had been removed by force.

Enter Martin Meeks, a retired Chief Inspector with the Special Branch, now enjoying the quiet life in Winterbourne Monkton. He was incensed about the chips and was determined to vanquish

them in whatever small way he could. In the process, Meeks became an unlikely poster child for the bin movement.

To provide context, one peculiarity of the British psyche – reflected even in judicial decisions – is the reverence paid to "ordinary, honourable and decent" citizens who selflessly take up arms against great odds to fight City Hall. Meeks was such a man.

Spearheading the local "Ban the Bug" campaign, Meeks was

---

37   Residents Revolt against Wheelie Bin Spies, the Evening Standard, 10 September 2006
       http://www.thisislondon.co.uk/news/article-23366337-residents-revolt-against-wheelie-bin-spies.do
38   The Mail on Sunday' 10th September 2006

photographed defiantly holding aloft the chip that he had torn from his bin. Ironic that a man who spent his life in one of the most secretive police departments now demanded transparency – but such is the nature of the privacy issue. Not since the postal stamp controversy of 1839 had Winterbourne Monkton witnessed such a drama!

All that remained was to find an official silly enough to respond in a hostile tongue. The Mail found just such a man. In a classic Own Goal, Kennet Council leader Chris Humphries indignantly declared: "These bins belong to the council. They don't belong to the people who hold them. They are interfering with a bin that belongs to somebody else."

That comment was sufficient to ignite another round of civil disobedience, stretching from the southern counties right up into Scotland.

Although no-one had thrown themselves in front of a train – or a horse – for the cause of Bin Liberation, the episode had a resounding impact on local government, and served to remind it of the crucial importance of openness. Bingate has now become part of the narrative of government and continues to be a benchmark of accountability in public service delivery.

Openness is everything. To provide context, consider the garbage situation in Belgium. There, the government has established the most riotously complex rubbish regime in history, breach of which results in 75 euro fine for even the most minor transgressions.

Belgium provides for several colour coded translucent rubbish bags. At first sight the system appears straightforward: yellow for paper and cardboard, white for general refuse, orange for food and blue for tins and plastic.

This situation, however, is far from straightforward. Does a milk carton go in the yellow bag for cardboard? No. Most apparently contain a microscopically thin aluminium lining and as such must be placed in the blue bag, but Bio cartons go into the yellow bag, even if they don't use the word "bio". Do eggs go into the orange food bag? No. Well, the shells have to go into the white bag and the rest into the orange. And what of food packaging? No-one knows. It seems generic packaging can go into the white, but what if there's a paper covering? Do householders need to spend hours peeling off the paper lining for the yellow bag? There is little hope for the millions of hapless visitors to the country. In time, a degree in biochemistry may be needed to understand the rules.

The Belgian authorities exploit this conundrum, and they routinely fine residents for breaches of the rubbish regime. The reason people are complacent about the situation is that the government has been at least vaguely open that this is a revenue raising exercise. One local told me "there's a hundred thousand bins in hotel rooms and a hundred thousand street waste bins that aren't subject to this farce. Us residents are just low-hanging fruit". Resistance in Belgium thus emerges not through bin-burning parties, but by people covertly hiding illicit material in approved receptacles to give the appearance of compliance. Generally though, people try to stick by the rules, which might have been the outcome regardless of fines and a nationwide snooping regime.

Of course the BinGate "campaign" did not stop the use of bin chips – indeed installation has risen steeply since then – but local authorities have learned to be far more inclusive and open about the technology.

Our team at the global watchdog group Privacy International – like all our colleague campaigning organisations – was taken completely off–guard by these events. Things were moving so randomly and at such speed that it was impossible to grab the tiger's tail. In pubs up and down the country citizens were slamming their fists on the table in fury at being treated this way. We could contribute little more than a comment or two to the media train. While residents were organizing "bin burning" parties in suburban streets across the country, all we could do was adopt the secondary role of "rent-a-quote".

There was no "campaign", at least not in the traditional sense of the word. Neither was there a controlling mind that coordinated or planned the activities (with the exception of the Mail on Sunday that performed the role of promoter and catalyst). The actions were spontaneous and local. In many respects it was the perfect "people's" strike against authority.

Having said that, the Bin Liberation movement is replayed every day, in different realms, somewhere in the world. Such actions have become a part of social, economic and political life. It is clear that the privacy issue comes to life in the most improbable way – and often from the most improbable people.

A rose by any other name

Bingate taught us much about attitudes to snooping, not just in Britain but elsewhere. As it was a "pure" action unsullied by central command, it sits as close as you will ever get to the genuine public psyche.

A scan of the press commentary and published letters reveals some killer elements to the Bin Bug phenomenon. Interestingly they are the same elements that occur time and time again in successful campaigns against government intrusion.

First among these is secrecy. While it is almost impossible in many countries to garner mass public support for, say, improved Freedom of Information laws, the public nerve can be touched whenever government tries to bury information. Secrecy is a trigger point in any campaign, in part because it underlines the second common factor: hypocrisy. Governments that constantly require their electors to yield their private life to official scrutiny should be equally open about their own activities. Citizens sense this principle, even if governments don't. For smart activists, it is a case of flipping the coin from protecting rights to fighting transgressions.

There's no doubt that these triggers have propelled the world of privacy to a huge extent over the past half century. Still, one question that sticks in my mind is whether the concept of privacy was the driving force behind the Bingate actions. Press reporting at the time ranks – in order of popularity – the terms secrecy, bugging, spying, deception, Big Brother, control, manipulation – and then privacy, at number eight on the list.

Be that as it may, all of the items on that list rest on the foundation of privacy. It does not matter so much how privacy is defined or expressed, as long as the expression is true to the core principles of that right. In the same vein, "justice" and "freedom" can be expressed in a hundred ways – and are all the stronger because of that diversity. "A rose by any other name would smell as sweet". Privacy is, in essence, a mechanism – a benchmark – that delineates the relationships of power and control between us and the world around us.

Meanwhile, across the Atlantic...

Unbeknown to the UK bin campaigners, activists in the US had been working on precisely the same issues for at least seven years – employing almost exactly the same principles.

This effort was spearheaded by Katherine Albrecht, who in 1999 became incensed about the use of spy chips in the retail sector. Together with Liz McIntyre, the two provoked public outrage at the way supermarkets covertly deployed the chips. Their dogged persistence sensitised a huge industry and led to greater awareness of when and how RFID should be used.[39]

Albrecht's success was due in part to her technical assessment. For her, a "foundation of evidence" was critically important. She worked with an extensive network of technical experts and hackers to identify precisely how these chips could be covertly used to track customers as they went about their daily business. Her ambit stretched way beyond a single application of the technology and extended to the multiple threats that it created. This many-headed approach blind-sided the industry. It simply couldn't keep up with her.[40]

She is quoted in "The Privacy Advocates" saying "I found myself with a wallet full of shopper cards . . . and one day it occurred to me that every one of those cards, every plastic card in my wallet, represented a database and information about me, everything from my library privileges (what books I had read), to my bus pass. And the ones that I found the most offensive were the ones that were actually keeping track of the food that I needed to live on, because to decide not to participate would have meant spending a lot more for my groceries. So in a pretty intense week . . . I just said I am going to put together a web site and I am going to learn everything there is to learn about this—I am going to dive in with both feet. And I put together the website at nocards.org, which was the founding website of CASPIAN.[41]

39 Wikipedia entry on Katherine Albrecht.
    https://en.wikipedia.org/wiki/Katherine_Albrecht https://en.wikipedia.org/wiki/Radio-
    frequency_identification (accessed August 11th[th] 2018)
40 Albrecht, Katherine, and Liz McIntyre. Spychips: How Major Corporations and
    Government Plan to Track Your Every Move with RFID. Nashville: Nelson Current,
    2005.
41 Bennett, C.J. The privacy advocates, p.46

Successful as it was, the UK campaign lacked this detailed technical expertise. The British actions hit their target at many levels, but they lacked the analysis that Albrecht could muster. While UK activists were burning their chips, similar movements in Germany and the US were analysing patent documents and conducting hacking workshops.

That early RFID campaign borrowed strategy from the environmental movement of the 1970's and 1980's. Back then, activists shifted their focus from rhetoric to analysis. Campaign groups hired technicians to conduct independent tests on sea water, animal life and air quality. This approach raised the stakes and forced companies to be more precise about their claims.

This process is no easy challenge. It is one thing to make simple declarations about the importance of freedom and autonomy – or even the future of the planet – but it is quite another to use detailed analysis to build a long-term foundation of resistance and change. Albrecht built a technically aware constituency by – for example – demanding why the industry did not acknowledge "sworn patent documents from IBM describing ways to secretly follow innocent people in libraries, theaters and public restrooms through the RFID tags in their clothes and belongings". Such detail made it possible for her to write for influential publications such as Scientific American.

It was an interesting contrast of approach. In the UK, anger was focused on the users of the technology. In the US, energy was dedicated to destabilising trust in the technology itself. In campaign terms, the latter approach was more sustainable.

Katherine Albrecht's influence on industry was made clear to me in the early 2000's, when I was invited to keynote an RFID meeting convened by the UK Department of Trade and Industry. Manufacturers and the retail sector attended in droves, as did the European Commission and other government departments. I uttered many provocative comments during my talk, but it was only when I mentioned Albrecht's name that the entire room let out a collective groan. It seemed she "just didn't get it". But the public got it – as did lawmakers.

As Margaret Mead observed: "Never doubt that a small group of thoughtful, committed, citizens can change the world. Indeed, it is the only thing that ever has."

The nature of the beast

There have been countless such campaigns, but it is no easy matter identifying precisely what this "privacy" thing is that they all represent. Like Bingate, it is likely that this is more than just a legal term. People will rally around privacy because it is a platform upon which rests many related issues of unfairness and intrusion. Privacy may be a passive word, but it has become shorthand for something far more powerful in the public psyche.

Consider the late 1960's. Back then, almost no-one "on the street" used the word privacy – let alone understood its legal meaning. These days, it seems, almost everyone has an opinion on the topic.

Walk into any bar in any of a hundred countries now and you'll encounter a dozen vastly different views on privacy. And the mere fact that you can trigger an argument on privacy in any bar – even with total strangers – supports the assertion that this is indeed one of the most vibrant and important subjects of our age.

I say this because in 2017 I made a bet with a colleague at the University of Amsterdam that I could get into a privacy argument in five local bars in three hours. I won that bet.

Communications surveillance, intrusion by government agencies, junk texts, identity requirements, social media profiling: these are issues that galvanise entire populations. Then there are countless other more specific privacy concerns (such as Bingate) that are sparked every second of the day at the level of community, street, workplace, club and family.

But what precisely is privacy? As I say elsewhere on this issue, I certainly had no clue when I got religion over the issue as a fourteen year-old. I saw it as a question of unaccountability and misuse of power.

This is not such an unusual scenario. Indeed it permeates even the most remote parts of the globe.

For example, in 2008 Gus Hosein and I were appointed as external expert advisers to the United Nations High Commission for Refugees (UNHCR) to audit the biometric security of refugee camps in Africa and Malaysia. The UN had embarked on a scheme of mass electronic fingerprinting and it was our job to determine whether the technology was fit for purpose and whether there were any serious privacy violations.

Indeed it turned out there were many major privacy and security issues at stake. As we toured the most desperate and dangerous places on earth it became clear that here was yet another technology being crammed into an environment in ways that were completely inappropriate.[42]

In the chaotic, fly-blown, dust-bowl camps in the far reaches of Djibouti and Ethiopia, we asked the refugee representatives how they felt about being electronically fingerprinted. The response was, for us, extremely interesting. While not understanding the word "privacy", they described almost every element of the concept. A few said they felt that something of themselves was being "taken away".

Definitions of privacy vary widely according to context and environment. As one write observed, "in one sense, all human rights are aspects of the right to privacy"[43] (see the legal chapter for more on definitions).

As I mentioned earlier, privacy is a little like freedom: the less you have of it, the easier it is to recognise. And, like the concept of freedom, privacy has at least a hundred wildly different definitions. Even after decades of academic interest in the subject, the world's leading experts have been unable to agree on a single definition.

Populations interpret the meaning of privacy in different ways. And it is often the case that those interpretations can shift according to current events.

Privacy protection is one way of drawing the line at how far society can intrude into your affairs. In that context, privacy is a question of power – yours, the government's and the power of the corporations. "The bedrock of civil liberties is the setting of limits on the power of the state to interfere in the private life of its citizens", Patricia Hewitt once observed (that was before she became Britain's minister for health and blotted her copybook on issues such as a nationwide surveillance regime over tobacco smoking).[44]

Privacy can be viewed as a measure of how much surveillance and

---

42 Davies, S and Hosein, I. Privacy Impact Assessment for the United Nations High Commission for Refugees: a late stage PIA for UNHCR's trial of an automated fingerprint identification system; 2009 (unpublished)
43 Volio, F. Legal personality, privacy and the family in Henkin (ed) The International Bill of Rights, New York : Columbia University Press, 1981.
44 Cited in Simon Davies "Big Brother; Britain's Web of Surveillance", London. Pan McMillan, 1994

control can be established over our lives. It is a measure of how much we should become subjects of the expanding information empire. Privacy can even be a benchmark to indicate how much autonomy a nation should have in the emerging international order. Canada, France, Northern Europe and some Latin American countries have demonstrated this approach in the past, establishing highly politicised actions to protect the national interest from data subversion by larger countries.

Colin Bennet explains: "Although there is no consensus on how to define privacy, even in English speaking nations, there is common agreement that privacy is something that every human being needs at some level and in some degree. This point is substantiated by a wealth of social psychological and anthropological evidence that has suggested that every society adopts mechanisms and structures (even as simple as the building of walls) that allow individuals to resist encroachment from other individuals or groups."[45]

Any review of the history of privacy reveals that the issue in the 1980s was seen (by those few who knew the field) as a key indicator of the strength of a democracy. However, apart from a handful of highly charged political campaigns against specific technologies, public awareness was still nascent. In the words of veteran privacy writer John Carroll, "Privacy was not a virtue in the greedy 1980s, nor is it a cause for concern in the needy 1990s".[46] The same cannot be said for the present day.

At one level, the case for privacy is a clear argument for restraining the use of information systems. Many such privacy arguments that made sense twenty years ago, might seem in the modern day to be paranoic and anti-social. From the perspective of the advocate for privacy, however, information is power – an equation that does not change from one millennium to the next. Lord Balish in the HBO series Game of Thrones goes at length on this matter. History demonstrates that information in the hands of authority will inevitably be used for unintended and often malevolent purposes. If any government is allowed, piece by piece, to assemble a complete linkage of computer technology, many of our traditional freedoms will be imperilled. The alarm will not be raised until the mechanism has become "indispensable". In that respect government

---

45   Bennett, C J, The Privacy Advocates.
46   Cited in Simon Davies "Big Brother; Britain's Web of Surveillance", London. Pan

becomes symptomatic of Lord Varis's web of spies.

Again, referring to the work of Colin Bennett:

> *Privacy plays important functions within liberal democratic societies by preventing the total politicizing of life; it promotes the freedom of association; it shields scholarship and science from unnecessary interference by government; it permits and protects the use of a secret ballot; it restrains improper police conduct such as compulsory self-incrimination and "unreasonable searches and seizures"; and it serves also to shield those institutions, such as the press, that operate to keep government accountable (Westin 1967, 25). In a similar vein, Paul Schwartz (1999) has advanced a similar theory of "constitutive privacy" to protect the ability of individuals to speak freely and participate in public life on the Internet.*

Privacy is one of the most important rights of a free nation. In many countries, we take it for granted. To understand why Privacy is so important, you only have to imagine life without it. People who have no rights of Privacy are vulnerable to limitless intrusion by governments, corporations, or anyone else who chooses to interfere in your personal affairs.

However it is important to note that privacy is not just an individual right – asserting the rights on one person – but it is a broader public right.

As Colin Bennett explains,[47] there have been attempts to realign, rather than abandon, the privacy concept. Priscilla Regan, for instance, has argued that privacy should be seen as a common value: "in that all individuals value some degree of privacy and have some common conceptions about privacy." It is a public value "in that it has value not just to the individual... but also to the democratic political system." And it is a collective value "in that technology and market forces are making it hard for any one person to have privacy without all persons having a similar minimum level of privacy." She contends that an individualistic conceptualization of privacy does not serve the privacy advocate well.

McMillan, 1994
47   Bennett, C J. The Privacy Advocates. P. 10

Her analysis suggests that privacy, framed in individualistic terms, is always on the defensive against arguments for the social benefits of surveillance. Privacy will always be in conflict with those social and collective issues, which tend to motivate general public and their representatives. We must, therefore, frame the question in social terms. Society is better off if individuals have higher levels of privacy.

Throughout the past century, many renowned experts have taken on the challenge of definition. They have achieved some more notable successes – complex as that archive may be. I would like to recap some of the more notable attempts.

I suspect the easiest prism through which to view all these definitions is to imagine a hypothetical employment situation. Apologies for the simplicity.

Let's say you are twenty-one years of age. it is your first year of work after university, but you are still living at home with anxious parents (who doubtless suspect that in your new "partying" environment, you will soon become a surprised parent, a drug addict or a criminal – or all three). They were always hugely supportive, but the current stress is more intense. It would have helped if your older sister hadn't been cautioned for possession of laughably bad-quality ecstasy.

The parents have become fixated on some of your mood changes. Plus that constant itch on your leg and the small lip rash. They want to know more. Sensible parents might have concluded that these symptoms are merely a result of work-related stress, but your folks have more lurid ideas. They are on your case at every opportunity, and even once (you suspect) searched your room.

How might the definitions of privacy work in your favour? This is of course, not a simple question. You will have a sort of Duty of Care to provide emotional support to your parents, but lines need to be drawn. It is predictable – though not in any way helpful – for them to invoke that old equation "If you live under our roof, you abide by our rules".

You could look back over 120 years for a response to this interrogation. In the 1890s, future U.S. Supreme Court Justice Louis Brandeis articulated a concept of privacy that urged that it was the individual's "right to be let alone." Brandeis argued that privacy was the most cherished of freedoms in a democracy, and he was concerned that it should be reflected in the Constitution.[48] That idea is a benchmark for privacy and permeates even the family space.

The Preamble to the Australian Privacy Charter echoes that position: "A free and democratic society requires respect for the autonomy of individuals, and limits on the power of both state and private organisations to intrude on that autonomy... Privacy is a key value which underpins human dignity and other key values such as freedom of association and freedom of speech. Privacy is a basic human right and the reasonable expectation of every person."[49]

The word "autonomy" arises routinely in such definitions.

At a more intimate level, Arnold Simmel argues, "The right to privacy asserts the sacredness of the person". He believes a violation of a person's privacy is a violation of their dignity, individualism and freedom, a view also reflected in the Australian Privacy Charter. This is a crucial perspective. It reflects the idea of "my body (and my psyche) is my temple".[50]

One of the most influential definitions in the past half century was coined by Alan Westin in his seminal 1967 work "Privacy and Freedom," in which he described privacy as the desire of people to choose freely under what circumstances and to what extent they will expose themselves, their attitude and their behavior to others.[51] Again, in our hypothetical scenario, that could be a crucial equation. Of course in the real world, there is inevitably a social contract involved. Certainly if this matter had been escalated to the level of a medical professional, one big question is the extent to which you might feel obliged to divulge areas of your life that you would probably prefer to remain private. And of course a doctor might advise that you are in some way "required" to divulge them because you might be "at risk to yourself or to others". This goes to the heart of the much ravaged principles of medical confidentiality. In that respect, Edward Bloustein defines privacy is an interest of the human personality. It protects the inviolate personality, the individual's

---

48 Warren, S and Brandeis, L. "The right to privacy", Harvard Law Review 4, 1890 pp 193- 220.
49 "The Australian Privacy Charter" (1994). published by the Australian Privacy Charter Group, Law School, University of New South Wales.
50 Nrold Stimmel. The fall of public space. 2001 https://www.sociologi.aau.dk/digitalAssets/210/210631_arbpapir-9.pdf
51 Westin, A. (1967). Privacy and Freedom. p.7.New York. Atheneum.

independence, dignity and integrity.[52]

"Dignity" is another word that permeates the definitions and the texts. In the above scenario, "dignity" is without doubt a key factor. Dignity is the inverse of embarrassment; threat or violation.

Ruth Gavison takes the analysis to another level in observing that there are three elements in privacy: secrecy, anonymity and solitude. It is a state which can be lost, whether through the choice of the person in that state, or through the action of another person.[53]

The Calcutt Committee in the UK was unable to find "a wholly satisfactory statutory definition of privacy." But the committee was satisfied that it would be possible to define it legally, and adopted this definition in its first report on privacy:

> *The right of the individual to be protected against intrusion into his personal life or affairs, or those of his family, by direct physical means or by publication of information.*[54]

From my own perspective, as a privacy advocate, the definition has to be at least as potent as the forces which oppose privacy. In 1996, the definition of my own choosing, and my own making, was as follows:

> *The right to privacy is the right to protect ourselves against intrusion by the outside world. It is the measure we use to set limits on the demands made upon us. It is the right we invoke to defend our personal freedom, our autonomy and our identity. It is the basis upon which we assess the balance of power between ourselves, and the world around us.*[55]

Power, autonomy and dignity sit at the heart of almost all of these definitions. This applied to my own work, even when I did not understand the word "privacy". For more than fifteen years after my campaigning escapades at school (which I recount elsewhere), I ended up running

---

52 Bloustein, E. (1964 Privacy as an Aspect of Human Dignity, [1964]. 39 New York U. L.R. 962 at 971

53 Gavison, R. Privacy and the Limits of Law, [1980] 89 Yale L.J. 421, at 428.

54 Report of the Committee on Privacy and Related Matters, Chairman David Calcutt QC, 1990, Cmnd. 1102, London: HMSO, page 7.

55 Davies, S. (1996) Big Brother : Britain's web of surveillance and the new technological order. Pan, London, (second edition).

campaigns all over the world. Workers' rights campaigns, drug law reform campaigns and land reform campaigns. At the core of many of those actions were the principles of autonomy and dignity. Those campaigns almost always focused on abuse of authority and the imbalance of power. These elements are all central to privacy, even though – in common with all my peers at the time – I still never used the word.

I'm curious about this dilemma. Privacy is an idea which has galvanised continents, but it is still passive. We don't have a Martin Luther King Jr in this field to find the right words. Yes, people describe their frustration about intrusion in terms of privacy, but is it just shorthand for something else? My own thinking is that the notion of privacy – as I discussed while recounting the Bingate campaign – represents four pillars of power: hypocrisy, secrecy, deception and unfairness. I asked some of my privacy colleagues for their thoughts.

The responses were interesting, not the least because not many had given this genesis a thought. I was surprised at how many resonated with my thoughts as a campaigning adolescent, fighting against unfairness and the imbalance of power.

Phil Booth, one of Britain's most influential campaigners, explained "privacy is the name of the field we're associated with; for me, this has always been part of a much bigger picture – namely, trying to ensure everyone is treated fairly and justly. Which requires, amongst other things, privacy – "the right from which other rights flow", especially informationally, and certainly in a society predicated upon data-under-information-processing – as a precondition; also stuff like not being assigned an official 'identity' or number (which tends to end with machetes, or in the ovens), or having your biometrics sucked into a giant Home Office-run database... "

Rikke Frank Jorgensen of the Danish Institute for Human rights explains: "To me the issue was always political – and always deeply embedded with power. Privacy for me has always been about setting limits to power – be it state or commercial power. Thus emphasising over and over again, that it's a fundamental premise for a free and open society – at both individual and societal level."

These reflections were mirrored by Katarzyna Szymielewicz from Poland's Panoptkon Foundation "Abuse of power and institutional hypocrisy played a big role in shaping my steps and determination to get involved in the fight against surveillance. It was not so much about privacy (as the end goal) but about 'opening the surveillance state' and questioning the dominating, fear-based narrative. I have seen (back then and still today) data protection and privacy used as a shield that we, as human beings, can use against oppressive state and other actors that try to control us."

Such thoughts underpin the concept of privacy. Those elements of power and deception are commonplace. They drive people to become advocates.

Chapter Three: The challenge of the technology environment

> *Is there such a thing as "high risk" technology, or is it just a matter of how we use ordinary technologies? Yes, there are many misused products in everyday use, but there are also systems that are deployed and sold specifically to repress populations. This has become a vast industry, controlled by Western nations. But what of the future? Is it possible to predict how far this will go? The answer is "possibly", and the prognosis is not good.*

It is tempting to dive straight into a discussion of the vast array of amazing new technologies that are shaping (or deforming) the world of privacy. There are now so many that any attempt to itemise them would be futile. And in some respects, the technologies themselves are secondary in importance to the trends that underlie them. These are the drivers that form the bedrock of nearly all tech developments.

Beyond the obvious aspects of the rapidly changing speed, capacity and diminished cost, there are a number of important dynamics to consider that affect nearly all forms of technology. Twenty – even thirty – years ago, many texts on privacy and technology identified three core trends that were driving the information society. I expanded a little on these in the first chapter.

The first is globalisation, which removes geographical limitations to the flow of data. The development of the Internet is perhaps the best known example of a global technology. The development of international technology standards is another.

Then there's convergence, which leads to the elimination of technological barriers between systems. Modern information systems are increasingly interoperable with other systems and can mutually exchange and process different forms of data. This is how, for example, techniques such as Entity Resolution can match data across a large number of previously isolated programmes.

And finally, there is multimedia – related closely to convergence. Multimedia fuses many forms of transmission and expression of data and images so that information gathered in a certain form can be easily translated into other forms.

These trends continue to drive us forward. And as you will know, the three intersect substantially, to the point where those categories are almost redundant. They do, however, provide a useful shorthand for how the world has changed.

By way of example, I mention later (in the chapter on visual surveillance) that CCTV is not merely a camera system any more. In the early days it was a fixed angle, single media system that connected a lens to an analogue recording device. Over the next few years the cameras were given mobility and could be moved around remotely. It also became possible to synch several cameras linked through a central monitoring location. Still, the technology was clunky, costly and inefficient. Hard-copy tapes were required, and authorities were overwhelmed when a search of the images was required. Automated motion detection was the next phase.

As the 1990s approached, the technology moved swiftly from analogue to digital, meaning that footage (to use that quaint analogue expression) could be quickly searched and interrogated. It became possible to store all images that were captured. With the development of high capacity communication, it was then also possible to quickly transmit those images to any authority that wanted them. Within a few years, the surveillance content was being broadcast in real time across the Internet. This trend began with fairly benign images of traffic spots and beach weather, but quickly moved on to crime scenes. As the price of surveillance technology plummeted, it became democratised as a game anyone can play.

This however wasn't just a change in technology; it was a change of "process". It was not a case of just adding another "bit" to the technological ecosystem. Manipulation, search and digital transmission went beyond the technology itself. A process means that the collection of technologies is greater than the sum of its parts.

This dynamic was never so evident as the period from the late 1990's, when digitisation fused with analysis software. This fusion ushered in an age when images could be interrogated and minutely scrutinised beyond any level of human capacity. Images could be "peeled back" to reveal behavioural and biometric aspects (biometrics relates to the physical characteristics of a person, such as face or gait). Interoperability of systems means that all these features can be combined into a national surveillance system. And soon we had drones to add to this equation.

The same applies to identity systems. There was a time when such objects stood alone as a technology of control. Now it is not just that cards contain chips and biometrics, but they are also merely the visible manifestation of a complex web of systems.

These trends make it almost impossible to speak of a single technology. There was a time when it was a simple matter to add CCTV to the growing list of potentially hostile technologies, but what happens when that classic technology fuses with images from camera phones? If images captured by ordinary citizens can be uploaded to an interface using geolocation and analysis software, it will be impossible to escape the net.

Another example of this process creep can be found with the telephone. Moving the landline phone system from analogue to digital presented some key challenges for campaigners. Before then, a telephone was just a telephone. Then, in the early 1990's, it all changed. The introduction of Caller Number Identification (or caller line identification, depending on which country you were in), opened up a substantial privacy threat. It was possible for anyone to see the number that was calling them – and in such cases that usually meant the person linked to that number).

The Electronic Privacy Information Center in the US spearheaded this issue, generating public awareness and forcing telephone companies to introduce a range of privacy safeguards that could provide some level of anonymity. US Congress intervened in this quest. However, digitisation provided a platform onto which could be loaded an infinite variety of new processes.

The convergence of data sources has also become a huge privacy issue. "Big Data" – the amalgamation and peeling back of a large number of disparate information sources to reveal data that are not readily visible – is one notable example.

Then there is the Elephant in the Room: Artificial Intelligence (AI).[56] The most potent definition I've encountered is from Stuart Russell and Peter Norving, which proposes that AI can be broken down into the following categories:

1) systems that think like humans;

2) systems that act like humans;

3) systems that think rationally; and

4) systems that act rationally.[57]

Most of us, perhaps unwittingly, have engaged with AI. One of the most notable examples is the mass deployment of "chatbots" which mimic human language and responses. These sit behind chat boxes in social media and commercial interfaces. They are also used increasingly at the level of voice interaction.[58]

Chatbots use a relatively simple code, but they now have the ability to fool an increasing number of people that they are actually human. Consider the following exchange that took place with a chatbot called "Eliza" that was programmed to ape a West Coast psychotherapist:

Woman: Men are all alike.
Eliza: In what way?
W: They're always bugging us about something or other.
E: Can you think of a specific example?
W: Well, my boyfriend made me come here.
E: Your boyfriend made you come here?
W: He says I'm depressed much of the time.
E: I am sorry to hear that you are depressed.

---

56 EPIC Artificial Intelligence page https://www.epic.org/algorithmic-transparency/

57 Quoted. in Committee on Technology, National Science and Technology Council, "Preparing for the Future of Artificial Intelligence" (Executive Office of the President of the United States, October 2016), 5, https://obamawhitehouse.archives.gov/sites/default/files/whitehouse_files/microsites/os tp/NSTC/ preparing_for_the_future_of_ai.pdf. Preparing for the Future of Artificial Intelligence.

58 Adams, T. The charge of the chatbots. How can you tell who's human online? The Observer. 18th November 2018. https://www.theguardian.com/technology/2018/nov/18/how-can-you-tell-who-is-human-online-chatbots

W: It's true. I am unhappy.

E: Do you think coming here will help you not to be unhappy?

W: I need some help, that much seems certain.

E: What would it mean to you if you got some help?

W: Perhaps I could learn to get along with my mother.

E: Tell me more about your family.[59]

That conversation took place in 1966. The technology has moved on considerably since that era, and now has true AI capability. Voice biometrics now make it possible for the machine at the other end of the line to mimic friends or employers.

Using such systems can result in the disclosure of vast amounts of sensitive personal information that is not covered by professional codes of confidentiality.

A recent study by Access Now concluded:

> *Many of the issues that arise in examinations of this area are not new, but they are greatly exacerbated by the scale, proliferation, and real-life impact that artificial intelligence facilitates. Because of this, the potential of artificial intelligence to both help and harm people is much greater than from technologies that came before.*[60]

Such reflections have been the motivation for EPIC to produce Universal Guidelines on AI.[61] This is an important step in the challenge to come to terms with one of the most complex and risky arenas of technology development.

Privacy regulators are struggling to deal with the possible implications of this process, but some have tried to be ahead of the curve. The UK Information Commissioner's Office published a report that made an effort to link AI to data protection.[62]

---

59 ibid

60 Human Rights in the age of Artificial Intelligence. (2018). Access Now.

61 Universal guidelines for artificial intelligence, 27th October 2018. Electronic Privacy Information Center. https://thepublicvoice.org/ai-universal-guidelines/

62 Big data, artificial intelligence, machine learning and data protection 20170904

So in summary, there are now processes that "link" data. There are processes that "fuse" data. There are processes that "interrogate" data and there are processes that create a superbrain over all the other processes.

There is a view commonly expressed by commerce and government that technology is neutral. "It's not the gadget; it's how it is used". In this respect, the vendors and users of surveillance and intrusion technologies are taking the line used by everyone from gun sellers to gambling machine manufacturers. I don't buy this argument. If such people are so worried about misuse of their "benign" systems they would hard-wire protections into them – but they rarely, if ever, do.

There are hundreds of surveillance technologies and techniques, but at the moment it is useful to focus mainly on the foundation parts that constitute them. It may be helpful to look at the next chapter on law, to see how these foundation stones are created.

A periodic approach to understanding surveillance

In 2013, while teaching at an Italian university, I attempted to create a model that might explain all the dimensions of surveillance. I ended up with a much truncated periodic table (otherwise known as the Elements Table).[63] You might remember the periodic tables from school – Helium, Hydrogen and so on. If you have ever seen the HBO series Breaking Bad, that table would have sprung instantly into your consciousness.

Version: 2.2 Information Commissioners Office. 2017.

63 'An exciting new periodic table reveals the elements of surveillance' The Privacy Surgeon, 12th November 2013 http://www.privacysurgeon.org/blog/incision/an-exciting-new-periodic-table-reveals-the-elements-of-surveillance/ (accessed July 5th 2018)

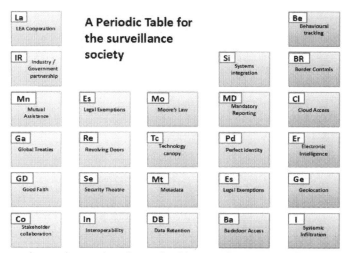

A Periodic Table for the surveillance society

La — LEA Cooperation				**Be** — Behavioural tracking
IR — Industry / Government partnership			**Si** — Systems integration	**BR** — Border Controls
Mn — Mutual Assistance	**Es** — Legal Exemptions	**Mo** — Moore's Law	**MD** — Mandatory Reporting	**Cl** — Cloud Access
Ga — Global Treaties	**Re** — Revolving Doors	**Tc** — Technology canopy	**Pd** — Perfect identity	**Er** — Electronic Intelligence
GD — Good Faith	**Se** — Security Theatre	**Mt** — Metadata	**Es** — Legal Exemptions	**Ge** — Geolocation
Co — Stakeholder collaboration	**In** — Interoperability	**DB** — Data Retention	**Ba** — Backdoor Access	**I** — Systemic Infiltration

For me, it was interesting that only thirteen of my twenty five elements related directly to technology. The remainder were to do with law, policy and social aspects.

If you judge the current privacy environment on the basis of media reporting of the past few years, you'd be excused for imagining that our panoptic situation is a compound of five elements: backdoor access to software (Ba), systemic infiltration (I), Metadata (Mt), global treaties (Ga) and industry/government partnership (Ir).

However, it is an unstable compound, that can react to sudden changes in the legal or political environment. The balance of the ingredients is too volatile. Stabilising elements are needed to resist public opposition. To fix this equation, three further elements are required: legal exemptions (Es), Interoperability (In) and Security Theatre (Se). (Security Theatre – a term coined by security guru Bruce Schneier – is the illusion of threat or the illusion of its resolution).

Now we have a seven-element compound that has the ability to neutralise most external influences. Global treaties create the foundation bond, industry/government cooperation provides the knowledge pathways, metadata is the raw elemental material, while interoperability (system compatibility) permits the free flow of material across sectors and organisations. These are elements that neither campaigners or the public can influence to any major extent.

Now, when you add two bonding elements – universal legal exemptions and security theatre – the result is a robust solution. Security theatre is the primary catalyst that combusts to create a false sense of urgency which in turn accelerates the formation of legal exemptions. In this reaction there is much vapour and heat. However the combination of exemptions and global treaties insulates this chemical activity. This results in the seventh element – systemic infiltration – becoming active, and indeed dominant. Edward Snowden made that ingredient quite apparent.

So now we have the raw surveillance compound. However its potency is limited. More elements are needed to ensure that there is a firm basis to ensure universality. The compound requires vast amounts of energy in the form of data and so Mandatory Reporting (Md) involving everything from financial transactions to health records provides a rich reserve of fuel. Data Retention (Db) and Geolocation (Ge), provide a potent double-bond that satisfies the needs of other elements.

Data flow is accelerated by institutional bonds such as LEA (La – Law Enforcement Agency) cooperation and Mutual Assistance (Mn) administrative assistance obligations. Meanwhile the Revolving Door (Re) between industry and government ensures that the compound's internal mixture is kept uniform and stable. Systems Integration (Si) becomes an efficient catalyst that with the right injection of security theatre enables a permanent state of growth for the Technology Canopy (Te).

I understand that this a somewhat cynical way of approaching the topic, but at least it simply illustrates the systematic way that our privacy has been attacked. I often wonder if somewhere in a government or corporate bunker this hasn't already been thought of – and of course converted into Newspeak.

Is it possible to identify all the high-risk technologies?

The short answer is "sort of". The Electronic Privacy Information Center provides an excellent reference list. However these technologies mutate and evolve, with older ones (such as CCTV, social media and mobile phones) becoming platforms for entire generations of new apps and gadgets.

I have spent several years publishing articles for my website, the Privacy Surgeon, and have tried to condense the spectrum of technologies as much as possible, primarily not to overwhelm the readers with endless tags. The index of actual technologies that I ended up with follows:

Biometrics, bodily privacy systems, border controls, cloud computing, communications surveillance, genetics, health systems, identity systems and social networks.

That's a riotously short list. In reality there are hundreds more, including countless apps, big data technology, data mining machinery, visual surveillance, Artificial Intelligence, GPS interception technologies, smart grids, smart roads, smart vehicles, drones, code breaking computers, stealth technology, cookies, keystroke loggers, geolocation and airport scanners.

There are some case studies that provide an interesting perspective on how feral technology development has become. Each of them underscores the risk that unfettered evolution can create extremely jagged edges for privacy.

The underbelly of location and tracking

The convergence of technologies and processes has given rise to some dangerous (and often relatively recent) threats to privacy. Among those is geolocation.

This process has become a vast commercial boon for apps developers. At its most basic level, such apps allow the user to find a local bar or shop – and of course to figure out the best way to a destination.

But the evolution of GPS and the smart-phone market has also spawned a macabre industry of surveillance apps designed to be covertly installed onto the cell phones of vulnerable employees, business associates, partners and children.

Products such as Flexispy[64] and Mobile Spy[65] – which by 2014 were allegedly used by hundreds of thousands of voyeurs – are chiefly marketed to paranoid parents and suspicious partners who want to invisibly monitor target phone activity – particularly real-time geolocation and call logs.

Such products are capable of allowing a third party to remotely view emails, messenger chats, text messages, phone contacts, memos, call logs and calendar appointments. as well as pictures, videos and music files saved in the phone. Many will allow subscribers to remotely listen in to voice conversations and view internet browsing history and saved bookmarks.

Indeed, the spy software has in the past few years extended its reach to Android tablets and iPads, opening up a significant new market and substantially increasing the threat to the privacy of millions of people.

These cross-platform apps can be loaded onto devices in about five minutes but generally require physical access to the target phone. Once installed the software can initiate alerts for the use of pre-set keywords in texts and emails, as well as entry or exit from designated locations (which one product describes as "Geo Fencing").

Regardless of the legal jurisdiction in which they are used, the apps have always been – at best – grossly unethical and perilous to trust. And recent product launches have moved the industry into outright violation of criminal law. A product called StealthGenie permits the covert interception and recording of voice calls as well as remote activation of the target device's microphone.

StealthGenie's terms and conditions include a bizarre requirement for obtaining the written consent of the target phone user – a condition that Professor Daniele Pica from Rome's John Cabot University describes as a blatant contradiction-in-terms, "The software uses default stealth mode but allegedly needs to be approved by the surveilled person. The latter contradicts the former. A question arises: is it stealth or is it transparent? Is this legal? Should it be legal? Regulators should move immediately to

---

64 This app may be he illegally helping people illegally spy on their spouses, Forbes. 22nd February 2017 https://www.forbes.com/sites/thomasbrewster/2017/02/22/flexispy-malware-spy-on-spouse-illegal-wiretap-act-offences/
65 Mobile Spy homepage http://www.mobile-spy.com/ (accessed 4th September 2018)

audit such services to preserve the dignity of people."[66]

The stealth nature of these apps flies in the face of efforts by parts of the mobile industry to ensure that active tracking software remains visible. GSMA, the international mobile industry association, has published apps guidance that includes recommendations on transparency.

Courts are, however, taking notice. A StealthGenie seller was fined half a million dollars in 2014 by a Virginia court and ordered to surrender the product's code[67].

US industry and government (generally) insists on maintaining a free market for intrusive apps. For example, a draft Code of Conduct published by the US National Telecommunications and Information Administration (NTIA) was condemned outright by privacy and consumer groups as a toothless mechanism that did little or nothing to improve transparency in the market.[68]

Gene Genie

Back in 2012, New Scientist reported[69] on a smartphone app that will allow you to carry around an encrypted copy of your genome. The magazine noted that with prices for DNA sequencing falling fast, this app may not be as futuristic as it sounds.

The app – named Genodroid[70] – was developed by a team led by Emiliano De Cristofaro at Xerox's PARC lab in Palo Alto, California. The team has been investigating how people might safely transport the personal information stored in their genome.

---

66   The world's most dangerous mobile phone spying app just moved into the tablet and iPad market; the Privacy Surgeon, http://www.privacysurgeon.org/blog/incision/the-worlds-most-dangerous -mobile-phone-spying-app-just-moved-into-the-tablet-and-ipad-market/ (accessed May 12th 2018)
67   Seller of StealthGenie Spyware app is fined $500,000. Engdaget. 1st December 2014 https://dl.acm.org/citation.cfm?id=2381980
68   Ferguson, T, 30th July 2013 http://www.mobileworldlive.com/ntia-app-code-of-conduct-attracts-criticism (accessed July 13th 2018)
69   Marks, P. New Scientist. Want to keep your genome safe? There's an app for that. London. 31st October 2012

The ability to keep our genetic profile in a pocket does present the potential to access a variety of personalised medicine services, such as a prescription for drugs tailored to our own genetic make-up, or – for more ordinary purposes – compare our ancestry with that of a friend.

"A digitised genome reveals a treasure trove of very personal data as well as information about your siblings and current or future progeny," De Cristofaro told New Scientist. "However, these wonderful advances and prospects are rife with serious privacy risks," he adds.

How right he is – and how refreshing for an app developer to sound the privacy alarm so early in the Venture Capital cycle.

The true "privacy problem" with nearly all information-based systems surfaces when a bespoke or single-purpose technology becomes a platform or a pipe designed for multiple purposes or even for universal application.

Take face recognition for example. When that biometric was confined to narrow functions in which the individual interacted on a time to time basis with a single system (say, a perimeter security system for a building) it remained a relatively harmless technology. There was little or no linkage or interoperability with other systems.

Then with the emergence of face.com, which created a face recognition "pipe" that fuelled platforms such as those in social networking, a whole new privacy dimension started to take shape. The capacity for universal use induced all the most aggressive privacy threats, fuelled by the loss of control by individuals.

The same applies with the genome app. While the technology remains under the control of its owner the privacy threats are limited (chaos protects privacy). Create a "platform" for universal usage and institutions start to demand compliance – and those same institutions start to share the data.

The developers have created a cryptographic base for the app, but the essential problem is that they see the world in terms of "good" and "bad" players. Good players have permission to access the code; bad players don't. This of course is a simplistic approach. Most people are likely to be concerned about third party access to their genome even if it is by a "good" player using the appropriate permissions.

Yes, the team is aware of the risks, but in creating the potential for universal use they will also create the gateway to a new market for genetic disclosure. That may be no bad thing, but limitations – technical limitations – need to be embedded right now. Legislative protections may be of little or no use.

Technology transfer and policy convergence

The macro-trends outlined above have had a particular effect on surveillance in developing nations. In the field of information and communications technology, the speed of policy convergence is compressed. Across the surveillance spectrum – wiretapping, personal ID systems, data mining, censorship or encryption controls – it is the West which invariably sets a proscriptive pace.[71]

Governments of developing nations rely on first world countries to supply them with technologies of surveillance such as digital wiretapping equipment, deciphering equipment, scanners, bugs, tracking equipment and computer intercept systems. The transfer of surveillance technology from first to third world is now a lucrative sideline for the arms industry.[72] [73]

According to a 1997 report entitled 'Assessing the Technologies of Political Control' commissioned by the European Parliament's Civil Liberties Committee and undertaken by the European Commission's Science and Technology Options Assessment office (STOA),[74] much of this technology is used to track the activities of dissidents, human rights

71 Davies, S and Hosein, I. (1998). Liberty on the Line in Liberating Cyberspace, Pluto Press, London.
72 Big Brother Incorporated, Privacy International site: www.privacyinternational.org (accessed May 12th 2018)
73 Privacy International has more recently published a comprehensive analysis of the global trade in surveillance technologies; "The Global Surveillance Industry", July 2016 https://privacyintyqcroe.onion/sites/default/files/2017-12/global_surveillance_0.pdf (accessed July 19th 2018)
74 Published by Science and Technology Options Assessment (STOA). Ref : project no. IV/STOA/RSCH/LP/politicon.1

activists, journalists, student leaders, minorities, trade union leaders, and political opponents. The report concludes that such technologies (which it describes as "new surveillance technology") can exert a powerful "chill effect" on those who "might wish to take a dissenting view and few will risk exercising their right to democratic protest". Large scale ID systems are also useful for monitoring larger sectors of the population. As Privacy International has observed, "In the absence of meaningful legal or constitutional protections, such technology is inimical to democratic reform. It can certainly prove fatal to anyone 'of interest' to a regime."[75]

Government and citizen alike may benefit from the plethora of IT schemes being implemented by the private and public sectors. "Smart card" projects in which client information is placed on a chip in a card may streamline complex transactions. The Internet will revolutionise access to basic information on government services. Encryption can provide security and privacy for all parties.

However, these initiatives will require a bold, forward looking legislative framework. Whether governments can deliver this framework will depend on their willingness to listen to the pulse of the emerging global digital economy and to recognise the need for strong protection of privacy.

It's not just the technology – it's how you use it

It is natural to view technology as a polemic. There are "bad" technologies used by "bad" people and agencies. Then there are "good" technologies used by, well, you and I.

If only it were so simple. As technology moves to a closer symmetry with our mind, our behaviour and our emotions, the definitions become infinitely more complex – and the repercussions become even more complex.

Consider the "like" function in social media. Is "like" a technology or a

---

75 Big Brother Incorporated; report by Privacy International, 1995.

technique? Is it a process in its own right, or is it inseparable from the rest of the social media platform? When does a line of code become a "feature", and at what point should it be regarded as a "technology"? And whatever name you give it, where does it sit on a scale of "badness"? Whatever the answer, few people would regard it as a dangerous technology (or function). How could it ever be compared to, say, mobile phone interception equipment?

The answer is not so cut and dried. Take the case of a colleague of mine, Simon Moores. Police in the southern England borough of Kent spent months in 2014 considering whether to lay criminal charges against him for "liking" the Facebook post of a colleague. The move signalled a bizarre twist in British policing from extending criminal evidence from content to context. This has the potential to create a serious chilling effect on free expression, but also has unexpected privacy consequences.

This episode was the latest turn in a heated dispute over a Tesco supermarket development in the town of Margate. Tory councillors Simon Moores, Mick Tomlinson and an unnamed colleague were questioned under caution by police over accusations of conspiracy to harass an opponent of the development.

Moores, who can best be described as a pacifist, was stunned by the allegation, but was even more surprised when police started using anonymous comments, made on his popular Thanet Life blog, under a statement on the development from local MP, Sir Roger Gale, to support the allegation.

However the most disquieting aspect of the police action was that the unnamed councillor also faced criminal charges for doing no more than "liking" a Facebook post of the former mayor of Margate, pointing out that an objector's artist's impression of the proposed Tesco development was in the wrong place, and of the wrong size. The development's opponent claimed this was "offensive" to her, and complained she was the subject of criminal harassment by the three prominent local councillors.

The police action could signal an extension of the traditional ambit of material evidence. This could mean that any public interaction with a post could expose a third party to the risk of prosecution without so much as publishing a single word.

There have been cases where Twitter users have been prosecuted for publishing offensive or threatening tweets, and one defence argument has been that Twitter, for some people, is a stream of consciousness rather than a systematic and methodical act of malicious publication. In some respects these grounds sit somewhere between suspended reality and temporary insanity.

"Likes" are in the same league, but are fundamentally different, both in meaning and context. They are transient – often instinctive – reflections of a mood or reaction. Prosecuting a "like" is perilously close to Thought Policing. A parallel in conventional policing might be to prosecute someone for groaning or smiling.

The Margate episode is not a precedent. Another case occurred in 2012, when an Indian woman was arrested and charged for liking a post criticising public sentiment over the death of a politician. The prosecution of "likes" is even more prevalent in less democratic countries. In 2014, an Egyptian man was arrested after liking Mossad's Facebook page.[76]

The case involving Moores et al is, however, one of the rare occasions in the democratic world that the 'act' of liking a post has been materially used by police. It entails a great number of implications for online free expression. It also presents a number of interesting legal challenges.

For example, a landmark 2013 first amendment decision by the 4th Circuit Court of Appeals case determined that the act of expressing interest on Facebook is the "internet equivalent of displaying a political sign in one's front yard, which the Supreme Court has held is substantive speech."[77]

Meanwhile, the lower court in that case had taken the opposite view, ruling that "liking a Facebook page is insufficient speech to merit constitutional protection," because it does not "involve actual statements."

Chief Judge William B. Traxler Jr., writing for a three-judge panel of the Fourth Circuit, said no such distinction existed.

---

76 Yasser Okbi, 16th March 2010 http://www.jpost.com/Middle-East/Egypt-arrests-Israel-lover-for-Star-of-David-tattoo-contacting-Israelis-on-Facebook-345517 (accessed August 12th 2018)

77 Palazzolo, J. 18th September 2013 The Wall Street Journal. http://blogs.wsj.com/law/2013/09/18/court-facebook-like-is-protected-by-the-first-amendment/ (accessed July 13th 2018)

> *On the most basic level, clicking on the 'like'*
> *button literally causes to be published the*
> *statement that the User 'likes' something,*
> *which is itself a substantive statement.*

The reason I have decided to go on at some length about this matter is that we are witnessing the emergence of techniques that can easily harvest and analyse likes, thumbs-up, thumbs-down, scowls, emoticons and any other form of non-alphanumeric engagement. It is entirely possible that in a matter of years, such technologies will be regarded as deeply hostile to privacy. The key question is when – and how – we draw the line.

The (almost) hopeless task of predicting the future of technology

It is a drizzly November day in 2049. Hello from the future.

I'm sending this message in the hope that you can learn from some of the choices that our ancestors made in the early 21st century, the period in which you are now living.

This is what life could be for your children and grandchildren. Maybe it will give pause for thought about why we should think carefully about the path we took.

In many respects, this is an exciting and beautiful period of human history – the bountiful horizon of information.

But for some of us, this is also a deeply distressing world. Technology feels like a living organism that wraps tightly around us, enveloping every second of our day, everywhere we go. it is not meant to be hostile, just helpful. However there is no space left.

Nothing is simple any more. Almost every item you buy has sensor technology that interfaces with something else. None of us can remember the last time we bought a frying pan or a toaster that wasn't connected by default into the electronic ecosystem. These sensors are locked through your identity into the mobile spectrum, ensuring that your safety is protected in the event of overheating or misuse. If you manage to switch off this interface for "critical" devices like hot water systems or kitchen ovens, your home insurance protection is eliminated.

If you have children, you are expected to exploit every connection possible. Failing to do so makes you a bad parent. The media remind us of this expectation every day through a litany of horror stories of children who drank out-of-date milk or played with a cat that wasn't authorised for contact. Health and safety control has become omnipresent. Yes, even perishable food packaging now has sensors that alert you to the use-by date and possible health risks – whether you want the information or not.

We learned that this technology was once called "The Internet of Things", but it is now so commonplace that it has no name. it is just a fact of life that interlaces everything. The chips at the centre of this empire of technology are now as cheap as a few grains of rice. Data Corp ordered three billion of them the other day, for less than the price of a nice yacht – which, by the way – all the tech executives seem to own these days.

The most intricate interface involves "high risk" activities such as recreational drugs, drinking, exercise, sports, and even some forms of sex. In all such matters, there's a legal obligation to link the items being used directly to the identity of the individual. In some countries you can no longer buy a bottle of whisky without its sensor being linked to your identity, and then – through the mobile spectrum – to your personal profile. It transmits the volume left in the bottle, the speed of consumption and a dozen other factors to your profile. If, for example, such items come into prolonged contact with any other item registered to a child, authorities might be alerted. Interference with the data is, in some cases, a criminal offence. The technology is fit for purpose only some of the time, but still enough of the time to make it a profound irritant. Hackers have marvelously subverted it.

Because driving is generally considered a "high risk" activity, we long ago gave up any idea of the "open road". There was a time when a person could get into a vehicle, and experience freedom. Now every movement – on the road and off – is minutely analysed and in many cases is linked to your profile of interactions with other high risk activities (such as the whisky bottle). All vehicles – even bicycles – have become surveillance devices that continually analyse and transmit data. Indeed many common items are manufactured as continuous surveillance devices, including almost all doors and windows, items of clothing, road surfaces and rooftops.

We once imagined that all this communication between people and things – and between things and things – could happen anonymously. And there was a brief period when such privacy was actually possible. If you bought a microwave device, there was a time when it wasn't necessary to link its vast output of data to your mobile network or your identity. That idea, however, never really took off. Now the ecosystem knows what you cook, when you cook, how you cook – together with all the dangers and variations in those patterns. it is all about convenience, safety and saving money.

In the 20th century, when people spoke to each other on the landline telephone they asked, "How are you?" Later, with mobile devices, it became, "Where are you?" Now it is, "What are you?" And the "what" is crucial. There are over nine billion people on the planet, and a billion of the poorest have invested all their money in technology to scam the other nine tenths. The only currency now is the credibility you acquire from your digital persona, and there are many intermediaries out there that provide automated references.

The early 21st century was focused on the danger of "smart grids" controlled by the utility companies, but critics rarely imagined that the real threat wasn't a grid, as much as the fine-lace surveillance of a hundred billion appliances.

For some of us, the most unsettling feature of our life these days is the fact that many people openly publish this information, not just to their own networks, but to the world at large. Full disclosure has become the accepted way to validate your character and integrity. And full disclosure is also the best way to achieve credibility with potential employers, future friends, insurers, banks, schools and commercial organisations. Indeed for many people, it is almost impossible now to build social and commercial relationships if people fail to disclose the most intimate details of private life. Around a tenth of all news media coverage is horror stories of rogue employees, romantic encounters that went wrong or tenants who skipped their rent. Integrity – or the image of integrity – is now the common currency.

Until a few years ago law enforcement and security agencies used to pay lip service to limiting their access to this information. But as the spectrum of data increased, that effort became too much trouble. In any event, the voluntary disclosure of so much information about so many people gave authorities free rein to do as they pleased with the information.

Now the world just accepts that police can see anything they choose to see. After all, parents who expose their children to high risk activities deserve all they get. And there's a public expectation that everyone from teachers and doctors to investors and even shopkeepers should be fully open about their lives.

People of course don't know what is being viewed by authorities, only that everything could potentially be seen. Yes, there are shades of '1984' (Nineteen Eighty-Four). We are all on our best behaviour. Interacting with police is now a terrifying prospect for anyone who has acted against the public interest.

It is not all bad. Wealthy societies are certainly safer and more orderly now, but they have also been pacified. For most people, this feels like a good development. But something is missing, and you sometimes see it expressed publicly. The idea that people could have freedom to do as they please and control what is known about them has almost disappeared. Of course there are those who try to go off the grid (known as "going feral"), but those people are excluded from most mainstream activities. Maybe they like it that way.

They used to call this idea "privacy", but there's little room for that idea in an era in which we spend our time figuring how to upload more data rather than less. For most people, to think otherwise was a luxury that applied in a different age.

* * * * *

Is this prediction over the top? Quite possibly but consider what is at stake. The partnership between humans and information technology is in its infancy, but already there are huge challenges for the protection of privacy. Ahead of us is the fusion of our digital personas with the machinery of commerce. We are only just beginning to explore a future of ubiquitous and ambient computing in which we become enmeshed in a technological ecosystem – the fusion of flesh and machine. The consequences for privacy cannot easily be overstated.

Gerald Santucci, formerly of the European Commission and who was responsible for advising policy on such matters, observes: "The issue… is the upcoming reality that smart objects endowed with intelligence and unprecedented self-configuring and self-healing capabilities will make choices for us or on our behalf. it is not just more data that will be generated, it is new kinds of data, i.e. data sensed by humans' artefacts and processed by the IT systems." [78]

This could well amount to a dystopia. The problem is that activism has become so fragmented and specialised these days that is hard to find the capacity to oppose such technologies. The temptation is simply to try having them regulated. That strategy rarely works. As I discuss elsewhere, there are limits to the effectiveness of regulation and we may be about to reach that threshold within the next decade.

The 2049 scenario above is not that far-fetched when you consider the inverse. If we travel back in time for a similar duration – thirty-one years – we arrive at 1987. It would have been impossible then to imagine the technological world in which we now live. Could most people even begin to conceive of the ubiquity of technology or the omnipresence of information? The mobile phone was still a magical mystery, there was almost no Internet and home computers were clunky items that – at best – operated off a twin floppy disk drive. I recall writing my first book in 1984, on the subject of preservation of historical sites. I used a typewriter in combination with thousands of sheets of "copy paper", which was the medium employed by journalists to manually move text around. The task of identifying a single paragraph was mammoth. None of us could have imagined a time – even though that time was just around the corner – when all those words could be located on a single document, within which a phrase could be found in a matter of a second.

Even George Orwell remarked that the world he described in '1984' (Ninety Eighty-Four) was not a prediction of the future: it was just one of

---

78 European Commission official warns that new thinking is needed for the future of Privacy, The Privacy Surgeon, 18th September 2013
http://www.privacysurgeon.org/blog/incision/european-commission-official-warns-that-new-thinking-is-needed-for-the-future-of-privacy/ (accessed February 12th 2018)

several scenarios.

Indeed, the longer term implications of our current trajectory are anyone's guess. Humans have always been hopeless at predicting the future. Indeed, if the past teaches us just one lesson, it is never to trust fortune tellers. Long range forecasts are overwhelmingly wrong. The few that endure do so, invariably, through good luck, or the simple law of averages. Or, as Arthur C Clarke put it, "The future is not what it used to be".[79]

In 1948, the founder of IBM demonstrated his visionary prowess by predicting that as many as twelve companies might someday have their own computers. According to the May 1967 edition of Popular Science, 75 per cent of all US college graduates would go, within a decade, into jobs in the computer industry. Little wonder then that we no longer fear the future. The prophets have let us down so often that we are cynical – and largely optimistic.

Nevertheless, many scientists and researchers are happy to dip their toe in the waters of the future, even if the stench from a millennium of dead prophecies has made everyone nervous. Most people now generally agree that the margin of viability in prophecy appears to be ten years.

John Naisbitt,[80] for example, wrote a magnificent best-seller in 1982 called 'Megatrends', in which he used complex research methods to identify forces which would shape our destiny. The book was widely viewed as a masterly study on the future, and for some years it seemed to be right on target. Twelve years later, mysteriously, his predictions started to go off the rails.

Naisbitt went for the Big Picture. He argued, for example, that short term thinking would become long term thinking, yet a world recession created business and political practices that reversed this. He predicted that centralisation would yield to de-centralisation – yet throughout the world, a new era of predatory corporate practices helped to kill this hope. As soon as a trend emerges, it instantly throws open a range of new forces that mutate it. The irony in long term forecasting of humans is that people deliberately go against the grain.

---

79 See https://ldsmag.com/the-future-isnt-what-it-used-to-be/ for a discussion of this theme.
80 Wikipedia entry for John Naisbitt https://en.wikipedia.org/wiki/John_Naisbitt

Closer to home, a consortium of high profile British organisations joined forces in 1994[81] to calculate what life would be like in the future. Recognising the fallibility of long range forecasting, they decided to opt for the safe bet of a five year prediction. Their project – 'Wiring Whitehall' – was a hard-nosed probe into the sort of technology that was likely to be in use by 1999, and the sort of society it was likely to create. The report makes interesting reading. Some of its predictions are optimistic: crime would be lessened, government would be more efficient, and people would have access to a vast range of services and information. Indeed, such was the outcome.

A decade after Naisbitt, in 1992, I myself wrote a privacy book that attempted to predict the future in ten to fifteen years. In some respects I got it right – projections of home shopping, mobile phones, smart cards and health technology – but in others, I was an abject failure.

> *For the technologically literate generation, the next ten years are going to be good ones.*
>
> *A top-of-the-range personal computer will, for example, most likely have the power of a basic present day military research system. It is likely that you will be operating your computer through voice recognition. Keyboards will be largely redundant. People will find more satisfying uses for their hands. A new generation of software will transcribe the human voice at the rate of 100 words a minute. The 'tuning' process will be fine enough to produce an accuracy just slightly worse than the average professional typist. Instant language translation using artificial intelligence will be in general use. The barrier of language will be removed.[82]*

Most of those predictions hardly worked out. Language translation, yes, but as for the rest the prophecies were on a very unstable path.

---

81 Cited in Davies, S. (1992). Big Brother: Australia's web of surveillance and the new technological order; Simon & Schuster, Sydney.
82 Davies, S. "Big Brother: Australia's web of surveillance and the new technological order; Simon & Schuster, Sydney, 1992

How about this one?

> *Powerful Virtual Reality (VR) systems will be*
> *commonplace, though they will then be cheap*
> *enough to suit the pocket of most households,*
> *and spectacular enough to actually deserve*
> *the name "virtual reality". Sensual and*
> *erotic VR will be extremely popular. Used in*
> *combination with designer drugs, it will*
> *provide an unprecedented form of recreation*
> *that makes computer games and television*
> *insipid and obsolete.*

I do know some people who live that sort of existence, but I fail to see the demise of computer games and television.

And finally, this hilarious bombshell:

> *The consensus among experts is that*
> *computer technology will have reached the*
> *point of total compatibility. Virtually all*
> *machines will be able to talk with each other.*
> *Around two hundred million people*
> *worldwide will be connected to the*
> *worldwide 'web' of computers, the Internet,*
> *which by the year 2005 will be so complex*
> *that one and two year university courses will*
> *be offered to help people find their way*
> *around the system.*

I rest my case.

Chapter Four: A brief legal primer

What are the elements of privacy? How do we analyse it and what does it "mean"? More important, how do we seek protection? Law provides some answers, but not all of them. After centuries of privacy evolution – some of which is covered here – there have been many efforts to give us some models of protection, including independent regulators, but the question is whether they are feasible. The key issue is whether law in itself is a sustainable equation in an era when information has become feral.

When I started lecturing on Privacy and Data Protection in the early 1990's, the legal dimension of the topic – even in that era – was daunting. There were few courses in the world that could provide inspiration. Even then, there was a complex interaction of international and domestic laws. There were sectoral laws and a vast web of treaties and conventions. Add to this the complexity of the growing fusion between privacy law and the laws of competition and consumer protection. And Europe was on the cusp of creating the world's most influential and wide-ranging privacy law. To some extent, we were sailing in unchartered territory.

There is no doubt that the laws governing privacy can be confusing – even for legal professionals. They are in a constant state of flux, even though their core principles remain immutable. Although there is a growing consensus about how these laws should be constructed, there is still a stark variance in the way some countries have gone about the task.

The trend, however, is very much alive. Almost every major country now has a privacy law (even China has adopted laws to protect financial information but has also more recently adopted more broad ranging laws[83]). The increasing sophistication of information technology with its

---

83   Where are we now with data protection in China. Lexology. 13th September 2018.

capacity to collect, analyse and disseminate information on individuals has introduced a sense of urgency to the demand for legislation. Furthermore, new developments in medical research and care, telecommunications, advanced transportation systems and financial transfers have dramatically increased the level of information generated by each individual. Computers linked together by high speed networks with advanced processing systems can create comprehensive dossiers on any person without the need for a single central computer system. New technologies developed by the defence industry are spreading into law enforcement, civilian agencies and private companies.

According to opinion polls over the past twenty years, concern over privacy violations is now greater than at any time in recent history.[84] Uniformly, populations throughout the world express fears about encroachment on privacy, prompting an unprecedented number of nations to pass laws that specifically protect the privacy of their citizens.

For at least two decades it has been common wisdom that the power, capacity and speed of information technology is accelerating rapidly. The extent of privacy invasion – or certainly the potential to invade privacy – increases correspondingly. Legislation is one way to provide protections.

I realise that not everyone reading this is a lawyer (and neither am I), so it could be useful at this stage to take a brief look at the foundation for privacy governance. I'll keep this as uncomplicated as possible, but it is important to gain an insight into how we are protected (and of course, how we are often not protected).

Starting at the macro level, privacy is a fundamental human right recognised in many international instruments: the UN Declaration of Human Rights, the European Convention on Human Rights, the International Covenant on Civil and Political Rights, and in many other treaties. They assert that privacy underpins human dignity and other key values, such as freedom of association and freedom of speech. These documents have helped build privacy into one of the most important human rights issues of the modern age.

---

https://www.lexology.com/library/detail.aspx?g=dbe04c03-7990-4e0d-8368-e0170637de08

84 Davies, S. "Re-engineering the right to privacy: how privacy has been transformed from a right to a commodity", in Agre and Rotenberg (ed) "Technology and Privacy : the new landscape", MIT Press, 1997 p.143.

Those instruments, together with privacy principles adopted by the Organisation for Economic Cooperation and Development (OECD) and the Council of Europe, have formed the foundation for the laws of many countries. In recent times there have been numerous other instruments such as the Madrid Declaration, sponsored by the Electronic Privacy Information Center.[85]

For most nations, the enactment of protections is a voluntary matter, whereas, in Europe, the 2018 General Data Protection Regulation (GDPR) not only requires all EU member states to adopt strong privacy laws, but also requires countries it does business with to do the same.

To confuse matters even more for the uninitiated, Europe and several other regions use the expression "data protection" instead of privacy. Data protection protects people by protecting their data, but those laws are in some ways a subset of the larger privacy domain. More on that shortly.

Nearly every country in the world recognises a right of privacy explicitly in its Constitution. Australia is a notable exception. At a minimum, these provisions include rights of inviolability of the home and secrecy of communications (echoing the wording of the international texts). Most recently-written Constitutions such as those of South Africa and Hungary include specific rights to access and control one's personal information.

In many of the countries where privacy is not explicitly recognised in the Constitution, such as the United States, Ireland and (until recently) India, the courts have found that right in other provisions.

This trend began in the early 1970s, when countries began adopting broad laws intended to protect individual privacy. Throughout the world, there is a general movement towards the adoption of comprehensive privacy laws that set a framework for protection. Most of these laws are based – as previously mentioned – on the models introduced by the OECD and the Council of Europe.

Europe's legislation – and the requirement for trading partners to have the same – has resulted in a wave of legislation, with many dozens of countries now having data protection or information privacy laws.

---

85 Madrid Declaration. 3ʳᵈ November 2009. Electronic Privacy Information Center. https://thepublicvoice.org/madrid-declaration/ (accessed 4ᵗʰ November 2018)

Around forty are in the process of enacting legislation.[86]

What are the different elements of privacy?

it is useful – though less so in the legal context – to conceive of privacy as four intersecting spheres. This is the traditional model of explaining the topic, though as we'll discuss later, it is increasingly theoretical:

- **Information Privacy**, which involves the establishment of rules governing the collection and handling of personal data such as credit information and medical records;

- **Bodily privacy**, which concerns the protection of people's physical selves against invasive procedures such as drug testing, airport scanners and cavity searches;

- **Privacy of communications,** which covers the security and privacy of mail, telephones, email and other forms of communication; and

- **Territorial privacy**, which concerns the setting of limits on intrusion into the domestic and other environments such as the workplace or public spaces.[87]

This model worked well for a couple of decades, but the emergence of the digital world caused a meltdown of the categories. Is social media communications privacy or information privacy? Is the use by law enforcement authorities of infrared technology to covertly inspect homes information privacy or territorial privacy? Almost every process these days rests on a digital platform. In other words, data.

---

86 Banisar, D. National Comprehensive Data Protection/Privacy Laws and Bills 2018', available at: https://papers.ssrn.com/sol3/papers.cfm?abstract_id=1951416 (last revised 25 Jan 2018)
87 Banisar, D and Davies S. (1999). Privacy and Human Rights. Washington DC. Electronic Privacy Information Center

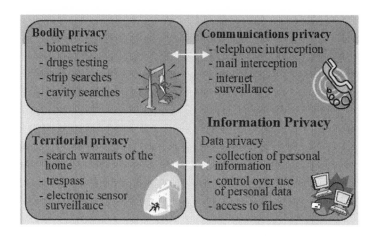

This is where data protection comes into play. This legal structure sets out a series of principles that create comprehensive protection across almost all domains of privacy.

The expression of data protection in various declarations and laws varies only by degrees. All require that personal information must be:

- obtained fairly and lawfully;
- used only for the original specified purpose;
- adequate, relevant and not excessive to purpose;
- accurate and up to date; and
- destroyed after its purpose is completed.

There are also other principles, such as the right to view your information and the right to have it corrected.

I hunted around for a simple, solid and articulate legal analysis of privacy. There are many, but I could find few more easily digestible than a report written by David Banisar that I co-authored in 1998, for the Global Internet Liberty Campaign (GILC). Some of its conclusions are outlined elsewhere in this chapter. That report was the predecessor to the Privacy & Human Rights reports, published annually by the Electronic Privacy Information Center (EPIC).

Those reports, regrettably, came to an end when they became so huge that they could best be described as ship's ballast! The 1999 edition[88] was a

---

88   ibid https://www.epic.org/bookstore/phr1999/

modest 167 pages. By 2005,[89] the report had ballooned to 1,151 pages, and showed no signs of atrophy. We figured, based on that trajectory, that by 2015 the guide would reach around 4,000 pages.

Nonetheless, the reports have stood the test of time, and their words are as meaningful now, as they were then. In 2018, Privacy International also published an excellent handbook on data protection policy, which explains all the key elements.[90]

One howling question is whether these laws actually make a difference. I address this at the end of this chapter. The brief answer is; they do, but there are vast gaps and shortcomings which may become even more pronounced as the years go by (see the following chapter on protections).

Even with the adoption of legal and other protections, violations of privacy remain a concern. In many countries, laws have not kept up with the technology, leaving significant gaps in protections. In some places, law enforcement and intelligence agencies have been given significant exemptions. Finally, in the absence of adequate oversight and enforcement, the mere presence of a law will not provide adequate protection. It may be merely cosmetic.

There are widespread violations of laws relating to surveillance of communications, even in the most democratic of countries. The U.S. State Department's annual review of human rights violations – even twenty years ago – found that over 90 countries engage in illegally monitoring the communications of political opponents, human rights workers, journalists and labour organizers (ironic, given the revelations of Edward Snowden). In France, a government commission estimated in 1996 that there were over 100,000 wiretaps conducted by private parties, many on behalf of government agencies. In Japan, police were fined 2.5 million yen for illegally wiretapping members of the Communist party.

Police services, even in countries with strong privacy laws, still maintain extensive files on citizens not accused or even suspected of any crime.

Companies regularly flout the laws, collecting and disseminating personal information. In the United States, even with the long-standing existence

---

89 Privacy & Human Rights (2005). https://www.epic.org/bookstore/phr2005/default.html
90 The Keys to Data Protection, Privacy International
https://privacyintyqcroe.onion/sites/default/files/2018-
09/Data%20Protection%20COMPLETE.pdf (accessed October 29th 2018)

of a law on consumer credit information, companies still make extensive use of such information for marketing purposes.

The list goes on at depressing length. Having said that, there is enough firepower both in the regulatory sector and the media to shame companies or to extensively fine them. The GDPR empowers privacy authorities to penalise companies to the extent of tens of millions of euros – possibly more. Whether there is a willingness to do so is another question.

Models of privacy protection

There are currently a number of major models for privacy protection and in some countries, several models are used simultaneously.

The regulatory model, as described in more detail in the following chapter, has been adopted by Europe, Australia, Hong Kong, New Zealand, Central and Eastern Europe and Canada – among many others. It is that of a *public official* who enforces a comprehensive data protection law. This official, known variously as a Commissioner, Ombudsman or Registrar, monitors compliance with the law and conducts investigations into alleged breaches. In some cases, the official can penalise an offender through an administrative process leading to a monetary fine or other demand. The official is also responsible for public education and international liaison in data protection and data transfer.

This is the preferred model for most countries adopting data protection law. It is also the model favoured by Europe, to ensure compliance with its new data protection regime. However, the powers of the commissions vary greatly, and many report a serious lack of resources to adequately enforce the laws.

Some countries such as the United States have avoided general data protection rules in favour of specific *sectoral laws* governing, for example, video rental records and financial privacy. In such cases, enforcement is achieved through a range of mechanisms. The problem with this approach is that it requires that new legislation be introduced with each new technology, so protections frequently lag behind. The lack of legal protections for genetic information in the U.S. is a striking example of its limitations. In other countries, sectoral laws are used to compliment comprehensive legislation by providing more detailed protections for certain categories of information, such as police files or consumer credit records.

In the past, there were some stark differences in the way Europeans deal with privacy, in contrast to the US approach. Daintry Duffy, writing in 2003 for CSO Magazine, described the difference as follows:

> *Where privacy is concerned, Americans distrust their government. But they'll gladly hand over their personal information to a corporation to get a deal on their groceries. Europeans, on the other hand, will give their government extremely broad surveillance powers, but they largely forbid private enterprise from accessing any personal data without their express written consent. In the corporate security world, this has translated into an ideological disconnect: U.S. executives think Europeans are missing the marketing opportunity personal data provides, and the Europeans, by and large, see their American counterparts as fast and loose, callous even, when it comes to their citizens' privacy.* [91]

This divide is slowly closing. US consumers are far warier now of corporate intrusion. A litany of major data breaches and privacy failures by major companies has changed the way Americans view the corporate sector. Meanwhile data protection and various court rulings are creating a small impact on the way governments handle information in Europe. Security services, however, appear largely exempt from this trend.

---

91   Duffy, D. "Simon Davies: Privacy's New Image", CSO Magazine, 1st August 2003 https://www.csoonline.com/article/2116256/privacy/simon-davies--privacy-s-new-image.html (accessed August 12th 2018)

The right to privacy

Privacy has roots deep in history. The Bible has numerous references to privacy.[92] There was also substantive protection of privacy in early Hebrew culture, Classical Greece and ancient China.[93] These protections mostly focused on the right to solitude.

In the modern context, privacy can be defined as a fundamental (though not an absolute) human right. Freedom from torture, for example, is an absolute right. The law of privacy can be traced as far back as 1361, when the Justices of the Peace Act in England provided for the arrest of peeping toms and eavesdroppers.[94] In 1765, Lord Camden, striking down a warrant to enter a house and seize papers wrote, "We can safely say there is no law in this country to justify the defendants in what they have done; if there was, it would destroy all the comforts of society, for papers are often the dearest property any man can have."[95]

Parliamentarian William Pitt wrote, "The poorest man may in his cottage bid defiance to all the force of the Crown. It may be frail; its roof may shake; the wind may blow though it; the storms may enter; the rain may enter – but the King of England cannot enter; all his forces dare not cross the threshold of the ruined tenement."

Various countries developed specific protections for privacy in the centuries that followed. In 1776, the Swedish Parliament enacted the "Access to Public Records Act" which required that all government-held information be used for legitimate purposes. In 1792, the French Declaration of the Rights of Man and the Citizen declared that private property was inviolable and sacred. And France prohibited the publication of private facts and set stiff fines in 1858.[96] As mentioned above, in 1890, American lawyers Samuel Warren and Louis Brandeis wrote a seminal piece on the right to privacy as a tort action describing privacy as "the right to be let alone."[97]

---

92   Hixson, R. Privacy in a Public Society: Human Rights in Conflict 3 (1987). See Barrington Moore, Privacy: Studies in Social and Cultural History (1984).
93   ibid. at 5.
94   James Michael, p.15
95   Entick v. Carrington, 1558-1774 All E.R. Rep. 45.
96   The Rachel affaire. Judgment of June 16, 1858, Trib. pr. inst. de la Seine, 1858 D.P. III 62. See Jeanne M. Hauch, Protecting Private Facts in France: The Warren & Brandeis Tort is Alive and Well and Flourishing in Paris, 68 Tul. L. Rev. 1219 (May 1994).
97   Warren and Brandeis, *The Right to Privacy*, 4 Harvard L.R. 193 (1890).

The present privacy benchmark at an international level can be found in the 1948 Universal Declaration of Human Rights, which specifically protects territorial and communications privacy. Article 12 states:

"No-one should be subjected to arbitrary interference with his privacy, family, home or correspondence, nor to attacks on his honour or reputation. Everyone has the right to the protection of the law against such interferences or attacks."[98]

Numerous international human rights covenants give specific reference to privacy as a right. The International Covenant on Civil and Political Rights (ICCPR), the UN Convention on Migrant Workers[99] and the UN Convention on Protection of the Child[100] adopt the same language.[101]

Legal definitions of the right to privacy have significantly expanded, with one influential judgement, which built on the international conventions, stating:

"The right to respect for private life does not end there. It comprises also, to a certain degree, the right to establish and develop relationships with other human beings, especially in the emotional field for the development and fulfilment of one's own personality."[102]

The Evolution of Data Protection

Interest in the right of privacy increased in the 1960s and 1970s, with the advent of information technology (IT). The surveillance potential of powerful computer systems prompted demands for specific rules governing the collection and handling of personal information. In many countries, new constitutions reflect this right. The genesis of modern legislation in this area can be traced to the first data protection law in the world enacted in the Land of Hesse in Germany in 1970. This was

---

98   Universal Declaration of Human Rights, <http://www.hrweb.org/legal/udhr.html>
99   A/RES/45/158 25 February 1991, Article 14.
100 UNGA Doc A/RES/44/25 (12 December 1989) with Annex, Article 16.
101 International Covenant on Civil and Political Rights,
       <http://www.hrweb.org/legal/cpr.html>
102 X v. Iceland, 5 Eur. Commin H.R. 86.87(1976).

followed by national laws in Sweden (1973), the United States (1974), Germany (1977) and France (1978).[103]

Two crucial international instruments evolved from these laws. The Council of Europe's 1981 Convention for the Protection of Individuals with regard to the Automatic Processing of Personal Data[104], and the Organisation for Economic Cooperation and Development's Guidelines Governing the Protection of Privacy and Transborder Data Flows of Personal Data[105], articulate specific rules covering the handling of electronic data. The rules within these two documents form the core of the Data Protection laws of dozens of countries. These rules describe personal information as data which are afforded protection at every step from collection through to storage and dissemination. The right of people to access and amend their data is a primary component of these rules.

These two agreements have had a profound effect on the adoption of laws around the world. The OECD guidelines have also been widely used in national legislation, even outside the OECD countries.

The unstable foundation stone: Consent

Over the past few years I've noticed a growing discord among my colleagues on the issue of consent in data protection. Indeed I'd go as far as saying that many believe that this pillar of rights is becoming a dangerous illusion. I'm starting to agree.

I don't say this lightly. All privacy advocates enter this field believing that the concept of consent is self-evident. It's one of three untouchable buttresses – the other two being proportionality and necessity. These principles form the foundation of our work. Indeed consent is defined variously as *explicit, informed* and *implied.* The first condition is seen as

---

103 An excellent analysis of these laws is found in David Flaherty, "Protecting Privacy in surveillance societies", University of North Carolina Press, 1989.
104 *Convention on the Protection of Individuals with regard to the Automatic Processing of Personal Data* Convention, ETS No. 108, Strasbourg, 1981.
<http://www.coe.fr/eng/legaltxt/108e.htm>.
105 OECD, *Guidelines governing the Protection of Privacy and Transborder Data Flows of Personal Data*, Paris, 1981.

absolute and unequivocal, while the third simply assumes that any action you take, such as visiting a website, gives the organisation a free hand to do as it pleases. The European legal framework has largely moved away from the implied consent model.

It's worth spending a little time on this issue. In my view, consent will become one of the most crucial legal debates over the coming two decades.

Many of us long ago gave up believing in the "fair and lawful" provisions of data protection which give limitless bias to whatever legislation happens to be in place. However it seems increasingly that even the most ardent data rights traditionalists are privately conceding that the consent concept is becoming unstable and largely unworkable. There have been countless articles and papers over the past few years challenging the notion of consent, ranging from the domain of Biobanks[106] through to employment.[107]

A similar condition applies to "notice", which is the sister pillar of consent. Notice requires organisations to tell you what they will (or may) do with your information. But even if you are able to comprehend the language in those policies (which I describe in more detail elsewhere), the task of reading all that documentation would be onerous. Researchers calculated some years ago that reading every privacy policy would require seventy-six work days a year.[108] The question of course is what mechanism could replace these?

This is not a mainstream conversation within civil society. It's possible that advocates believe to do so could be seen as giving ground to the data vultures. Making any concession on consent could weaken an already fragile framework. At least, that's one view from the advocacy community.

All the same, we all regularly bemoan the decay of consent – even if it is

106 http://www.lsspjournal.com/content/11/1/1
107 Consent process empowers data. Taylor Wessing. http://united-kingdom.taylorwessing.com/globaldatahub/article_consent_process_emp_data.html (accessed July 16th 2018)
108 Madrigal, A. 1st March 2012. Reading the privacy policies you encounter in a year would take 76 work days. The Atlantic. https://www.theatlantic.com/technology/archive/2012/03/reading-the-privacy-policies-you-encounter-in-a-year-would-take-76-work-days/253851/ (accessed 12th October 2018)

usually in private conversation. The principle has been corroded over the years through an array of public interest and economically pragmatic carve-outs. The twitching data carcass that's left is ravaged by circuitous arguments about the difference between explicit, implied, informed and unambiguous consent. Still, all of us hold on to the idea of consent, even if it's just to remind us that the data subject has at least some inalienable rights.

Of course none of this should detract from the PRINCIPLE of consent – absolutely not. Consent is rightly a cornerstone of data protection. It's just a question of whether the principle has any meaningful value.

I tried testing out my views by starting a conversation on Twitter (hardly scientific, but a useful litmus test). All the responses expressed concern over the instability of consent in the current framework. The vast majority of respondents argued for a technological /mathematical solution. Others expressed the view that the current focus on consent should be shifted to a stronger effort to control the "use" of data by organisations.

These are useful perceptions. However, the two issues that concern me are:

- Will it be even possible in a few years to maintain any practical consent framework, and
- Will the surveillance required to enforce consent become a worse invasion than the original processing?

I'll address the latter challenge first.

My take on this issue is that most consent mechanisms were conceived in the pre-dawn of the Internet age. They were developed at a gentler time in history – a time when it was possible to build a simple flow chart of personal data relationships. Say, in the 1970s, that might be your bank, supermarket, telephone company, utilities providers, video store, employer and "hire purchase" company. That list has now been magnified a hundred fold.

We had a chance at tracking such a finite number of data collectors. Not so these days. Data has become such a labyrinth that consent enforcement has now shrunk to a focus on the activities of global online household brands. Almost every other entity does more or less what it pleases as long as its processing is not controversial in nature.

At its most basic level, I'm sure colleagues will resonate with the fact that this week alone I've pointlessly unsubscribed from more than twenty junk email streams, most of which laid some hollow claim to justify the invasion. Many people don't take such a risk, fearing that the unsubscribe feature is merely a validation trap – which it usually is. But even those entities that should know better are playing fast and loose with consent.

As a case in point, a few years ago I foolishly requested a brochure for the University of Salford's online international commerce law course – which, by the way, incorporates data protection. In response, I received no fewer than seven marketing emails from various parts of the university before I finally called a sensationally worded stop to the menace. If business schools are incapable of respecting consent, what hope is there for anyone else?

It goes without saying that the overwhelming view of large swathes of business is that consent is something you respect in the "unambiguous opt-out" – hardly a view that chimes with the more robust interpretation of consent. To be frank, I'm coming to the view now that "legitimate interest" is the way to go. At least that way, there can be a tighter focus on how data is used. More on that later.

But even if consent was respected and followed, the key question is whether the remedy might become worse than the malady. To illustrate this point we need look no further than the notice and takedown requirements on providers (Notice and Takedown is a legal requirement in many countries that establishes a condition, where, when a provider is "put on notice" that content is illegal or damaging, that content must be removed or the consequences for the publisher will be magnified.)

I was interested to read an analysis[109] on that subject by Daphne Keller of Stanford University's Center for Internet and Society. One of Keller's key arguments is that Europe's new notice and takedown framework is so poorly conceived that it becomes not only an unnecessary threat to free speech, but it also morphs into a vast surveillance mechanism.

We face the same problem when enforcing consent. Any online user in Europe will be familiar with the last bungled effort to achieve this

---

109 Keller, D. Notice and takedown rules are bad news for free expression but are not beyond repair. https://cyberlaw.stanford.edu/blog/2015/10/gdpr%E2%80%99s-notice-and-takedown-rules-bad-news-free-expression-not-beyond-repair

outcome. In summary, the EU Cookie Directive[110] requires most websites to seek explicit consent from users. This imposition not only proved to be an utter pain for all parties, but it severely damaged the integrity and reputation of data protection. And providing a clear audit trail of consent would require significant additional processing.

The cookie farce is a clear example of analogue thinking. Tackling the cookie issue with such a blunt instrument has become counter-productive. A proper audit and compliance element in the system could require the processing of even more data than the original unregulated web traffic. Even if it was possible for consumers to use some kind of gateway intermediary to manage the consent requests, the resulting data collection would be overwhelming.

I wonder why we're even going down this road. Some colleagues have suggested that a vast opt-in regime serves to sensitise business to the need for data compliance, but this seems to me a little like the reasoning behind public floggings.

I mentioned elsewhere that in an essay published recently in the Privacy Surgeon, the European Commission's Gerald Santucci expressed grave concerns that the current data protection framework is entirely unsuited to the emerging information age – and particularly the INTERNET OF THINGS. In the wake of a vast new generation of complex data streams, he argued, how can consent be meaningfully managed? In this view, the data overload of the coming decade risks turning much of consent into little more than a symbolic effort.

Perhaps someone could enlighten me on how precisely at any practical level we can enforce consent in a decade's time? When your refrigerator becomes a data intermediary for processing and disclosure to your doctor or supermarket, I wonder at what point the data subject has a chance to be involved. In the end, like the Cookie Directive, we end up with a meaningless box-checking exercise that merely irritates countless consumers.

There are two obvious paths that can be taken. One is to go down the health and safety road. The other is to adopt mathematical solutions.

---

110 Wikipedia entry on the EU Directive on Privacy and Electronic Communications. https://en.wikipedia.org/wiki/Directive_on_Privacy_and_Electronic_Communications (accessed July 3rd 2018)

In the health and safety road, the onus for protection would be removed from the citizen and placed squarely onto the organisation (the data use approach). With rare exceptions, employees no longer have to bear the responsibility for workplace safety, nor do they need to consent to the consequences of dangerous work environments. The same could apply to processors.

In the mathematical model, powerfully encrypted "black box" technology would create a technological lock-down to guarantee privacy protection. I discuss this concept in more detail elsewhere in the text. However neither of these approaches has evolved over the past decade, largely leaving the consumer responsible for self-enforcement of rights.

Returning to the new General Regulation, there's a clear conflict between consent and the equally crucial matter of data minimisation. Entities are required to fulfil a number of conditions, including consent and prior relationship. In the wording of the Regulation, this requirement necessitates the collection of considerable amounts of data on customers. This surely was not the intention of the Regulation, but the legal enforcement aspect will ensure that data will be archived, simply to cover the backs of data controllers.

One thing is clear. The present moment for European data protection should not be wasted passing fruitless and counter-productive rules. This should be an opportunity to create constructive and meaningful laws that support online growth while also genuinely protecting rights.

So, does law offer us any hope?

The short answer, of course, is "yes – to an extent". But to answer the question thoroughly, it's essential to look at weaknesses both in "protective" laws (such as privacy) and also in "restrictive" laws that have an impact on freedoms. In reality the two hemispheres converge markedly. For example, a law that enables the creation of a nation-wide CCTV canopy would be regarded by some people as protective. Equally so with measures to increase the powers of security authorities.

The laws that protect us and the laws that constrain us are the end point of a complex process. And it is often the case that the best laws are those that have a well-considered and sensitive gestation. Others are concocted in the heat of a public scandal and rushed through parliaments without adequate consultation, debate or analysis. What can result is a maze of badly constructed privacy laws – and even more badly constructed security laws. Even laws that have a sound pragmatic foundation can be compromised by a chaotic development process.

I mention numerous examples throughout this book of well-meaning public policy efforts that ended up compromising the right to privacy. Security and police law is not alone. From tobacco legislation to medical privacy the effort to maintain strong privacy has historically been a struggle. Without adequate oversight, accountability and enforcement, the mere presence of a law will not provide adequate protection. It may be merely cosmetic. Data Protection law is particularly vulnerable in that respect.

Between 2014 and 2016, I led an international initiative called "The Integrity Project".[111] Its aim was to discover the failures of law-making and to create a set of standards that should apply to the creation of any law – but particularly laws that have an impact on freedoms.

A similar exercise was conducted in 2015, led by the Institute for Information Law at the University of Amsterdam.[112] That report resulted in ten recommendations for the conduct of security agencies, including seamless accountability and layered transparency, independent and complete oversight, prior assessment, an adversarial principle in oversight, adequate resources for oversight bodies and expanded rights for bodies to publish data on surveillance activities.

During the Integrity Project process, hundreds of rights campaigners, legal experts, NGOs, journalists and officials from a wide range of professional bodies met across Europe to find a way to encourage politicians and governments to speak the truth when they propose intrusive security and policing measures.

The project was motivated by concerns that lawmakers and key elements

---

111 Davies, S., Denmark based initiative could be the most important step for human rights. 6th May 2016 http://www.privacysurgeon.org/blog/incision/a-denmark-based-initiative-could-be-the-most-strategically-potent-step-yet-for-privacy-rights/
112 http://www.ivir.nl/publicaties/download/1591.pdf

of mainstream media have promoted new surveillance measures through rhetoric rather than evidence. Many surveillance initiatives have been fuelled – at least in part – by irrational, false or populist assertions. Only on rare occasions have such measures been based on a solid foundation of reason and evidence. Importantly, even fewer have been subjected to any form of structured risk assessment or test.

Demands for measures such as data retention, information sharing, electronic visual surveillance, identity systems, urban militarisation and police checks are therefore often driven by assumptions that are unstable or illusory. Increasingly, these dynamics are global in nature, with governments replicating the poor practice of other nations (a syndrome variously known as "policy convergence" or "policy laundering").

This rationale has degenerated to the point where law enforcement and security agencies such as GCHQ and the NSA have lied outright to Congress and to Parliaments.[113] Such behaviour not only deeply imperils civil liberties, but it could also create actual harm to genuine public safety. Importantly, the fragile trust between the public, security organisations and law enforcement agencies could be further damaged. These failures are endemic. Even the September 2016 Swiss referendum on expanded security powers was characterised by rhetoric about national sovereignty rather than cogent analysis that might provide clarity about genuine threats to public safety.[114]

The project (which at the time of writing has not completed its work) concluded that all laws must be guided by an international framework of benchmarks, including risk assessments, research on alternative options, independent assessment, international comparative research, structured public consultation, the creation of a statistical foundation of evidence and the development of comprehensive transparency and accountability.

In the absence of such measures, it is natural to focus on the inadequacy of law – and there are indeed many gaps and failures in law. But if anyone wants proof of the relevance of privacy as a foundation for law,

---

113 Davies, S. Why it is time for NSA campaigners to target the lies and deception of Britain's spy agencies. The Privacy Surgeon.
http://www.privacysurgeon.org/blog/incision/why-its-time-for-nsa-campaigners-to-target-the-lies-and-deception-of-britains-spy-agencies/
114 Switzerland votes in favour of greater surveillance. The Guardian 25th September 2016.
https://www.theguardian.com/world/2016/sep/25/switzerland-votes-in-favour-of-greater-surveillance

they need only reflect on the fact that over the past few years, almost every government and corporation on earth has been repeatedly forced to address the issue. Law is just one consequence of such underlying factors.

Wherever you turn, for the big international institutions – WTO, WEF, IMF, the UN, the ILO and even Bilderberg – privacy has become an enduring topic. And, crucially, the conversation is slowly shifting from deflection to engagement.

This is a fascinating process which carries a sense of the inevitable. If you map the ascendancy and entrenchment of many issues – the environment, slavery, anti-discrimination, child exploitation by corporations – you can see the current privacy trends mirrored almost precisely.

That's not the same as saying everyone is galvanised by a zeal to strengthen privacy rights. It merely signals that – like the environment or Corporate Social Responsibility – smart leaders know the issue isn't going to go away.

This shift isn't exclusively a response to the Snowden revelations – though that chapter has accelerated the trend. Leaders have watched carefully as media scandals have unfurled over privacy issues. They've seen shares crash,[115]corporations burn[116] and CEO's fall on their sword[117]. And, by degrees, privacy is being drawn not just into corporate risk models, but also into ethical frameworks.

Where reputation is the only game in town, privacy has emerged as a genuine threat. Importantly, if current trends hold, it's only a matter of time before privacy is broadly viewed as an opportunity rather than a liability.

This wasn't always the case. There was a time – not so long ago – when organisations viewed privacy almost exclusively through the prism of legal compliance. If the legal department didn't flag a privacy issue as a compliance risk, there was little or no hope of change. The idea that brand reputation may suffer, or people may change their vote – or their

---

115 http://www.heinz.cmu.edu/~acquisti/papers/acquisti-friedman-telang-privacy-breaches.pdf (accessed July 8th 2018)

116 News of the World closes. July 7th 2011. The Guardian, London. http://www.theguardian.com/media/blog/2011/jul/07/news-of-the-world-closes-live-coverage (accessed July 12th 2018)

117 The US bank data scandal and the grand uncle of PRISM. The Privacy Surgeon. http://www.privacysurgeon.org/blog/incision/campaign-notebook-2006-the-us-bank-data-scandal-and-the-great-uncle-of-prism/ (accessed June 1st 2018)

shopping preferences – on the basis of privacy concerns, was until recently an aberrant notion.

To better understand this shift it may be useful to consider the changed dynamics of privacy campaigners and advocates – those individuals who have been responsible to no small extent for the transformation.

Scroll back ten or fifteen years. Then, privacy advocates suffered continuous, ad hominem attacks on their integrity. From the earliest days of the privacy movement, advocates were routinely characterised as extremist, self-interested, bleeding-heart liberals who were out of touch with reality. This was the default mindset of most powerful institutions. Former UK Home Secretary David Blunkett described them as the "Liberati".[118]

This polemic has shifted. I'm not suggesting that antagonism toward privacy has disappeared – far from it. But governments and corporations are no longer inclined to instinctively marginalise privacy issues. Indeed privacy is now a core risk issue for many sectors and has moved from mere legal compliance to an unstable core threat.

It wasn't so long ago – indeed as recently as the 2000's – that legal professionals were institutionally suspicious about the policy competence of privacy campaigners, while many in the IT sector regarded almost anyone in the privacy sphere as technologically naïve. Such positions are no longer sustainable.

Having said that, there are still many dinosaurs out there who harbour an anti-privacy pathology. Increasingly however, they are being pushed into the margins. Their "shoot the messenger" philosophy no longer resonates with the emerging narrative of governments and corporations.

To provide a brief example, it's now hard to imagine that in the 1990s, the handful of campaigners working[119] to expose the NSA and GCHQ mass surveillance programs were generally looked on by mainstream opinion-makers as tinfoil hat-wearing paranoiacs. We just kind of accepted the slur, just as we accepted the ridicule from authorities that

---

118 Personal interview with David Blunkett on the Privacy Surgeon "Privacy Channel", 2012 www.privacysurgeon.org

119 A lesson from history for those who strive to bring intelligence agencies to account. The Privacy Surgeon http://www.privacysurgeon.org/blog/incision/a-lesson-from-history-for-those-who-strive-to-bring-intelligence-agencies-to-account/ (accessed July 2nd 2018)

followed our early-warning campaigns against CCTV, government-issued identity, crypto controls or data retention.

It's equally hard to believe that as recently as 2004, those of us who warned[120] about the dangers of Google's ascendancy were mauled and humiliated by countless techies who had become blind to the risks of global data capture.

Such extreme responses are now vanishing as privacy concerns move from the fringe to the mainstream.

This activity indicates a growing maturity and confidence within the privacy community – an evolutionary step that no-one in power can afford to ignore.

Contrary to the image frequently promoted by its antagonists, the field is populated by highly informed and well-connected experts who have built a foundation of evidence for privacy campaigning. Indeed the privacy community (perhaps more accurately described as a network of networks) rigorously polices itself on matters of factual accuracy. There's a hive awareness that assertions must be solid if the credibility of advocacy is to be maintained.

These are early days, but there's every indication that privacy has achieved a critical mass that will propel the issue indefinitely. The dinosaurs will continue to resist this shift, but in time they will become more isolated and exposed.

Law evolves in response to such dynamics. The big question of course is whether it can keep pace – and keep pace adequately. But as long as the underlying drivers are there, it is still relevant to trust in the Rule of Law, however inadequate it may sometimes be.

---

120 Privacy International files complaints against Google Gmail. Search Engine Journal. 2004. http://www.searchenginejournal.com/privacy-international-files-complaints-against-google-gmail/464/ (accessed July 10[h] 2018)

Chapter Five: Who will protect us?

We might imagine that when our elected representatives pass a law and appoint an independent regulator, our privacy problems will be addressed. But this is not necessarily so. All the approaches to protection are deeply flawed. Whether the model is self-regulation or an official commissioner, there are many problems that need to be solved.

It is June 2010, and I'm sitting in a bleak operations office in Scotland Yard, the headquarters of the London Metropolitan Police (otherwise known as "The Met").

Scotland Yard clearly has no concept of workplace comfort or *Feng Shui*. The place is desolate and depressing. Grubby off-white walls, hard chairs and a few pictures of local maps and depressed-looking wanted persons. Still, anyone in a mug shot or a passport photo is required to look depressed by order of the guidelines (one is not permitted to smile or show any emotion when taking a passport picture in many countries).

Opposite me are a couple of senior police – at Detective Superintendent level I believe. One might have been an Assistant Commissioner. They are looking extremely perplexed and confused. And they are slightly annoyed, because I'm late.

I am late for a good reason. I had managed somehow to arrive by the back door. That's one effect of being almost blind, I guess. Walking innocently past security I had blundered along some secret underground corridor until, finally arriving at a restricted internal checkpoint, I was then discretely ushered out by a small army of embarrassed police. It was an uncomfortable start to what inevitably would be an uncomfortable meeting.

Scotland Yard has asked me here because I'd just lodged a criminal complaint against Google – two actually.[121] The issue was the company's unlawful mass collection of personal Wi-Fi data as part of its Street View project. Almost every connected house in Britain had had its Wi-Fi coordinates – and sometimes passwords and "payload" content of communications – harvested and the matter was sparking controversy (the Google operation soon became known as "Wi-Spy").[122]

This wasn't the first time such an action had been taken. UK internet privacy campaigners had filed criminal complaints against British Telecom over claims of unlawful computer intrusion for targeted advertising.[123] The complaints were largely ignored, but the action itself generated significant press coverage.

I had learned that the UK data protection authority (called the ICO) had given Google a clean Bill of Health following our complaint to them on this matter. More worryingly, it was about to follow the Irish lead by destroying all of the illegally acquired material that Google had supplied to them. This, in my mind, was a disaster. We needed that data so we could push for an independent audit, but the UK was adamant that destroying it was the lawful thing to do. Ireland had also exonerated Google and had already destroyed the data.

I went straight to Scotland Yard and lodged a formal complaint that Google had breached two criminal laws, including the Wireless Telegraphy Act, by harvesting a mass of Wi-Fi data without consent (crime reference number 2318672/10). I then immediately emailed the UK regulator and warned that any attempt to obliterate the files would be a criminal offence of destroying evidence. The police, for once, agreed with me. I sent a note in similar terms to every other privacy authority in the world. At least this action had the effect of stopping the data carnage, until German authorities could conduct a proper audit. They did so and ruled that in some respects the Google project was unlawful.

If a DPA is adequately resourced, if it has independence and if it has the

---

121 Privacy International press release on Metropolitan Police investigation of Google; 22nd June 2010 http://www.privacyinternational.org/article.shtml?cmd[347]=x-347-566448

122 Google finally admits that its Street View cars DID take emails and passwords from computers, Mail Online, 28th October 2010, http://www.dailymail.co.uk/sciencetech/article-1323310/Google-admits-Street-View-cars-DID-emails-passwords-computers.html

123 Christopher Williams, 27th October 2010. The Register. http://www.theregister.co.uk/2010/10/27/cps_bt_phorm/

courage and motivation to do its job, then the regulatory approach can work. But that's a very big "if". US advocates tend to look fondly upon the predominant EU regulatory model, but there are cautionary tales to be told. Many of our complaints to data protection authorities had fallen on deaf ears.[124] The failures below are by no means symptomatic, but they represent a large enough problem to warrant attention. it is important to provide context for how two of the models of privacy protection – criminal law and privacy regulators – often function in the real world.

* * * * *

On 23rd June 2010 police confirmed to news outlets that they would be investigating Google[125] but not before calling me into Scotland Yard for a quite interesting discussion.

Part of the conversation went as follows:

> **Them**: "So how do you propose we go about this? Who do we even interview? We haven't done anything like this before."

> **Me**: "Why not start with the UK Managing Director of Google, and work out from there?"

> **Them**: "We don't have the resources for this. It could be huge. You're a friend of the Attorney General *[then Dominic Grieve, who had been working with Gus Hosein and I on establishing a formal Parliamentary group on privacy]*, why don't you ask him to get us more funding and stop cutting what we have?"

All the same, they did pursue an inquiry, but it went nowhere. Police had told media the initial investigation would take around ten days, after which it would be passed to a specialist team if it was established that Google was in breach of the Regulation of Investigatory Powers Act

---

124 Privacy watchdog clears Google Street View; ZDnet 1st August 2008
    https://www.zdnet.com/article/privacy-watchdog-clears-googles-street-view/ (accessed 4th June 2018)
125 Google under investigation by Met Police, BBC News, 23rd June 2010
    https://www.bbc.co.uk/news/10391096 (accessed 4th June 2018)

(RIPA) or the Wireless Telegraphy Act. As far as I know, it never got to the level of a specialist team. The police had already signalled to me that it would be hard to find a controlling mind in the UK, and they certainly had no intention of escalating the matter to Google HQ. My guess is it took even less time for police to make this decision than it had taken the UK privacy regulator to do so.

The outcome should have come as no surprise to anyone. Legal issues aside, if the DPA's were at a loss to understand the Google technology, the police stood even less chance. Still, the process bought us much needed time.

This was by no means the first investigation of its type. In the US, Connecticut's Attorney General was leading a 30-state investigation and had demanded Google "come clean" about how the Wi-Spy code came to be incorporated in its Street View system.

The action of the UK Information Commissioner's Office to our complaint was even more telling than the police response. It played out much the same way. The office had a collective moan about Privacy International, decided in advance that Google was off the hook – and then for cosmetic purposes sent a couple of technologically untrained staff to Google's London office so the advertising giant could plea that it had acted lawfully. That's to say: "it was all a big mistake". At that point, the DPA decided to delete the data. Their action was thwarted, thanks to the police complaints.

How the Irish dealt with Edward Snowden

In July 2013, the Irish Data Protection Authority gave Apple and Facebook a clean bill of health over the transfer of illegally acquired PRISM data to the US National Security Agency. The secret transfers had been revealed by whistleblower Edward Snowden not long before. But, according to the Irish DPA which had carriage over such matters, the practice was entirely legal, and those companies were free to ship the personal data of Europeans across to the spy agencies.

The Austrian-based campaign group Europe v. Facebook had brought a complaint in 2013 alleging that the transfer of personal information to the US was unlawful. The subsequent Irish decision followed a process that the press variously described as a "probe", an "investigation", and an "inquiry". [126]

One has to feel at least some pity for the Irish Data Protection office under these circumstances. This was a massively complex legal quagmire, and the office was handicapped by an almost total absence of serious legal advice, resources or information. Add to that the complexity that Facebook is a big employer in Ireland and there is tacit pressure not to rock the boat – in the same way that Irish consumer regulators are encouraged to turn a blind eye to the borderline criminal trading practices of RyanAir.

The end result is that there never was an investigation – let alone a "probe". Europe v Facebook knew it, Apple knew it, and every privacy regulator in Europe knew it.

There might have been a "poke", but there's no way that an office as small as the Irish DPA could ever have resolved a legal issue as complex and far-reaching as this within a month. For one thing, the office didn't even have the raw facts at its disposal. Apple and Facebook would have made sure that disclosure of any technical evidence would have taken months – if ever.

Based on my understanding of similar cases in the past, here's what happened:

After receiving the complaint from Europe v. Facebook, a couple of the staff at the office sat down with the Commissioner and had a grumble about the campaign group – which understandably they regarded as an interfering troublemaker. After ten minutes everyone agreed on the outcome of the "probe" and the rest of the time was spent writing the appropriate two-page response. Maybe the office made a couple of telephone calls. End of story.

This summary isn't meant to sound dramatic – it is just the reality of how such matters often play out.

In the case of the UK regulator's "investigation" of Google following our

---

126 Europe v Facebook page http://europe-v-facebook.org/EN/en.html

complaint on the matter, that office has more resources, so it was able to send a longer letter of response. However it all boiled down to the same position: "We asked the company, it said it was acting lawfully – and we have no reason to doubt its word".

No-one's best interest is served by such a process. Privacy protections are circumvented, consumers feel cheated and companies become resentful. Regulators might feel smug that they escaped having to conduct a proper investigation, but every time they pull such a stunt, public trust in them – and in the law – takes another tumble.

Case study: A more ordinary story of regulatory failure

There's a catchy line from *Hamlet* that – in modern times – is usually truncated to *"There's something rotten in Denmark"*. Certainly, until very recent times, that quote could well apply both to Danish data protection, and to the national authority that supervises it.

Perhaps it's not fair to single out that delightful kingdom, but I will do so anyway. True, there's something rotten in many European states, in terms of the way data protection authorities go about their business. Some of them are becoming increasingly timid, isolated and invisible to the public. Others are simply aloof.

Denmark deserves special mention, in part because from 2015, its government appeared to be running amok on surveillance initiatives. Denmark embarked on the sort of surveillance and control agenda that some other EU states have pursued (particularly France, Belgium, Netherlands, UK, Spain and Italy). The intelligence services have been expanded, data retention is being extended, anti-terror packages are being introduced and police powers increased. These include new powers for the Danish Defence Intelligence Service to monitor Danish citizens abroad without the need for a warrant.

Beyond the realm of police and security, there has been strong criticism about the level of data protection generally in Danish public institutions.

In summary, government authorities in Denmark are lining up to brutalise protections, while the general population appears increasingly chilled about the collapse of their privacy rights.

Given the Copenhagen shootings in 2015, perhaps it is natural for a nation in shock to take such a road. However something is amiss when such measures are adopted without substantial debate – particularly when Denmark routinely boasts a claim to being at the pinnacle of human rights.

But where was Denmark's DPA in this dangerous situation? In terms of legislated government powers, its profile is opaque at best. I looked at a summary of the office's activities over that year and there are only one or two elements that offer any hope whatever. Yes, this DPA has engaged police and some authorities over intrusive technologies, but the language and process it uses is sterile and uninspiring to anyone outside the legal realm. People who should, in normal events, be fellow travellers with a data protection watchdog overwhelmingly described it as toothless, aloof and compromised.

Perhaps one explanation is that it's hard to know where the Danish Ministry of Justice ends and where the Danish DPA begins. There's a revolving door between the two. Technically, the agency is independent, but if you populate a hen house with enough foxes, it soon ceases to be a hen house – regardless of what you call it. This goes to heart of the question of independence, and why that element is so important.

The highly respected Danish Institute for Human Rights also appears to have concerns about the DPA. In a report earlier that year it slapped the authority over its handling of social media complaints. To be fair, the DPA does issue a warning that it doesn't normally deal with complaints about the likes of Facebook, preferring instead to refer complainants to the Irish authority or to Facebook itself, but that's beside the point. And of course, complaining to Ireland about a company with its EU headquarters based there has traditionally been futile.

This jurisdiction deficiency, in my view, is absurd. I earlier described the Danish DPA as dysfunctional, and the Facebook situation is one reason why I chose that word. Denmark has the highest proportion of Facebook users of any EU country. The place is steeped in social media culture. Facebook penetration in Denmark in 2015 was almost fifty percent greater than the EU average of 38 percent and yet the Danish DPA, certainly until recently, saw no reason to advocate on behalf of this huge sector.

The Danish DPA – like several other such agencies – is far too insular and inward looking. I tried several times to meet the agency but hit a brick wall every time. In the present era it is crucial for such agencies to look beyond their borders. I could just as readily criticise such countries as Slovakia and Romania on the same grounds, though matters are slightly improving there. By 2012, the Estonian, Slovenian and Italian DPA's saw the folly of an insular attitude and changed course to a more global outlook.

To be honest, if that agency was ruthlessly effective within Denmark's borders, I might have been more empathetic – but it isn't as effective as it could be. A report by the Danish Auditor General (Rigsrevisionen), from 2013 and 2014, revealed that several state institutions have inadequate protection of personal data. In other words, the Danish DPA only partially did its job.

The story is repeated across the world. There are laws and supervisory authorities, but there are substantial gaps and weaknesses. It is possible that the new General Data Protection Regulation will remedy such shortcomings, but the healing may take some years. In the meantime there have been some excellent episodes where DPAs have made a real difference. The chapter on banks goes into detail about one such case. The Heathrow Airport case detailed elsewhere in the text is another instance where a regulator can make a real difference.

* * * * *

Returning to the challenge of investigating multinational companies. the harsh reality is that many US companies distrust European-style data protection law and they certainly have little intention of wholeheartedly complying with either the letter or the spirit of an investigation. This applies in particular to Google, which quite blatantly believes those protections to be archaic and unworkable (and also – in another erroneous view – to get in the way of maximising profit). Whenever a regulator "investigates" a complaint, such companies often close ranks. Regulators learn almost nothing about the intricacies of data processing, business models, security techniques, monetisation practices, contractual arrangements, forecasting outcomes or future planning.

There has to be a better way. Even for those regulators who do conduct meaningful investigations (and there are a few) there's probably an elastic limit to the traditional model of external investigations. As the world moves to the cloud and as information becomes ubiquitous and ambient it may be impossible within a decade for regulators to conduct any precise examination of data practices. I do think in the circumstances it is worth exploring some novel regulatory ideas even if they end up failing a reality check. Supervisory systems can easily fall into disrepute if they are not tested with alternative approaches, as witnessed by the systemic corrosion of the UK telecommunications regulator OFCOM in its failure to uphold consumer rights.

How to complain to a privacy regulator

All that having been said, if you decide to take personal action and complain to a privacy regulator, it may be worth considering some fundamentals. After making several hundred complaints over the decades, I learned from bitter experience that the road may not be as smooth as you might imagine.

Of course, as with so many such issues, there's a "why" that precedes the "how". Why should you send a complaint to a data protection or privacy authority? Well, because it might make a difference. And it probably takes less time to write a letter than it does to spend hours table-thumping in the pub to your friends about a privacy issue that irritates you.

The first point to understand is that in most jurisdictions, every person has a right to send a letter of complaint to their local data protection authority (DPA). And some data protection authorities actually read those letters.

It is best to be realistic though. The odds of a DPA taking action on your complaint are slim. Most DPA's are under-resourced and overwhelmed with work and such letters are, frankly, a waste of their time. DPA's know their priorities, and if your issue isn't on that list, you're likely to receive one of the following template responses:

- It is not in our jurisdiction;
- You have no standing;
- We are unable to substantiate your complaint;
- The complaint falls outside our mandate;
- We have already dealt with a similar complaint.

Being aware of these five template responses will give you ammunition for an effective complaint. Then, research is everything.

You should clearly state at the beginning why you have a direct interest in the complaint. DPA's like to deal with people who have been affected by a violation. Sending a complaint about something that you overheard on a bus is less likely to receive attention, than if you were actually hurt by an abuse of law. And some DPA's simply won't look into a complaint unless it is from the person who has been aggrieved.

However you should add something about the broader public interest. In a sentence or two, explain why your issue is also of concern to thousands or millions of people. You might want to consider stressing the impact on vulnerable people or children. That should put your complaint further up the queue.

Unless you really know your legal stuff, don't play amateur lawyer. You'll just irritate the reader. You can make oblique reference to proportionality or fairness, but don't quote specific bits of law or you might find the complaint will be handled narrowly in that context. Let the DPA do the work of figuring out the legal logistics.

Now for the body of the complaint. Write an introductory section that sets out the background, history and context. Who or what exactly are you complaining about? What happened? What was the chain of events and what consequences arose? Be as specific as you can. If you can include screen shots or hard evidence, do so. Just saying "yeah, I went onto Google and it sucks coz they rob all my data" won't cut it.

Do a quick search of the DPA's to check whether they've ruled on your issue in the past. It doesn't matter which side they ruled on, but just make sure to reference previous cases. It makes you look intelligent and committed, and it nudges them in the right direction.

Other approaches to protection

With the development of commercially available technology-based systems, privacy protection has also moved into the hands of individual users. Users of the Internet can employ a range of programs and systems which will ensure varying degrees of privacy and security of communications. Questions remain about security and trustworthiness of these systems. The European Commission evaluated some of the technologies and stated that the tools would not replace a legal framework.[127]

There's no doubt that NGO's and consumer groups can also offer some degree of broad protection, though the resources available to these groups is constantly under stress and they rarely have the capacity to take on individual cases. And even in circumstances where they can take on a case, this usually involves shepherding the matter through courts or regulators.

However, there are many fun ways that people can protect their privacy, even at a day-to-day level. I spent nearly twenty years as a university lecturer unsuccessfully trying to figure out a way to make identity authentication an interesting and popular topic, but only recently did I crack the problem (identity authentication is the process by which you prove that you are who you say you are). It's all about "pull" and "push" and making people in call centres read out hilariously stupid words from their screen. I call it "negotiated authentication", but more on that later. First some background.

As any security professional knows, one of the main problems with authentication is that it's usually a one way street. Organisations operating online or via a phone demand that individuals provide identity data, but they rarely reciprocate to prove their own legitimacy. This

---

127 Opinion 1/98: Platform for Privacy Preferences (P3P) and the Open Profiling Standard (OPS). <http://europa.eu.int/comm/dg15/en/media/dataprot/wpdocs/wp11en.htm>.

creates a risk of identity theft. Anyone can call your mobile and demand a password, date of birth and address, and most people will willingly give out the information – particularly if the alleged reason for the call is "security".

As a rule there's far too much "pull" of personal information going on. A safer mutual authentication system that provides confidence to both parties will involve much more "push" of information, requiring the other party to confirm the accuracy of known data, rather than the customer being required to disclose the information up-front. For example, why on earth should I be handing over my address details to an alleged health provider when surely it's they that should be telling me my address so I know they're not fraudsters? We live in strange times.

Good progress has been made on technologies for Web-based and electronic transactions, allowing the consumer (or the consumer's machine) to be more certain that an organisation is what it claims to be. But most phone-based interactions between organisations and customers still rely on instinct and trust, with individuals required to give out bits of their personal data to a purported company or agency. Even if the technology was available, it would be only a partial answer to the much larger problem of social engineering by fraudsters. As Bruce Schneier says: "If you think technology can solve your security problems, then you don't understand the problems and you don't understand the technology." It's all about social engineering.

Keep an eye out for organisations that move from a pull to a push system. They're often the ones that are trying to put their security promises into action. For example Barclay's bank recently adopted a new push-based telephone security system. It sends you a message that reads out four possible dates of birth (month and year) before asking the customer to choose one and then submit a day of birth. The odds against a fraudster randomly guessing a correct combination of month and year are around 200 to one. The problem of course is that there are countless ways to reduce those odds – even by using publicly available demographic data. And once a customer starts giving out personal and identity information, more often than not they'll continue giving it out.

All the same, no matter how long the odds might seem, the risk to the customer is great. A scarily large percentage of the population use the same password for all purposes, so asking a customer for a password for, say, a book retailer may provide the same password used for a bank. One survey indicated that 61 percent of people use the same password for all their online accounts whenever they can. A 2018 survey showed that 59 percent do the same.[128]

But what if the customer were allowed to turn the tables by challenging the calling organisation to produce information that only a legitimate supplier would know? I recently tried such a method with T-Mobile, which has always made a habit of calling me from a variety of numbers if I'm a few days late with my mobile phone payment.

Having become heartily sick of arguing the toss over who should provide information first, I discussed the dilemma with a helpful call centre manager and we figured a solution.

It turns out that nearly all call centre systems have a "special instructions" field that allows operators to add useful comments about calling times, payment instructions or special customer requirements. Or just whether they are a total bastard. Into this field we placed a word. I must say it's the most hilariously camp and silly word ever to grace an otherwise tedious financial management system, but it is memorable and unique. Now whenever I'm called by T-Mobile, I demand that they read out the word before they get any information from me. The mutuality works for both of us, and we all get a giggle. I've changed it now, but it used to be "Poopsy Poo".

It's an infectious idea, and now my friends and I try to implement the system with every organisation that calls us. Sometimes we meet with success, sometimes not. HSBC Bank, for example, refused point-blank to institute the idea, even though they have a special instructions field. Their reasoning is that any new field of data presents unknown security risks. They could well be right, but neither have they come up with an alternative to their current fallible system.[129]

This is a small step to resolving a much larger problem, but it's a potentially useful measure that could help overcome the current imbalance in the authentication arena. And importantly, it will help

---

128 Security Boulevard. https://securityboulevard.com/2018/05/59-of-people-use-the-same-password-everywhere-poll-finds/
129 Why making a call-centre worker say "poopsy-poo" will strengthen your security, August 17th 2017 http://www.privacysurgeon.org/blog/incision/why-making-a-call-centre-worker-say-poopsy-poo-will-strengthen-your-security/

strengthen consumer trust by establishing a more genuinely mutual process.

Mutuality is crucial. On a larger scale, in recent times there have been calls to create a more cooperative relationship between civil society and

The drivers for privacy

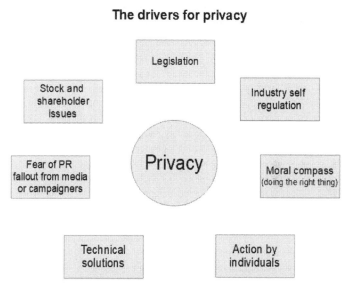

the corporate world so advocacy might be strengthened.[130] [131]

Data protection can also be achieved – at least in theory – through various forms of self-regulation, in which companies and industry bodies establish codes of practice. However, the record of these efforts has been disappointing, with little or no evidence that the aims of the codes are regularly fulfilled. Adequacy and enforcement are the major problem with these approaches. Industry codes in many countries have tended to provide only weak protections and lack enforcement. Still, this is currently the policy promoted by the governments of the United States, Singapore and Australia.

---

130 See the Civil Engagement project www.civilengagement.org

131 Davies, S. An advocacy storm is coming: could it water your garden? IAPP Opinion, 2016 (unknown publication date) https://iapp.org/news/a/an-advocacy-storm-is-coming-could-it-water-your-garden/ (accessed July 14th 2018)

That's not to say that individual companies don't care about protecting privacy; many do. The common mechanism to achieve protection is through Data Protection Officers (the European term) or Chief Privacy Officers (which is the US term). While these people tend not to deal directly with aggrieved customers, it is certainly their job to figure out where the company went wrong and whether it is legally compliant. The best privacy officers strive to achieve good practice and they evangelize for privacy across the company.

Positive stories of corporate in-house privacy protection

In 2006, Privacy International received a complaint from a supporter, along the lines that it seemed impossible for eBay users to delete their accounts. We sampled a number of people, none of whom were able to discover a link for account closure. This was unlawful under the Data Protection Act. Customers have the right to close their accounts.

After years of dealing with big organisations we had become battle-scarred. To us it seemed hardly worth the effort of confronting some invisible PR company, which in the end would do no more than read out a screen message telling us "XYZ cares about the privacy of its users." So we took the best course of action at our disposal and triggered an investigation by the UK Information Commissioner's Office (ICO) over our claim that eBay had fundamentally breached data protection principles. Once we had received a positive response from the ICO, all that was required were some well-timed calls to the press.[132]

The following day the story played loudly in the papers, both in the UK and overseas.[133] 'eBay under investigation' was a nice coup for us, even if it was a tad overhyped.[134]

---

132 ibid
133 Watchdog to investigate eBay over data privacy allegations 31st August 2006. The Guardian. https://www.theguardian.com/technology/2006/aug/31/news.newmedia
134 Graeme Wearden,31st August 2006 http://www.cnet.com/news/ebay-amazon-take-heat-on-privacy-practices/ (accessed July 2nd 2018)

Within a few hours eBay's global privacy lead, Scott Shipman, reached out to us ("reach out" is corporate-speak for "contact"). Rather than taking a defensive position, he offered to work with us to help fix the problem. This offer, for us, was a rare experience. Scott convened a working group of engineers and set up conference calls, to which we were included. He even informally brought on Facebook at one point to help crack the problem. It turned out that account closure was indeed possible, but that the pathway to that link was obscure.

It took nine months to resolve the issue, a task complicated further by the multiple languages that the company operated in. However, the result was – once again – a clear win for privacy.

Such engagement is possible, but it is relatively rare. I recall Microsoft postponing the launch of Bing *Streetside* (Microsoft's answer to Streetview) after we had suggested some security improvements. In that case it was a simple matter of us proposing stronger third-party audit provisions to obviate the sort of PR and legal drama that Google had faced over Streetview. Microsoft's then UK National Technology Officer Jerry Fishenden trusted us enough to provide advance notice of the launch, and that relationship allowed our advice to be circulated around the company. Microsoft responded quickly, and privacy was the clear winner.

But as I mentioned earlier, individual customers may not achieve that level of penetration into a company. If a complaint to the local data protection authority yields nothing, then it might be worthwhile asking an established advocacy group to represent you.

Case study: the negative side of in-house privacy protection

It is instructive to examine the role of company CPO's and DPO's in the aftermath of the Edward Snowden revelations about national security. Where were the privacy staff in private sector companies such as Verizon throughout this entire affair? To at least some extent, these officials are supposed to protect the organization by protecting the consumer, and yet increasingly it seems their role is cosmetic.

The situation offers two possible scenarios. Either privacy officers are subjected to the Mushroom Syndrome (fed on shit and kept in the dark), or they might indeed have known what was going on and said nothing (or been told to say nothing). Neither is a healthy state of affairs.

In a rare moment of public reflection on this topic, Alex Fowler, the CPO of Mozilla, wrote an opinion piece for the International Association of Privacy Professionals (IAPP), urging his colleagues to consider the wider ethical obligations on privacy officers.

> *All of the companies caught up in the news that complied with secret court orders to hand over bulk user data have privacy officers and dedicated teams of privacy professionals. Yet the extent to which any of these privacy teams were involved or were aware of these orders is unclear. This simple irony provokes reflection on the role of privacy professionals and our associated ethical and social responsibilities.*

These points are relevant to more than just an arcane professional sector. The IAPP has 45,000 members in 83 countries,[135] and these people – at the policy and at the operational level – collectively represent the credibility of the privacy field.

IAPP does deserve a special mention here. It has – in the space of less than twenty years – become the default privacy education platform worldwide. Consider that in such a short space of time IAPP has attracted almost half the membership of the Association of Computing Machinery (ACM), which throughout more than half a century before had built 100,000 members.[136] The ACM is the largest professional computing organisation in the world.

IAPP has an apparently policy-neutral position, as has ACM, but any organisation that creates an education platform cannot be totally immune from policy. Without doubt, IAPP fulfils all its legal responsibilities for

---

135 Wikipedia entry on IAPP
    https://en.wikipedia.org/wiki/International_Association_of_Privacy_Professionals
    (accessed July 8th 2018)
136 Wikipedia entry on ACM
    https://en.wikipedia.org/wiki/Association_for_Computing_Machinery (accessed July 7th

openness, but the time might have come for the organisation to go that extra mile and to declare its processes more rigorously in the increasingly complex environment in which it swims. I have argued to its leaders that the organisation needs to build a more robust and more transparent ethical foundation if it is to take on global leadership. To the best of my knowledge, this advice is being taken seriously.

On the IAPP site, Fowler raised foundation questions that should have been resolved long before the current crisis forced that debate:

> *As privacy professionals, do we have ethical obligations to the people whose data is our professional responsibility, or only to our employers? How do we handle conflicts of loyalty that arise? Does public safety trump privacy in every case and in any circumstances? Do we have obligations to report – even secretly, under legal requirements – our objections?*

At the moment there are few answers, but there is a certainty that over the next few years more attention will be paid to privacy professionals. It is in their – and the public's – interest to resolve such questions swiftly and courageously.

2018)

135

Chapter Six: Why do people start caring about privacy? Some personal stories

> *I have always been intrigued about why people start caring about privacy. I begin this quest by looking at my own campaigning experience as a fourteen year-old and then recount a number of examples of a similar effect on privacy advocates. I also relay anecdotes from some of my professional colleagues. What are the triggers that ignite passion in this field?*

A few years ago I got to know – sadly, too late to help her – a high school student who, alone, defied her school's policy of fingerprinting all students. The institution – one of top girls' schools in England – had decided fingerprinting was a useful initiative, even though the authorities were at loss to explain why it was needed. Monitoring the consumption of school meals and "security" seemed somewhere on the agenda.

The girl thought differently. To the astonishment of her friends and family, she refused to be fingerprinted. To her, fingerprinting was an affront; the last choice of a dead administration that had lost its way. Until that moment, she had never given such issues any thought whatever.

The school retaliated by imposing punishments on her entire class for "failing to provide peer support", and then removed her privileges. Her parents reacted with anger, saying their daughter was spitting in their face. She held out against all these pressures but finally called me a couple of weeks later and wept, as she told me that the school had threatened expulsion just before her exams. In a final act of defiance, she filed her fingertips down and presented the bloodied mass to the machine.

Now she evangelises for student privacy.[137]

Contrary to popular imagination, most people – people like her and I – become human rights advocates not by sitting in on a local meeting of radicals, but through such day-to-day life experiences. The spark might be mismanagement of a shopping centre or a sudden awakening that it is wrong for the police to collect DNA from everyone in an entire area. Some people become activists because their children came home from a camping trip with industrial waste on their clothes and others because of losing their job in a multinational takeover.[138]

These are people who can often be defined as ordinary folk with extraordinary beliefs. They are characterised by institutions as subversive but are more often what one judge in a recent UK trespass case over environmental protection described as *"decent men and women with a genuine concern for others"* who *"acted with the highest possible motives"*.[139] This idea must go to the DNA of many people.

Taking action – or even just becoming an advocate for any cause – can be daunting. However it is fair to say that radical action is probably far more common than most people imagine. The radical spirit in us wants to pursue a respectable and justified cause. Annoyingly, it is so often the case that "other" people's rebellions are simply selfish and pointless, but not those of our own. it is not surprising therefore that activists and campaigners are often portrayed so badly. The stereotype of the radical as a corrosive, left-leaning obsessive is far from the truth. In reality, activists are found right across the human spectrum, and often in the most surprising guises.

Just to ruminate on this theme for a moment, I've always believed there are very few people who can go through life without challenging authority in one way or another. Even those who appear submissive by nature have probably taken a stand. At a certain moment, even the most anally retentive conformist will resist forces that threaten a quiet life.

Standing up to authority is one of the defining processes of a healthy mind. Taking steps to challenge regressive or unfair power is a natural

---

137 Davies, S. Ideas for Change. (2018) Irene Publishing. ISBN 978-91-88061-23-2
138 Smith, Robert E. War Stories: Anecdotes of Persons Victimized by Invasions of Privacy. Providence, R.I.: Privacy Journal, 1993.
139 Lewis, P & Prakash, N, 5th January 2011
    https://insideclimatenews.org/print/6892?page=2

response for any reasonable self-respecting member of society. Indeed through the course of human history every step forward required a challenge to rules and conventions. The great movements that shaped society were made possible because a mass of people supported a radical idea and abandoned the way things used to be done.

To defy unfair power doesn't make you "a radical" or "an activist", it just means you took action in support of something in which you believe. The stereotype is a convenient way for entrenched power to devalue those who seek to reform bad practices. Doing something controversial does not define you; it enhances you.

it is impossible to accurately profile the advocate (or even to differentiate between the advocate and the activist). I once met a gentle great grandmother who caused hell for her local council for months by standing with a placard that read "City hall thieves... Give my house back", on a busy street corner every day. I've had tea with others who occupied a rubbish dump outside Manila and turned it into their home, defying military and police efforts to remove them. I knew a family who stood by their father as he defied his employer over discrimination and watched helpless as the bank took away their home.

I'm pleased to tell you in all those examples the underdog eventually won, though victory is often at the end of a long and painful road. How you define such people depends on how you resonate with them.

Perhaps it is not surprising that there's a radical persona lying just under the surface in all of us. We were influenced in childhood by an empire of films, plays, books, philosophies, ideologies and folklore, all celebrating the lives and legend of lawbreaking individuals who took hold of powerful ideas, and, against great odds, influenced and improved the world. They tell us much of what we cherish, including our rights and freedoms, was made possible because of the maverick activist. But in our mind, those were fairy tales.[140]

---

140 Davies, S. Ideas for Change

* * * * *

Almost every advocate recalls a spark – a trigger – which changed their life – and the lives of people around them. For example, following the Finchley Road dramas mentioned before, both Jones and Cameron became ardent privacy advocates. They came to understand the principles that underpin trust and dignity. Such is the experience with so many people.

As a boy, struggling into adolescence in the late 1960's, I had no clue about privacy. My school teachers never discussed it. The media were vacant on the topic. And privacy was surprisingly sparse as a theme in popular culture. True, as the sociologist Garry T Marx has observed, film and music were peppered throughout the past century with privacy references. We ordinary kids, however, were not tuned into that cultural heritage. We were obsessed with either the Bee Gees or Jimi Hendrix. Neither end of that spectrum was offering privacy insights.

Still, you don't need to understand the definition of privacy to instinctively know its importance. I conducted my first privacy campaign at the age of fourteen, even though I never used the word. That brief episode changed my life and caused me to embrace the world of privacy.

As the 1970's dawned, I was blundering and dodging my way through an authoritarian church schooling. It was a terrible place, characterised by mental and physical punishments that only the old church is capable of dreaming up. The concept of "student rights" hadn't yet been imported from the more evolved US schools and it would be years before our feelings could be expressed by anthems such as Pink Floyd's 'Another Brick in the Wall'.

We were, however, well aware of influential protest songs about the abuse of authority. Ranked high among these was 'Ohio' by Crosby, Stills, Nash and Young, a powerful piece of work commemorating the Kent State shootings in 1970. Perhaps curiously, those of us who cared about privacy-related matters were motivated by war, brutality and free expression rather than the domain of personal autonomy. Computers were not even on our radar – nor was state or corporate intrusion into private life.

That's not to imply that the potential threat from computers and databases was unknown. Concern about omnipresent Big Brother was well established – George Orwell made sure of that. It is just that Orwell had little visibility for people of my age and in my educational sphere. I kept hearing the phrase "this is Orwellian" but had no clue what it meant.

Ironically, nearly forty years later, I organised the London gala to celebrate the 50th anniversary of '1984' (Nineteen Eighty-Four). Orwell's reclusive son, Richard, had agreed for the first time ever to speak as did Michael Radford, who had directed the film of the same name. John Hurt, who played Winston Smith in that film, was also on the hook. Of course I had to pretend that I had known about the book since childhood.

Bizarrely, Orwell's publishers – Penguin and Secker & Warburg – controversially boycotted the event. Speaking to the press on this snub, Sir Bernard Crick, Orwell's official biographer, described the publishers as "money-making Philistines who have no care or thought for the great titles they own". Crick's response was justified, given that Penguin's statement on the matter was, "Just because some people wanted to have a party, it doesn't mean we should have to pay for the crisps". I guess thirty million sales never gave them a margin of profit for nibbles.[141] I had asked them for only two hundred pounds. I was in the hole for two thousand pounds.

Many of my colleagues tell me that exposure to certain technologies can – in time – trigger an interest in privacy. I remember, back in 1966, being intrigued by the amazing new technology of the IBM "golf ball" typewriter. I wondered then, even as a ten year-old, what technology would have in store for us. A year later, when the Roneo stencil printer gave way to the photocopier, I was convinced that technology would rule the world and that we needed to get in control of it. All it took was contact with that new technology. Imagination does the rest.

The cultural vacuum regarding privacy was certainly the case for my peers until a pivotal moment arose in my school. It was also the moment when The Doors released a noteworthy privacy-themed song called 'The Spy'.

We had been waiting for months to hear the 'Morrison Hotel' album, on which that song was featured. Many of us had only just listened to its haunting lyrics, when a gruff teacher – notorious among us boys for his

---

141 Publishers snub Orwell celebrations. The Independent on Sunday. Unknown
   publication date

sadism and various subtle perversions – took to the assembly stage, and bluntly announced that the school was launching a "crackdown" on what he dramatically described as "criminal behaviour that is destroying the school's reputation". Systematic body and bag searches would be introduced, along with routine interrogation of anyone suspected of being complicit in – well – anything the school chose to demonise on any particular day. Lockers and toilet cubicles would no longer have locks.

It seems the root of this action was the discovery of a joint under a desk in a senior classroom. The culprit disappeared from sight soon after – presumably in the church equivalent of a Black Bag operation. But try as it might, the school could not hide from view the discovery of three of its students in a gay night club. These two events were testimony to a moral decay that would surely bring about the demise of the Church of England.

I was not so certain. The school's response seemed, to me, completely unreasonable. It was an abuse of those in power, with the end goal of subduing us, the peasants. Even a fourteen year-old understands such things.

I responded with a call to reason. Meeting with the more liberal of the school governors, I explained that the unwarranted searches would destroy trust between students and staff. It would diminish the moral authority of the school. More important, it was neither appropriate nor fair.

In a legal realm far away – unknown to me – those very ideas were being distilled in data protection law as the principles of "proportionality" and "necessity". Indeed, at the moment when I was using those parallel terms, the German Landa of Hesse was promulgating the world's first data protection law based on those very principles.

My call to reason to the school fell on deaf ears, so I started militating.[142]

The school's plan soon backfired magnificently. Boys smuggled in porn magazines, scattered tobacco in hallways and planted open flasks of whisky in staff offices. I never even had to precisely coordinate all such antics. Students were randomly standing up in solidarity with their friends. Like Bingate (which I describe elsewhere), a great campaign cannot – and should not – be micro-managed.

---

142 Eliza Krigman; Privacy Activism: Turning threat into opportunity. Data Privacy Leadership Council. 2016

As foreshadowed, the locks were duly ripped from lockers and doors. Children were lined up for body searches. Students disappeared for hours for questioning as staff paranoia soared. But despite the growing rebellion among students, we were losing.

Discovering the Alinsky Factor

Finding the spark of privacy is just part of the equation. One needs a more knowledge-based foundation if that spark is to endure. I needed help to win this battle, so I immersed myself in the public library. The name Saul Alinsky appeared time and time again. Alinsky was a genius of community organising and had been an inspiration for grassroots activism in the US. He demonstrated how creative ideas can undermine the authority of even the most powerful institutions (as an amateur theologian, this resonated with me in the story of Jesus Christ overturning the tables of money lenders in the temple). If I was a better researcher – and not so academically inept – I would have spotted Alan Westin's seminal 1968 work "Privacy and Freedom",[143] but the library keywords didn't match my world view at the time. We need a better indexing system. There are countless activist networks operating in the political space, but many do not receive the recognition they deserve.[144]

Alinsky deserves more than a passing mention. He has inspired thousands of activists to an extent that is unprecedented in the modern age.[145]

It was as a Chicago criminologist, working in the 1930s in the then grey area of social work, that Saul Alinsky took his first steps into the arena of radical activism. During the course of his studies into the demography of organised crime he arrived at the South steel mills of Chicago's west side. Here, Alinsky took the bland notion of community organisation and turned it into a rallying cry for social justice and equality.

Alinsky was a man of fierce imagination. He pioneered a generation of

---

143 Westin, A. Privacy and Freedom, Atheneum, New York
144 Keck, Margaret, E., and Kathryn Sikkink. Activists Beyond Borders: Advocacy Networks in International Politics. Ithaca: Cornell University Press, 1998.
145 Alinsky, S. (1971) *Rules for Radicals*, New York. Random House.

social and civil rights campaigning based on colourful tactics, ingenious resourcefulness and a radical approach. These tactics rested on a broader foundation: the development of a "civil society" based on strong community partnerships.

One such action took place in Rochester, New York, a town noteworthy for two features: the vast complex that serves as HQ for the Eastman Kodak corporation, and the city's world famous symphony orchestra. Indeed, in 1963, Kodak, Rochester and its celebrated orchestra had become a *ménage a trois*. The Kodak magnates enjoyed a lavish lifestyle. They employed much of the town and kept some 40,000 people at as little cost as possible. Profits cleaved off the back of the immigrant workforce were siphoned into Rochester's innumerable middle class institutions

Kodak had gained an unsavoury reputation within the emerging civil rights movement. One rights campaigner described the city as "a southern plantation moved north" and added "the only thing Kodak has given to race relations is colour film". Throughout the previous year, Kodak had survived mass demonstrations, violent rioting and merciless lampooning in the national press, but its most formidable challenge came in the form of a conservatively dressed middle aged activist.

Alinsky, who had gained a reputation as a firebrand for workers' rights, had been brought from Chicago to Rochester by local community organisations to bring Kodak to heel. Kodak was right to go to amber alert: Alinsky created trouble wherever he went, forcing corporations to do the right things by their employees.

Alinsky's first strike against Kodak took place amidst the velvet surrounds of its directors' favourite concert hall. As the bosses took their seats, they gazed in bemusement at the sight of a hundred working class coloured people – all Kodak employees – seated directly in front of them. As the Rochester Symphony struck the gentle chords of Beethoven's Pastoral, a score of Euphonic blasts echoed around the hall. Thanks to a generous three-hour feast of baked beans, the workers loudly farted their way through the entire performance. The town's elite was scandalised. Alinsky, seated anonymously in the back row, was delighted. He saw ridicule as a vital tool for beating the backsides of unyielding corporate bosses.

The Rochester bean feast was the latest in a string of colourful Alinsky antics. Still fresh in the memory of corporate America was an action that went down as the most daring blackmail threat in Chicago's history. At stake was the security of the world's busiest airport – and the reputation of the entire Chicago administration.

The threat was uncompromising and simple: either City Hall met the demands of the blackmailers, or a small army of urban guerrillas would bring O'Hare airport to its knees.

These momentous affairs at the time were known to only a handful of people, and negotiations were confined to two parties. On the one side was Mayor Richard Daley, head of a vast and corrupt city administration. On the other, Saul Alinsky.

Daley faced a stark choice. Either he reformed the City's perverted housing policy, or Alinsky would give the green light to a thousand waiting supporters to squat in every cubicle and urinal in the airport. With its facilities blocked for even an hour, the Great Hub of Chicago would be a zoo; within two hours it would become mayhem.

At the eleventh hour, the administration caved in. The mere threat of the shit-in was sufficient to guarantee meetings to discuss improvement of the slum areas of Chicago. Ed Chambers, then Alinsky's right hand man, recalls: "We knew that power was not necessarily what you had or what you did, but what the enemy thought you had. If they think you are going to destroy the plumbing system or the Beethoven symphony, then they will have to act".[146] The Kodak and O'Hare actions galvanised Alinsky's reputation as the most innovative community activist in recent American history.

On to battle!

Inspired by Alinsky, it then took less than a week before I devised a plan appropriate to the man's legacy. On a dreary Monday morning, I formally announced the creation of a Students Representative Council (SRC). This

---

146 Cohen, Alex; Horwitt, Sanford (January 30, 2009). "Saul Alinsky, The Man Who Inspired Obama". *Day to Day*. NPR.
http://www.npr.org/templates/story/story.php?storyId=100057050

idea was anathema to a conservative church school and was sure to bring the issue to a head – one way or the other. We used two songs as anthems for this unprecedented mutiny. One was 'The Times they are a Changin' and the other, appropriately, was 'The Spy'.

I thought for one moment that my campaign's *Piéce de Résistance* had been when we subverted the school's public address system and played those songs through a hundred megaphones across the precinct (we beat the Shawshank Redemption by nearly a quarter of a century). But we ended up doing a little better than that.

I had organised a "public" meeting one afternoon to debate the SRC. The school was incapable of shutting down the meeting, chiefly because I was using the patronage of a rival church for the event. Thank you, Saul Alinsky, for your early analysis of "thinking out of the box".

Knowing that absolutely every staff member would attend, I then rapidly built and trained a SWAT team of a dozen trusted students to deliver the *coup de grace*. While the public meeting was in full swing, my team replaced the toilet locks. More significant, on every cubicle and on every locker (courtesy of the unattended school duplicators), they placed the following notice:

> ***Do unto others as you would have them do unto you.***
> Luke 6:31

In doing so, we unknowingly enacted the principles of transparency and accountability, while also celebrating Alinsky's principle that we should always "make the enemy live up to its own book of rules".

Despite my attempt at plausible deniability (I was intentionally speaking at the public meeting at the time of the action), the headmaster proclaimed the following day that, "If it smells like manure and tastes like manure, it probably is manure". I was expelled without appeal, but that episode changed me – and many of my friends – forever.

It was a seminal period for me. My SRC action caused a domino effect, with schools across the country taking similar action over issues as diverse as corporal punishment to prohibition of political beliefs. My peers met me regularly to discuss Alinsky and his strategies.

The Great Duck Scandal

But even these days as a seasoned campaigner, such precise triggers still affect me on a regular basis.

Consider the Great Duck Scandal of 2014, during which I was travelling on the ferry train from Hamburg to Copenhagen. On this occasion the trip was not as convivial as usual. Thanks to various reactionary government edicts, border controls throughout the European region have been ramped up (though there is, as some reports describe it, a glimmer of hope that a few EU borders are being relaxed).

There's a presumption in the Schengen Border Agreement of the EU that there should be unhindered travel, but countries such as Sweden and Hungary opted for a derogation. In some parts of Europe, moving between countries is returning to an era before the Union was formed. Many people in countries such as Sweden and Denmark, which in the past had been at war since the 17th century, were scandalised that these measures were being imposed. Or, more precisely, re-imposed. Denmark in turn stepped up its controls on Germany.

So, on that trip to Copenhagen it came as little surprise when three border officials approached me on the train and "requested" to search my bags.[147]

Until then I had paid little attention to internal borders. Sure, I had campaigned against US-VISIT[148] and the fingerprinting of all visitors to America. I had campaigned against "Electronic Borders" in countries such as the UK and Australia, but I had never found the motivation to look at what happens to some people when they cross internal borders within a region.

There was nothing of interest in my bags until one officer discovered a small hand carved wooden duck, which was given to me as a gift by a conference in Norway. It was my Good Luck Duck.

It was a beautiful item, doubtless carved by rustic artists from an ancient spruce tree on the shores of a remote exotic fjord. Someone had gone to

---

147 The scourge of humiliating luggage checks, the Privacy Surgeon.
   http://www.privacysurgeon.org/blog/incision/bag-searches-at-borders-reveal-more-than-ornamental-nipple-clamps/ (accessed 14th July 2018).
148 Gerald Nino, 11th December 2007 https://commons.wikimedia.org/wiki/File:US-VISIT_(CBP).jpg

the trouble of daubing it with art-nouveau yellow and blue circles, just like ducks aren't.

The officials were intrigued. "What is this?" one asked, slowly turning it around like an antiques expert. Admittedly, it was a typically Norwegian abstract duck made to look like a rugby ball with a pair of wooden scissors sticking out of one end. Fellow passengers also seemed curious to know. After all, they had become part of this show. "Why do you carry this?" he continued, in a voice loud enough to be overheard in Romania.

They prodded that duck. They held it to the light, shook it, tapped it and meddled with its bits. "Are there drugs in here?"

I explained that it was just a duck, but they persisted. Of course, they were bending all the rules to breaking point. Then he started banging it against a metal pole. At that point I became visibly angry. Then they went through all my papers, loudly enquiring why I had visited Russia.

I was irritated that this Security Theatre had overridden the basic right of free travel. On my return to Amsterdam I called a number of EU officials who I worked with and built a solid and detailed complaint to the European Commission. I quoted section 16 of the Schengen Border Agreement at them:

> *Internal borders may be crossed at any point without a border check on persons, irrespective of their nationality, being carried out.*

As I suspected, it was a hopeless exercise. Very few complaints to the Commission end up favouring the complainant.

I guess it is fair to say that this one tiny incident of duck banging turned me into a campaigner against the abuse of internal borders.

But back to the broader issue of why people become interested in privacy. I'll recount some stories a little later of colleagues who became full-time advocates, but I'd like to start with the experiences of three people who went through personal conflicts that changed their world view of privacy and which turned them overnight into advocates.

Case study one: the Great Canadian Chocolate Drama

I was travelling with my friend David (let's call him David Smith) en route from the US to Canada. I had some speaking engagements lined up there.

David was an Oxford University student, and was with me from New York to Halifax, Nova Scotia, when he made the mistake of failing to declare on his customs form that he was carrying seven Maltesers across the border.

For the benefit of the uninitiated, Maltesers are a confectionery product manufactured by Mars Incorporated. They consist of a small, roughly spherical malt honey flavoured centre, surrounded by milk chocolate.

The young Oxonian was unaware that these items might constitute dairy products and are thus a controlled substance.[149] This was despite precise government advice that dairy products mean "cheese, milk, yoghurt and butter", and thus by apparent logical inference, chocolate.

It is not that chocolate – if indeed chocolate is included in the definition of "dairy products" – is banned. Far from it. You can bring in 20 kg of the stuff. You could argue – maybe irrationally – that David was a borderline case, given that seven Maltesers weigh a combined 14.679 grams or 0.073395 percent of the allowable amount.

Having confessed this oversight to the border official, David was sternly lectured. Then, rather than taking the sensible route of asking him to simply throw the offending material into the nearest bin, the official told David to report to Canadian Customs on the way out of the airport. She wrote "CHOCOLATE" loudly on his form, as if to signal impending danger to Canada.

All this got me to musing that if airlines coming into Canada are permitted to peddle chocolates, then surely they should label all packaging with a customs declaration warning.

Then unfurled the second bizarre episode in this litany of oddities. There seemed to be no communication between border control and customs. David could have simply walked past Customs – they would have been none the wiser – but he dutifully reported to them. Big mistake.

---

149 http://www.beaware.gc.ca/english/brirape.shtml

Customs asked David whether I – as his travelling companion – had also been told to report to them. They didn't ask me, they asked him – the suspect. When he said no, that was good enough for them and I was told to leave.

They just let Mr Big go free! I had supplied David with the Maltesers, and in fact had two small bags of them on my person. Now I was free to roam the streets, trafficking my Maltesers to innocent Canadians.

I was not permitted to stay to support my friend in the impending grilling – Canadian Federal Privacy Act and all that. Canadian government officials always want you to know they are aware of the Federal Privacy Act. They usually tell you very loudly and repeatedly. The Federal Privacy Act – like the Data Protection act in the UK – has become a device to deny information or assistance to the public.

To the casual observer, Customs in Halifax might give out every sign of being an indolent, overstaffed, underworked bunch of time-servers, but don't you believe it. When confronted with the menace of chocolate trafficking they spring theatrically into action. Within minutes, the officers were all over David, doubtless convinced that a person who would carry confectionery might also be an arms dealer. Or, more accurately, an arms dealer without a state licence under the Export and Import Permits Act (R.S.C., 1985, c. E-19) to deal arms.

By way of background, the Canadian border does not enjoy a reputation for human kindness. In 2007 – in what was one of the most shameful incidents in RCMP and border security history – Robert Dziekanski was tasered to death for a crime no greater than being confused and agitated. Nor does the border agency enjoy a reputation for common sense. In a decision a few years ago, the Canadian International Trade Tribunal gave a severe slapping to the Canada Border Services Agency, for indulging in a Kafkaesque farce for many years over a simple administrative error in the labelling of boxes of imported Cheetos.[150] The signs were not good.

Mindful of this – and frightened as he was – David kept his cool.

Still, all the border agencies have beautifully crafted Charters. The Canadian Border Services Agency proclaims its commitment to ensuring

---

150 Barrie Mckenna, 9th January 2013 http://www.theglobeandmail.com/report-on-business/industry-news/the-law-page/in-a-bureaucratic-box-cardboard-cheetos-and-the-canadian-border/article7129030/

'respect and courtesy' and 'Fair application of the law.'[151] Oh, and privacy. Let's not forget privacy.

I left the customs area and waited for David. Half an hour... an hour... ninety minutes. By this time I was freaking out.

I asked a border cop for an assurance that David was OK, only to be loudly told, "Federal Privacy Act – I cannot talk to you." Then he added, "But I can tell you, the flight is not cleared." Well, I mean, talk about stating the obvious.

I informed the cop, that I was merely asking for non-personal information, and that he surely could at least give an assurance that David was alright, but he repeated "Federal Privacy Act", so the entire terminal could hear, and then added even more loudly, "SIR". Saying "sir" so assertively in Canada is a prelude to trouble. "SIR" means "back off". They learned this verbal tactic from the US. Of course.

I then finally managed after nearly two hours to speak to the Superintendent of Customs – a fearsome lady with more insignias than a Formula One racing car – who told me in, marvellously crafted tones of sarcasm, that she couldn't say anything to me because of the Federal Privacy Act.

It is a little known fact that although a course in the Federal Privacy Act is mandatory for all federal public servants, there are two possible related merit badges that officials can earn. One is in 'FPA assertiveness' (you have to learn to say "Federal Privacy Act" very loudly at anyone who dares ask for assistance) and then there's a more prized 'FPA condescension' badge, which qualifies you to make the enquirer feel humiliated and intimidated. The Superintendent of Customs clearly had a Level Three merit badge in FPA condescension. I think that might have been one of the insignias on her shoulder.

I told her I wanted to be with my friend because he would be scared, and I perhaps could provide support and advice. She said no. I then asked that she tell David that I would be here for him when he was released. She gruffly replied, "He can phone you when (if) he gets out."

The Federal Privacy Act apparently prohibited any further attention to the

---

matter, and no amount of insistence that I actually knew the Act made the slightest difference to the situation. Level Three merit badges are used against troublemakers like me.

She did however crack at one point and admit David was in "secondary examination". Secondary examination is one of those brilliantly meaningless terms that implies "special treatment". Was he having a heart attack? Had he been turned away at the border? It was such inhumane disinterest that had laid the foundations for the killing of Robert Dziekanski. I waited in utter ignorance of the proceedings, but at least she did assure me that he would be informed of my presence. I chain-smoked in the ice and snow of a bus shelter outside.

Meanwhile, here was what was going on behind the scenes.

Having secured the chocolate admission, the officers did a full search of David's possessions. Irritated at their continuing failure to find anything of interest they decided to do a swab procedure on his baggage. David's profile and demeanour of a wholly innocent traveller was clearly evidence of his guilt – over something.

How the system followed the Federal Privacy Act's principles of purpose specification and proportionality by elevating a chocolate admission to a drugs swab is beyond me. It stretches "just cause" and "reasonable suspicion" to a level I could not have contemplated.

In any event, they discovered traces of cocaine. Then the system went into hyperdrive.

"Traces of cocaine" might sound ominous, but it is worth remembering that cocaine traces are found in ninety percent of US banknotes,[152] and even in the air across several Italian cities.[153]

The officials microscopically inspected David's belongings, then they told him to strip – piece by piece like some macabre pole dance – and minutely inspected all his clothes. Then they went through the contents of his computer. That in itself should set alarm bells ringing in the ears of anyone who cares about proportionality and just cause.

Still having discovered absolutely nothing of interest apart from the

152 , http://www.guardian.co.uk/world/2009/aug/17/cocaine-dollar-bills-currency-us (accessed 12th July 2018).
153 Pfeiffer, E. 25th October 2012 http://news.yahoo.com/blogs/sideshow/traces-cocaine-

traces, they went medical. Ordering him to part his buttock cheeks, he was required to do a sort of weird naked Cossack dance in front of them, before having to perform various acts like lifting up his scrotum.

In the end, nothing. Of course. And by nothing, I mean not even an apology or an utterance of regret over what had happened.

The experience was traumatic. He still has nightmares, but it converted David to the cause of privacy. He is currently an assistant to a privacy network.

Case study two: The Gatwick debacle

This is the story of Jonathan, who in 2015 was detained and interrogated for more than seven hours at the UK border. The man was subsequently refused entry and forced back to mainland Europe on grounds that can best be described as bizarre and unstable.

Jonathan wrote a blog on the Privacy Surgeon some time ago about his experience. It casts a harrowing distinction between the government statistics and the harsh reality.

"So this is it. I'm suddenly in a bleak airport security detention room alongside a bunch of terrified people who seem to be what the government views as suspected criminals, over-stayers and terrorists. The daunting, heavy door closed behind me.

"I'm terrified. This is something I've never experienced before, but it's odd how you bond with people under such pressure. One guy, a very despondent New Yorker, had come here to see his girlfriend. The border police told him that he would be deported and that there's only a 50/50 chance that he'd see her before that moment. He knew that was a lie.

"A lovely woman from Nigeria, with family here, took me under her wing and worked hard to walk me through the process. She receives this horrible treatment each year when she visits, inevitably to be let into the country after the harassment is legally exhausted.

---

marijuana-found-air-eight-italian-cities-220044243.html (accessed 14th May 2018).

"The story repeats itself. Good, ordinary people with friends, family, relationships here. Brutalised and intimidated because they don't 'fit' the UK's standard. I'm next, and I can feel the tears building up."[154]

That action underscores an increasingly inhumane and unlawful UK border policy. It also highlights the utter chaos of the broader EU border management regime.

The management of European borders frequently leads to uncertainty and conflict. Different visa systems operated by the UK, Ireland and mainland Europe have created a situation where travellers are exposed to the risk of overstaying, with the consequence of detention and interrogation.

The primary arrangement in the EU is called "Schengen", an agreement that in theory creates a borderless region comprising 26 European countries. Schengen is an important agreement primarily because freedom of movement and the elimination of internal borders are central to the European ideal.

To satisfy this ideal, Schengen was designed as a vast "passport free" zone. Or, it *would* have been a passport free zone were it not for the fact that it isn't. The laws of most Schengen countries require you to carry identity documents at all times. In other words, you would be illegal if you didn't carry a passport.

All of which would not matter so much if there were no actual border checks, but there are. Indeed border checks involving demands for disclosure of identity are permitted by the Schengen agreement, so every country conducts border checks.

Here's the background to Schengen.

· The idea is that the system comprises a "hard" outer border encapsulating all member countries, and then "soft" internal borders so EU residents and tourists have "freedom" of movement. The logic is that it's hard to sneak into the Schengen area, but easy to move around once you're in it.

I should add a caveat. The deal that governments cut in return for having "soft" internal borders is that national authorities can often detain you at will and demand identity in a wide range of circumstances (and require

---

154 'Forced detention, interrogation and £20 Nicorettes… Welcome to Britain'
   The Privacy Surgeon; March 15th 2015
   http://www.privacysurgeon.org/blog/incision/forced-detention-interrogation-and-20-

your passport in situations like booking a hotel room). Much of this data feeds into a vast panopticon called the Schengen Information System. In this way, Schengen is being constructed as the world's largest zone of surveillance.

But there is a core problem. Even now, no-one – least of all the actual border authorities – has an agreed way of calculating this equation. In theory, officials should work backwards and count the number of days spent in Schengen to see whether the 90 allowable days has been spent. In reality, busy border officials look for the first (or sometimes the last) Schengen entry stamp and then count forwards. Indeed the Danish Immigration service advises using a calendar to count forward from the last date of entry into Schengen. This confusion triggered the problems encountered by Jonathan.

Jonathan, for the record, is a young, white, working class, partly Jewish, small-town American with a back injury and no criminal record. He had made two trips to Europe, one short journey in September 2015 and another extended trip in late November. The UK believed he had thus overstayed his welcome.

But with this in mind, Jonathan still took the decision to see friends in the UK, which he attempted to do on March 11th.

The first I had heard about Jonathan's predicament was a message via a friend to call the border authorities at London's Gatwick Airport. Jonathan was being detained and questioned – and had been in that state for almost five hours. He had told the authorities that I was a good friend and they should call me to verify that he wasn't planning to abscond forever into some remote English forest. It seemed a reasonable request. No-one wants to be in a remote English forest because of the hordes of backpackers and tourist buses.

I advised the border officials that there was no question of Jonathan breaking UK visa rules. Indeed he had already booked a flight to the Netherlands the following week. He would be staying with – and supported by – close friends during his short stay (those friends were actually in the airport and confirmed this situation directly with the authorities).

Despite these interventions, UK officials took the decision after seven

nicorettes-welcome-to-britain/

154

hours to remove Jonathan from the country and place him on the next flight to Copenhagen – his most recent point of origin.

The *Notice of Refusal of Leave to Enter* that was handed to Jonathan is nothing short of mystifying. It states that the reason for refusal is that Jonathan demonstrated *"a willingness to flout the immigration rules of another country"* (i.e. Schengen). This assertion stretches credulity to breaking point.

As a result of that experience, Jonathan is now a volunteer for a global privacy organisation. He also had the image of his deportation stamp tattooed on his chest as a permanent reminder of the saga.

Case study three: identity idiocy

Ridiculously overpriced whisky isn't the only reason why San Francisco's International House of Wine & Liquor is famous. Anyone of any age who buys a packet of cigarettes there is required to show an identity document. A sickly luminescent pink sign on the front counter of this Geary Street checkpoint advises that the policy applies to all customers.

As a bald, respectable-looking middle aged man, this is an imposition David Reynolds did not expect. To the titillation of queuing customers he announced that this was the most absurd requirement in the known world and that they should reconsider.

They didn't budge. Aggressively, the guy at the front counter shouted back that this was "company policy", in a tone that suggested he was an idiot for not realising that Company Policy trumped law. But more worryingly, he tried to assure everyone in the shop that this requirement was "police policy".

If anyone knows any legally sustainable police policy in this vein, please do enlighten me. Come to think of it, what is "police policy" anyway? Is it an administrative condition where police arbitrarily advise local businesses what they should do? Is it like the legally dodgy concept of "community policy"?

Indeed, there's a valid reason to require ID at licensed places in case someone is under 21. But at the age of fifty or sixty? The hilarious justification is sometimes that the policy avoids discrimination.

David promptly conducted a vox pop of a neighbouring business to make sure the police had not imposed this requirement, and the bemused staff said they had never heard of such a thing. They observed that people would vote with their wallets, which – in this case – they most certainly did.

This ludicrous irritation wouldn't have concerned David so much if it hadn't become so prevalent in the US – and elsewhere. Earlier that year while visiting Washington DC he had decided to visit a now-deceased club called Omega and had been clobbered with the same requirement. Then, a stony faced and now-unemployed bouncer had presented him with the startling news that age identification for all patrons was "DC law".

Americans have gone nuts over photo ID ever since 9/11. They can't get enough of it. AMTRAK insists on such documentation, even though the company doesn't have a clue what to do with the ID. People working at the reception desks of just about any office building require it. One friend was asked for photo ID when he tried to purchase some gardening equipment "in case the digging items are used in connection with explosives". You know, that whole "garden spade-fertiliser-bomb" connection. Logical really.

At least Britain sort of got it half right. There, to make life easier for stores selling age-restricted items, there's a "Challenge 21" programme, so anyone looking 21 or under is asked for ID, even if the products are available to over-18s. Tesco and other large chain stores then championed a "Challenge 25" programme, just in case someone slipped through the net. Finally some idiot in the seaside resort of Blackpool came up with the idea of "Challenge 30", which is roundly lambasted across Britain. All the same, Britain – like America – is terrified of alcohol, even though most of its culture, art, literature and music has been enabled by it.

But at least the UK outlets demand high-integrity forms of ID such as driving licences. In the US you can show a picture of your dog pasted on the back of a chocolate biscuit and they're likely to accept it. That's because no-one really knows – apart from bars and liquor outlets – why they are asking for ID in the first place, and no-one up the chain tells them, mainly because they don't know either. Everyone just goes through the motions. There's no way to verify the validity of ID, so everyone just plods along with the security theatre.

I have tested the limits of this procedure. Once I was asked for ID at the reception of a large office building in New York. I asked the security guy why he needed it and his reply was, "Don't know – they never told me. It's in my job specs".

So, I dutifully showed the guy my ID, which in this case was an out of date London School of Economics pass-card that looked like it was created with fingernails and pointed sticks in a Guatemalan prison. He looked at the dog-eared item and returned it, only to be asked, "So how do you know this isn't fake?"

The beleaguered security man repeated what he had said earlier, so I asked to see his supervisor.

The supervisor, confirming he didn't know why his people were collecting ID's or how they would validate them, said: "It's just a requirement they made in the work contract".

I went on up the chain, until finally, I had several security people, two supervisors of the security company and the contract manager for the building in a confused cluster, all agreeing that they didn't know why they were demanding ID's.

This insanity really does have to be evaluated. It is the identity equivalent of the old "loitering" laws. At best it is a public nuisance; at worst it is a threat to genuine security. The occasions where identity disclosure has real value are relatively rare, and in those cases, there needs to be a properly constructed and privacy-sensitive policy in place. Right now anyone, with access to a corner-stall two dollar document printer, can gain access into almost anywhere they choose. My dog photo will get me into everywhere else.

This is one of those many circumstances where a privacy Tsar would be of real use in the US. Such an official could set out standards and guidelines, so everyone would understand both the limits of their responsibility and the real meaning of the law.

David now evangelises for identity reform in the US.

* * * * *

Such is the case with many privacy advocates. Kirsten Fiedler from European Digital Rights (EDRi) recalls, "There was a very specific trigger that I remember. That must have been in 1999 or so. In any case, I wasn't even 20 years old when the city of Bonn, where I was studying philosophy at the time, started to put up surveillance cameras everywhere, especially in the subway stations. I remember getting very angry about this massive invasion – I felt very concretely that my freedoms were restricted".

For sociologist Gary Marx, that trigger was the Watergate scandal and the social movements that followed. For Steve Wright – who two decades later went on to trigger Europe's interest in the spying activities of the NSA – it was a brutal police action. "It was the special branch raid on Lancaster University in 1977 (motto: *'Truth lies open to all'*) when I realised that the capacities for monitoring had stepped beyond meaningful comprehension".

In a similar vein, David Christopher from Canada's OpenMedia recalls the spark being the eastern Europe revolutions of 1989. "I paid very close attention to this (yes, I was a political nerd even at the age of 12 years old — plus I had a brand new short wave radio to listen in on faraway broadcasts in those pre-Web days!). The revelations about the Stasi and the Securitate probably left a lasting impression on me that there needs to be very strict boundaries around government surveillance of their citizens' activities."

Likewise for Katarzyna Szymielewicz of Poland's Panoptykon Foundation. "My trigger in 2008 was the discovery of how governments worldwide, including Poland, used the 'war on terror' narrative to exclude individuals and groups of people from 'any' protection, to undermine the very concept of universal human rights. That was the year when we discussed secret prisons in Poland, and we felt that there is no way we can force government to become more accountable, if we do not question the whole narrative, and the surveillance machinery behind it."

For Robert Beens, the CEO of privacy technology company Startpage, it was in 2005 when he was reading 'the Google Story'. It described how data mining personal data of its users would soon become the 'inside monster-motor' of their business model. It also described the blind spot almost all techno-idealists seemed to have – "only seeing advantages to their technical innovations, but no negatives."[155] [156]

The more legally minded folk often find that court judgments provide a trigger. Former Berlin (Brandenburg) privacy commissioner, Alexander Dix – one of the heroes of the privacy movement – recalls, "Thinking back on what triggered my engagement in/for privacy, I remember my time as a law student back in 1970, when I first read a famous judgment by the German Federal Constitutional Court ('Abhör-Urteil'), dealing with an amendment to the Constitution and allowing for telephone tapping without judicial warrant by intelligence services. These powers until then had been reserved to the Allied Powers, and Germany passed emergency laws to get rid of them, and to join the western Alliance. These amendments were challenged before the Constitutional Court who – by a majority of 5:3 – upheld them as constitutional. I was particularly interested in the opinion of the three dissenting judges who – for me convincingly – took the view that "even in times of emergency (today we would add: in times of terrorist threats) certain fundamental human rights are not to be sacrificed."

---

155 http://www.nytimes.com/2006/08/09/technology/09aol.html
156 http://www.not-secret.com

PART TWO

STARTING THE MOVEMENT AND TAKING ON GOLIATH

Chapter Seven: Identity frolics

My first major campaign in 1987 against the Australian national identity card, and what the greatest civil resistance movement in the nation's history taught me. Narratives of similar campaigns against national identity systems from Thailand and the Philippines to India and New Zealand. And an overview of the UK national card campaign and the price advocates sometimes pay for success. Identity systems are more than just 'a card'; they are the visible manifestation of the surveillance state.

The Australia Card: a nation awakes

It is September 1987 and I'm sitting nervously in my tiny, cluttered bedroom in Sydney, Australia, watching TV images of a huge demonstration outside the State Parliament of Western Australia. At least 30,000 angry people have gathered to protest the introduction of a national ID card.

As the State Premier's car sweeps into view, it is attacked by the mob, which almost succeeds in overturning it. Were it not for the intervention of two van loads of police, they would doubtless have done so.[157]

I'm viewing these remarkable events while conversing on the phone with the Leader of the Federal Senate, Janine Haines. "This is amazing, but we can't have violence," she warns. "Do something! Call them off for a

---

157 The Australian, 24 September 1987 reported that a car carrying the Western Australian Premier was attacked by demonstrators in Perth and required police assistance.

while".

"Call them off?" I hardly even know who "they" are. Well, I kind of know, to the extent that one of the organisers called me a while back asking for speakers, but this event is completely out of my control. Still, Haines is right. The national mood is turning nasty and it is only a matter of time before someone gets killed in the growing furore. As recently as the previous day, newspapers had reported that even the Federal Labour Party Caucus (the governing body of the government party) had reached the point of violence over the ID issue.[158]

The phone keeps ringing. Next, it is the greatest sports hero of the age, Ben Lexcen, whose famous "winged keel" design had – for the first time ever – recently snatched the America's Cup yacht race from the US.

"Bloody brilliant!" he yelled. "You did it! We have them by the balls!"

But I hadn't done it. All I had done was to design the rocket and light the fuse for the movement. That, and hopelessly attempting to plan a national political strategy on rapidly shifting sands. Nine tenths of what was going on was entirely outside my control as campaign director. Events were moving now at such speed that I could barely even keep up with the day's news. I learned back then that sometimes you need to lose control over a campaign in order to win it.

Still, I had been a fool. I should have sensed that the writing was on the wall and that events in Perth would unfurl this way. The strength of public feeling was palpable. Only ten days earlier I had been at the podium of the AMOCO Hall in the central New South Wales town of Orange, where 4,000 furious people had gathered. To put the numbers in perspective, that's one in five of the city's adult population. Other towns across the country were responding in a similar way.

Organising mass demonstrations wasn't really my thing, but why not try! A couple of weeks later, fuelled with optimism from the Perth event, I called Sydney City authorities with a request to use The Domain, a vast stretch of parkland behind state Parliament House. I was guessing that with a sunny day and the right collection of speakers, we would bring in maybe 200,000 people – if The Domain could even support such numbers. And to be frank, there most likely was not a single public figure who would refuse to speak. I had already been on the phone to every famous author, artist and musician in the land.

Word travels fast. Within an hour the phone rang again, and it was a commander of police on the other end. "Ah, I see you're thinking of a demo," he nonchalantly began. "Indeed," I affirmed.

Five seconds of silence.

"We need to think a little about it," the man continued in a deadpan voice. "It might be a larger-than-normal thing".

"Larger-than-normal" was possibly the grandest understatement of the year, by any police officer. Even the cop agreed that 200,000 was a reasonable figure, while I was pushing the estimate to a quarter of a million. "I need to make sure I have the back-up," he continued.

"It could be more, who bloody knows. And then we need to seal off MacQuarie Street, but we have those road works on George Street, so it will fuck things up royally".

In a further desperate resort to logic, he added, "You know, we have all these expos coming up, and the Asian government thing so it might be useful to hold off for a while, and I can let you know a good date".

The man clearly thought I was an idiot.

"Anyway, we could always prevent you, if that's necessary", he continued, with a newfound vigour in his voice.

Under the circumstances, this was not the right move for him to make. "And just how do you actually plan on stopping me?" I went on. "This is public parkland. You can't stop all those people – and if you even tried it would be civil war."

"OK, maybe we can't, but we can shut off the power".

This hilarious threat wasn't going anywhere, so in the end, bizarrely, he agreed with my point, but added, "Look, it's not so simple. What if they went on the rampage? Like hit the streets and smashed cars and windows and things. Be fair: you can't disclaim liability for that – and what if people get hurt?".

I instinctively wanted to remind him that if people got hurt, it would probably be at the hands of the notoriously brutal local police. Back then,

New South Wales was little short of a police state. Cops did whatever they wanted with impunity. Just in the last two weeks I had seen friends beaten up by those thugs, and others who were extorted for money. Still, I remained silent on that point.

"Come into the department, and we'll talk about this".

"Ha!" I exclaimed. "So you can arrest me as some sort of threat to public order?" (I was advised that this was a new arrestable offence, even though I hadn't been able to find the actual legislation).

"We know where you live," responded the cop. "If we wanted to do that, we could do it now." I felt foolish.

"Can you give me a week?" he pleaded. "I just need to, erm, line things up at this end."

He didn't need a week. Within three days, the government relented and scrapped the card.

During those last three days the phone had been ringing off the hook from federal and state cabinet ministers from the left and the right, all assuring me they were opposed to the scheme. I was getting bored with the customary recitation "this conversation never happened, right?" But it was interesting hearing intimate details of the unsavoury arm-twisting going on from the Prime Minister.

As a final note to show just how far the gyroscope had turned, we held a riotous celebration party the following week at my house. Several hundred of our key people attended and we broke every noise ordinance in the book. To my subsequent embarrassment, there were some local complaints, but police just patiently waited around the corner for three hours until the last guests left at 6AM. They then strolled casually into view, asking, "Is everything OK?" before adding, "And bloody well done!"

* * * * *

By way of background, the Australian government had pledged to introduce this "Australia Card" scheme in 1985. Indeed it had been its primary election platform. After the senate had blocked the proposal, a federal election had been called over the plan, but neither the government or the Opposition bothered to mention the Card during the campaign period. Yet like every other ID scheme throughout future decades, it was to be a surveillance and tracking mechanism.

This credit card sized document was to be carried by all Australian citizens, permanent residents and tourists. It would initially contain a photograph name, unique number, signature and period of validity, As later events were to prove, it was to go down in history as one of the most notorious acts of policy folly of all time.

The public had initially accepted the idea without question. The plan was, after all, a simple matter of weeding out tax evaders and welfare fraudsters. "Only cheats and criminals would oppose it," chanted the government. "Law abiding citizens will want to support this," insisted the media. In time, "Nothing to hide, nothing to fear" became a sort of national mantra. Few people wanted to stand in the way of efforts to catch the guilty. Early opinion polls showed an eighty per cent support for the card. Later that became ninety percent. The other ten percent either remained silent, or had their opinions censored by mass media.[159]

Indeed, so popular was the idea that the government agencies wanting to use the card as a basis for their administration leaped in six months, from three to thirty. The proposed card was extended to catch assorted miscreants and illegal immigrants, and was to be used for financial transactions, property dealings, and employment. The list grew and grew. Health benefits, passport control, housing. This blow-out in unintended purposes was later to be given a catchy name by privacy advocates: "Function Creep". A billion dollars or more a year would ultimately be saved by the ID card system, or so the story went. The card number would be the link between all agencies. This was the subtle but crucial difference between this system, and the more traditional paper-based card systems that existed in Europe.[160]

At the time I wasn't much interested in the scheme. Historic sites

---

159 Davies, S. (2004). The Loose Cannon: An overview of campaigns of opposition to National Identity Card proposals, Published in Roger Clarke's site https://www.privacy.org.au/About/Davies0402.html

160 Roger Clarke; Just Another Piece of Plastic for your Wallet: The 'Australia Card' Scheme http://www.rogerclarke.com/DV/OzCard.html

preservation,[161] police and drug law reform[162] were my dominant concerns back then. Sure, I'd run many small privacy-related campaigns in previous years, but those had little to do with computers. Mainly they were employment and police-related actions – illegal wiretapping, trades union infiltration, police corruption and so on. And anyway, the country seemed to back the plan, and like almost everyone else, I just went with the media flow.

On reflection, computers were not on most people's radar screen in those days. I was still hunched over an Olivetti typewriter like some Raymond Chandler character, and the Internet was barely in existence. Computers were magical items used for stuff like car rentals and airline bookings. Nothing sinister there. How difficult then to imagine a world of computerised surveillance. When the Great Revelation did finally occur some time later to many of us, it amounted to what the British film industry is fond of describing as a "mind fuck".

Then in June 1987 a colleague, Tim Dixon, convinced me to attend a protest rally in Sydney's Martin Plaza (then Martin Place) organised by Senator Paul McLean.[163] I reluctantly agreed, arguing that if his surveillance conspiracy theories were so solid, then surely I would have heard about it. Or, at the very least, someone in a pub would have mentioned the ID plan.

It was a sad event. Fewer than a dozen people showed up (plus an uninterested dog). This in itself rang alarm bells in my head. Surely any national scheme of this magnitude should attract more interest? Something wasn't right.

The rally's failure worried me. But what to do? How does anyone reverse such overwhelming public opinion?

There was only one solution, and that was to gather together as many high profile public figures as possible. I felt – based on Tim Dixon's

---

161 See the Islands of Sydney Harbour, Davies, S. Hale and Irenmonger, 1984. This book ended up forcing the state government to make the seven islands open to the public for the first time in two hundred years.
162 For example, the Australia & New Zealand Foundation for Drug Policy was founded by Simon Davies in 1987and involved patrons such as former Australian Prime Minister Sir John Gorton and other former Prime Ministers and Governors General of both countries. This followed the publication of "Shooting Up: Heroin Australia"; Davies, S. Hale & Irenmonger, Sydney 1986.
163 ibid

analysis – that if I could just get five minutes with each person, then I could convince them to oppose it.

But that action in itself inevitably would not be enough to swing the trend. These national figures needed to be located right across the political spectrum, to the point where even bitter opponents linked arms. In this strategy, government could not dismiss the initiative as "just the usual suspects".

I cannot overstate just how daunting that challenge was for an ordinary person like me. Some people are accustomed to dealing with power, and some have to take the route of trial and error.

In any such impossible campaign, research is everything. I called over a few friends to a local bar to ask advice. It was crucial to identify and secure the first target so that other public figures might be more inclined to join the campaign. Ideally, I wanted a domino effect.

"OK", I started. "Let's say, hypothetically, that this ID card is a bad idea. Like, it is not what you think it is, but much worse."

They went along with this fiction, seeing as they were all were supportive of the scheme.

"And let's say it wasn't just a card," I continued. "What if it was something that could massively increase the government's power? What person might change your mind if that was the case?"

To their credit, they actually did give this question some serious thought. A few public figures were suggested, but the poll winner was Alan Jones, the country's second-top radio broadcaster and coach of the world-beating Australian national rugby team.

"I heard him saying something about this the other day on his show," remarked one friend. "But I sort of switched off in my head."

Miraculously, I caught Jones at his hotel during training (back then people would give you such location details without a second thought). I was somewhat on edge, given that Jones had a reputation for being – diplomatically speaking – extremely blunt.

I barely needed to evangelise the issue. "Put my name down. I don't like the thing," he snapped. "Do you want me to call anyone else?"

He did call some colleagues, as did I. One by one, as the critical mass grew, they joined. Within two weeks we had assembled an extraordinary coalition. If there is such a thing as Creative Visualisation, this was it.

One problem was that I didn't really know what this action was all about. Unfairness? Power? Un-Australianism (if there is such a word)? It took a call from Professor Graham Greenleaf of the University of New South Wales to distil this question.

"You know this is privacy, right?" he declared. "This is all about privacy."

This was all news to me, but it kind of made sense. I had never encountered that word before, and I hated it because it sounded so meek and passive.[164] Like, "Please leave me alone, please please". It turned out that the great advocate Justice Louis Brandeis had articulated the word "privacy" in similar terms a century ago, in US law.

I was also ignorant of the vast intellectual foundation against the card that had been built up by Greenleaf,[165] Professor Roger Clarke, Professor Geoffrey de Q Walker, the New South Wales Privacy Committee and others. Media had simply not reported on their efforts. It turned out that many people had tried to defeat it, from business leaders to trades union leaders, but nothing had made a dent on this juggernaut.

I arranged a meeting on 28th July 1987, at Jones' inner city home, of people from wildly different edges of the political spectrum to plot the card's demise. The meeting involved well-known libertarians, communists, academics, lawyers, mainstream political party leaders, media figures, and business, music, medical, farming and community leaders.[166] Never had there been such a diverse gathering.

Still, it was a diplomatic challenge. Senator Janine Haines and Australian Surgeons Association president Michael Aroney despised each other. The communists despised the libertarians. The farming representatives despised the left. Running that campaign was like walking on egg shells laid out on a tub of nitro glycerine. Still, everyone agreed to set aside their differences for the common cause. it is interesting how privacy cuts

---

164 Why privacy is such an awful word, Privacy International blog, November 3, 2011
   https://www.privacyinternational.org/blog/why-privacy-such-awful-word
165 Greenleaf, Graham. "Quacking Like a Duck: The National ID Card Proposal (2006)
   Compared with the Australia Card (1986–87).'' 2007. http://austlii.edu.au/~graham/
166 An account of this meeting was published in the Sydney Morning Herald on 5 October
   1987

right across the political spectrum.[167]

We made sure the meeting itself was the worst kept secret of the era and media went crazy in an effort to discover the identities of everyone involved. We stayed silent, then launched our initiative in the plush ballroom of the Sebel Townhouse. People queued around the block to be there. Hundreds attended. All the Prime Minister could exclaim in the evening news was, "A strange bunch of bedfellows".

The Prime Minister, Bob Hawke, had become obsessed about the Australia Card. For him, it was the Great Idea that would transform the whole country (in that summation we were in agreement, but for different reasons).

It was all very surreal for me. Only five years earlier – 1982 – when I was just 25 years of age, Hawke and I had very publicly linked arms on my project to build hundreds of Kibbutz-type communities using fallow land owned by the State (of which there were millions of acres). He had even given the keynote at the International Labour Organisation (ILO) in Geneva and evangelised our plan as the way that society would be revolutionised.[168] Now we were enemies.

The Prime Minister had drunk the industry Kool-Aid. From the time years before when we dreamed of communities built on strong trust and enduring relationships, he moved to a policy of a technologically imposed central authority for trust.

Not long after the campaign meeting in Sydney – and the accompanying media interest – the situation changed markedly. The public started to debate the downside of these cards. Questions about the civil liberties implications remained unanswered. Doubts were cast. More and more prominent Australians from the left and the right warned that this card was not a path of least resistance to solve societal problems, but a slippery slope to a totally regulated society and even to a police state.

Attention was focussed on the extensive reporting obligations throughout the government and the community, the automatic exchange of information throughout the government, the ease of expansion of the

---

167 Davies, S. (2004). The Loose Cannon: An overview of campaigns of opposition to National Identity Card proposals, published in Roger Clarke's site https://www.privacy.org.au/About/Davies0402.html
168 A Kibbutz stirs the national psyche, the Sydney Morning Herald, 27 June 1983

system and the encouragement of the private sector and state governments to make use of the card and its number. Like the British Poll Tax plan some years later, where Prefects would be appointed in each house to report to the State, the Australia Card would require mass reporting by individuals and organisations. All finance sector employees would have been forced under threat of jail to report suspicions to the government.

As the Australia Card Bill was subjected to increasing scrutiny, the surveillance nature of the scheme received more attention. Graham Greenleaf described the components of the Australia Card as "the building blocks of surveillance".

Still, public opinion was well in favour of the scheme. In my view, the answer was to keep building this unprecedented coalition of leading figures across the political spectrum, to instigate a campaign of opposition under the banner of the Australian Privacy Foundation.[169] I could never have known that this action was to be my first of many major privacy campaigns across the world. Our beginnings never know our ends.

It took a few weeks for the public to recognise the importance of the mechanisms behind the card. People no longer accepted the interpretation that the card was merely a "simple piece of plastic". The spectre of a complete linkage of all information became a frightening prospect for many people.

There were also pragmatic concerns of a different nature. It was estimated that up to five percent of cards would be lost, stolen or damaged each year. Tens of thousands of people would suffer serious and prolonged disruption to their affairs.

Once these well-known figures had stated their opinion, other highly respected Australians rapidly joined the condemnation of the scheme. Former Westpac Bank chairman Sir Noel Foley stunned his colleagues with the blunt assessment that the card would pose "a serious threat to the privacy, liberty and safety of every citizen". Australian Medical Association president Dr Bruce Shepherd went as far as to predict: "It's going to turn Australian against Australian. But given the horrific impact

---

169 Australian Privacy Foundation history; Roger Clarke;
    https://www.privacy.org.au/About/Formation.html

the card will have on Australia, its defeat would almost be worth fighting a civil war for." Fuelled by the unique alliance, newspapers and talkback shows recorded an exponential increase in public concern.

More Australians joined the Privacy Foundation to voice protest at the scheme. Right wing academic Professor Lauchlan Chipman, communist author Frank Hardy, former Whitlam Government minister Jim McClelland and left wing economist Professor Ted Wheelwright all linked arms with their ideological foe to fight the scheme.

Justice Michael Kirby, then President of the NSW Court of Appeal, became more of a support than he may know. His patronage was invaluable and became a sort of bedrock for us. We were regularly invited to his chambers for lunch to discuss the complex ethical dimension of the card. As I recall, white fish and white wine were routinely on the menu. And string beans.

Within weeks, a huge movement was underway. Rallies were organised on almost a daily basis. Although these were described as "education nights", the reality was that most were hotbeds of hostility, rather than well-ordered information giving sessions.

Roger Clarke provides an excellent description of these events. He recalls that the letters pages of most newspapers reflected the strong feelings of Australians. "We won't be numbers!" was a typical letters page headline, with others such as "I have no intention of applying", "An alternative is the ball and chain", "Biggest con job in our history", "Overtones of Nazi Germany", "I will leave the country" and "Passive resistance gets my vote".[170] The cartoonists contributed to the strong feelings, with some constantly portraying Robert Hawke in Nazi uniform. Paul Zannetti of the Daily Telegraph was possibly the most effective of all cartoonists.

Historian Geoffrey Blainey compared the extraordinary protest to the Eureka Stockade. "The destruction of the licences at Ballarat, and the stand at Eureka Stockade was a rebellion against the erosion of personal liberty associated with the Australia Card of that era".[171] The card had touched a nerve in the national psyche, by cutting across what many saw as the national character."

Within weeks of its commencement, the campaign had galvanised

---

170 West Australian, 12 September 1987
171 Daily Sun, Brisbane, 8 September 1987

Australia against the Card. Despite elements of hysteria, the average Australian came to understand that the introduction of such a scheme would reduce freedoms and increase the power of authorities. Indeed, "freedom" would come to mean the freedoms granted by the card. As the Financial Review so eloquently observed, Australia's rights and freedoms are far more fragile than those of its older counterparts. A government should be committed to strengthening those freedoms.

* * * * *

it is odd how occasionally an entire nation can change its view on rights in a relatively short time. I recall just four years earlier I had been taking a late night stroll down York Street in the city centre of Sydney, on my way to present a radio show. I spied a huge pile of cartons that had been dumped outside the Department of Veteran's Affairs. Intrigued, I took a moment to look inside.

To my astonishment, they were filled to the brim with confidential documents: bank statements, investigation files, medical records, details of security arrangements, computer printouts of paymasters' transactions – the list went on and on.

I grabbed a sample handful and the next day visited the editor of the Sun Herald, then the biggest selling newspaper in the country. Bizarrely, the response was that the story was interesting but not particularly shocking. The subsequent article was less than two hundred words and was placed fairly well back in the paper. I wasn't even asked to secure an official response. These days, such a bland scenario would be impossible to imagine.[172]

In contrast to the situation in 1987, it was near impossible to get serious traction for privacy stories in that earlier era. In 1982, for example, I wrote an exclusive article for the Sun Herald which blew the lid on illegal phone tapping by NSW police. My informant – who, by the way, went fully on the record – was Justice James Staples, a senior federal court

---

172 "Confidential files dumped in street", Davies, S. The Sun Herald, 11th August 1984

judge.

"The critical issue", he warned, "is that an illegal intelligence operation unknown to the government was, and maybe still is, being run by the NSW police."

He described the activity as a "para-military operation" and called on the police minister to sack the officers involved or resign. The paper ran this story as a medium-sized piece on page five.[173] Almost nothing transpired as a result of these disclosures.

Staples' claim should have caused a storm, but it didn't. Infuriated by the lack of response to his allegations, I continued campaigning on police corruption and intrusion. Matters improved slightly toward 1987, after the first state Ombudsman was appointed. I had occasional wins, one against the Internal Police Security Unit[174], but the overall standard of oversight by government was appalling compared to other Western countries. Having a strong regulator is crucial, and activists should consider relentlessly using such officials. For privacy, it took the ID card fight to usher in a Federal Privacy Commissioner. Regrettably, the initial legislation was exceptionally weak. Still, the new Federal Privacy Act was one up-side to the campaign that I initially didn't anticipate. After all, Australia is unique among advanced nations in that it has no constitutional right to privacy and most other human rights.

The Australian Privacy Foundation soldiered on regardless, winning numerous privacy battles. One was the Federal credit reporting legislation. I had been campaigning on that one for a while. We were concerned, for example, that the entire credit reference regime was controlled by a monopoly organisation, the Credit Reference Agency, and that that organisation was about to introduce "positive reporting", which would have massively discriminated against ninety percent of the population. In response, the CEO of the association had my files put in paper form in a safe in his office and required that anyone making an enquiry about me had to go directly through him. I'm not sure whether that made me feel safer or more vulnerable. Nearly a decade later, when the UK government proposed doing the same type of filtering for VIP's, I

---

173 Davies, S. "Judge attacks the police over phone tapping", the Sun Herald, 1982 (unknown publication date)
174 Simon Davies and Andrew Keenan; "Ombudsman slates police unit", Sydney Morning Herald, 24th June 1987. Report on Simon Davies' complaint to the state Ombudsman over police corruption.

kicked up a storm. I should have done so, back then in Australia.

* * * * *

The Hawke Government made several key mistakes in its preparations for the Australia Card scheme. First, it had made assumptions about the right of government that simply did not match community expectations. People felt that the government did not have a mandate to do as it pleased.

Second, the resort to patriotism – calling it the Australia Card – was resented hotly (It became widely known as the "Auschtralia Card" – a vicious pun on Auschwitz). Finally, and perhaps most important, the Government was simply not able to establish that it and its law enforcement agencies could be trusted with the mechanism.

Even after such a short time, the sophistication of public debate was highly developed. Letters to newspapers and calls to radio stations put the argument that with the implementation of the card, the onus of proof in day-to-day transactions would be reversed. Trust within society would be replaced by the demand for formal identification. The government appeared unable to understand people's concern that there would emerge a shift in the balance of power in the relationships between citizen and the state. According to academic experts and privacy advocates leading the campaign, the card would suffer "function creep" and would find its way into many aspects of life. Such fears could never be countered by government assurances.

That campaign has been variously described as a "revolution", a "rebellion" and a "revolt" by the people against the government. Whichever term you apply to it, those events were remarkable. There have been few occasions in my life when I could confidently stand on any bar room table and galvanise the attention and support of everyone in the place – and even fewer occasions when I knew I could lead a crowd to open battle.

Meanwhile across the Tasman...

Governments can often be so ill informed. Less than four years after the Australia Card bit the dust, the New Zealand government decided to follow suit (New Zealand is the closest country and closest political partner to Australia). Idiotically, in the same discredited resort to patriotism, they dubbed it the "Kiwi Card". The same IT suppliers that bid for this project were those that did with the Australia Card.

NGO's and activists urged me to travel across the Tasman to deal with the situation. I did. It was possibly the fastest demise of any national ID card in history. I recall it took 48 hours.

After landing, I went immediately to a meeting with the Maori Affairs minister. Following the traditional Kia-ora nose rubbing ceremony he expressed his concern about the scheme. Later that night we held a packed public meeting in the Wellington Town Hall. The vote against the cards was unanimous.

The following evening I had a live television debate with the justice minister on the most watched TV news programme. He lost it completely. I asked, "How can you prove this will not destroy civil liberties?" The presenter let me get away with that question, and the justice minister could only respond, "Well, that's just typical Australian exaggeration". He stuttered and stumbled his way through the remainder of the interview.

The scheme died the next day. Sometimes a single media interview actually can make a difference. It is rare, but it does happen.[175]

There can be little doubt that, in addition to the problems listed above, several very substantial privacy and data protection fears were established with the cards both of Australia and New Zealand. These included matters of data security, function creep, incursions related to data matching, improper use and disclosure of data, erroneous data, the establishment of central control and tracking and the possible development of an "internal passport". Coupled with the government's inability to establish that the system would actually tackle major problems such as the underground economy, even the most ardent

---

175 Back in the day: Kiwi Card criticised for shaming beneficiaries
https://www.tvnz.co.nz/one-news/new-zealand/back-in-the-day-kiwi-card-criticised-

government supporters became sceptical.

There was a very real fear in the Australian community in 1987 that the fundamental balance of power was shifting. As Justice Michael Kirby assessed: "If there is an identity card, then people in authority will want to put it to use... What is at stake is nothing less than the nature of our society and the power and authority of the state over the individual".

Six years later, in 2003, I was delighted to read in a Canadian Federal Parliament report the confirmation that the campaign had resulted in "nearly destroying the Australian government".[176] And interestingly, Bob Hawke's autobiography[177] reveals that the ID card failure was his greatest sadness as Prime Minister. He didn't regret the scheme – only its collapse.

Looking back on that experience, it all seems so surreal. I ran that campaign from my bedroom; an 8 metre squared cube in a suburb. One telephone – later two – and obviously no Internet or mobile. It is possible to achieve change even with the most meagre of resources. Activists have done so throughout history.

Sadly, that campaign was the Last Hurrah of a free country. The following year the government successfully introduced the Tax File Number (TFN) scheme, which was almost equally dangerous to privacy. Since then – in the eyes of many people – Australia has degenerated into one of the western world's most puritanical and controlled societies. True, its record on gay rights and equal opportunity is strong, but it is a governed nation beyond even the likes of Norway and the Netherlands.

In the end, the most notable outcome of the campaign was the introduction of a Privacy Act and a Privacy Commissioner – for all the limited benefit that created, which was far less than we had hoped for.

Still, that revolution lives on in legend and folklore, despite the almost impossible task of finding references to it on the major search engines. One day, when the country wakes up from its authoritarian slumber, it may resurrect those dynamics in a sort of South American way.

---

for-shaming-beneficiaries-6365839
176 House of Commons, Canada, A national ID Card for Canada, 2003,
    http://www.idsysgroup.com/ftp/cimmrp06-e.pdf
177 See https://trove.nla.gov.au/work/6492495

If at first you don't succeed, target the developing world

In 1991 I sat on the throne of the King of Thailand. I really – very seriously – shouldn't have been on there, but the king's staff had foolishly left me alone in the throne room in a hurry for a quick meeting with the king. I gazed at the throne and it gazed back at me. I could have been executed for this crime, but – like farting in the reception lounge of a defence armaments fair – the action has to be done once it springs to mind. As I nervously climbed the three jade-studded steps and sat on the red velvet, my main thought was, "My god, this thing is so uncomfortable". There's a ripe market for ergonomically designed thrones.

I'm was there because the Thai government had embarked on a highly sophisticated national ID card – one which was infinitely more intricate than the Australian version. The same suppliers and contractors had been hovering over that scheme for the past three years.

But how did I get there?

I had actually started this particular voyage of discovery far away to the north. Just after the New Zealand campaign, there I was, in the outer regions of Chiang Mai in Northern Thailand. Then – as probably now – this was a place of ancient customs and fixed values. Along the endless stretches of forests and rice farms, rural workers (or in European terms, "peasants") work with much the same crude technology that their ancestors used for centuries. The intricacies of the automobile were known only to a few. For some, the telephone was still magical. Here in the outskirts of Chiang Mai, some people neither knew nor cared to know about such things.

The farmers of Chiang Mai were, nevertheless, unwitting travellers on the information Superhighway. Since the 1990's – to their unending bemusement – they had all been issued with high-tech, plastic identity cards which they usually hung around their necks with a light chain. The card was part of national strategy to computerise the Thai government and to keep track of the population. Every Thai adult has a machine readable ID card containing a digitised thumbprint and photograph, details of family and ancestry, education and occupation, nationality, religion and information relating to taxation and police records.

The card could be scanned by any police or government official to activate a sophisticated nationwide network of computers throughout the Thai government. By using a person's population number, registered in all agencies and banks, it was possible instantly to secure information from police, social welfare, taxation, immigration, housing, employment, driving licence, census, electoral, passport, vehicle, insurance, education and health record databases. This remarkable system was called the "Central Population Database". Back then it was the world's second largest relational database, surpassed only by the system in Salt Lake City owned by the Mormon Church.

For a parliament obsessed by the urgency of economic growth, this system was a cornerstone of national development. From the perspective of the military controlled government, it offered an opportunity to monitor and track the entire population. An ID card is the visible part of the technology, and the only part that most Thai people understood. Behind the card lay a strategy to construct a web of information to bind every aspect of a Thai citizen's life.[178]

Of course no-one spoke about the added benefit of tracking the northern insurgents. That thought might inflame passions and ideas.

There were few people in Thailand fretting over these developments. Bangkok yuppies were anxious to ape the most sophisticated features of western life. Politicians were anxious to show the world that Thailand was a truly advanced society. The military wanted more information. Ordinary working people were too preoccupied with mere survival even to care.

At the time, media were still not convinced that such a massive information system would pose any threat whatever to the rights of citizens. One dissenter, the English language paper The Bangkok Post, published a two page investigative article on the project twenty-nine years ago. It warned: "The population database will considerably strengthen the power of the Interior Ministry, already the most powerful and largest government agency in the country, and of the police, who are also governed by the Interior Ministry."

---

178 Pinkaew Laungaramsri, Chiang Mai University, Harvard Yenching Institute. Working paper series: crafting citizenship cards colours and the politics of identification in Thailand. https://harvard-yenching.org/sites/harvard-yenching.org/files/featurefiles/Pinkaew%20Laungaramsri_ReCrafting%20Citizenship.pdf

The Bangkok Post had every reason to sound the alarm. The new database system had the potential to retard Thailand's already fragile democracy. A "Village Information System" monitored information at a local level. It was linked to electoral information, public opinion data and candidate information. Such a mass of related information in the hands of any government would put the opposition at a fatal disadvantage.

Political and economic factors such as these have been the key motivation behind the establishment of official identity cards throughout the world. The type of card, its function, and its integrity vary enormously. Around ninety countries including France, Germany, Italy, Spain, Portugal, Greece, Belgium, the Netherlands and Luxembourg have official, national ID's, that are used for a variety of purposes. Among those which do not have a national ID card are Britain, Sweden, Finland, Austria, Ireland and Denmark. There are many and varied reasons why a country chooses not to have an official ID card. Some are cultural, some are constitutional. One Irish official explained to the Daily Telegraph, "There has never been any attempt to introduce one because no one would ever carry it".

In most cases, the cards have become an accepted part of life. In Asian countries, for example, people are proud to show their ID card. In Singapore, the card is like an internal passport, necessary for every transaction. In Germany, many people say they like the card because it helps streamline day to day activities.

Interestingly, the more the card is "requested" by a burgeoning number of authorities, the more "convenient" it becomes.

* * * * *

So there I was in the outskirts of Chiang Mai. A local civil rights group had asked me to come. I had accepted, but I needed to see how this scheme might affect the vast majority of Thai people outside the elite urban areas.

Still, I also needed to travel to Bangkok, the capital. That's where all the action was happening. I was fortunate enough in the early weeks to be staying with the assistant prime minister, Mechai Viravaidya, who the previous year in London I had escorted on a "George Orwell tour" of the city. He is a true supporter of people's rights.

I launched into a media campaign, resulting in the aforementioned coverage in the Bangkok Post. I'll say it up front. It was a totally disastrous campaign. Well, it wasn't even a campaign. It was some idiot foreigner stumbling around making a fool of himself. And that's even before getting all publicly hysterical about a veiled death threat.[179]

I made a nuisance of myself with officials and in the press and then, one day, ended up being invited, by what I thought was pure fluke of circumstance, to the royal palace, where I spent a lot of time with a couple of the King's senior staff. We didn't talk politics, but I learned much about his exercise regime.

It seems my visit to the palace didn't go down well with some in the military, and I was "invited" to join who I think – but cannot in any way be certain – was the deputy head of Thai military. He was certainly very senior to have the city's top hotel cordon off its Chinese restaurant for eight people. Putting two and two together, I'm guessing the stakes were rising, and they were worried about mightier forces than they were becoming involved in scrutinising the card scheme. They were probably getting a big cut of the money. it is what the big accountancy companies used to run as a line item called "market facilitation." Not bribery.

The big man ignored me throughout the meal, focusing on his generals, but then turned and bluntly introduced the second part of the equation: the opportunity and the danger. Apparently if I worked with them, life would be an "endless party". Otherwise I would be in trouble. I won't bore you with details of the threat, because it involved body language and some silver chopsticks. Silver chopsticks were the way people in power used to determine if there was poison in their food. He remarked, "We wouldn't want anything bad to happen to you, my friend, would we?" Well, you'd have to have been there, I guess.

Then things got complicated. My room was raided at the hotel, and stuff was stolen. My access to local language papers was blocked. Money

---

179 Elmer-Dewitt, P/ Peddling Big Brother. Magazine June 24, 1991
    https://content.time.com/time/magazine/article/0,9171,973251,00.html

transfers stopped arriving. I figured they'd won this round.

The only person I really knew was the assistant Prime Minister, and I could hardly ask him for advice. I really did want to complete this mission though. I'd been in Bangkok hunting around for weeks. There was almost no information on the system and I knew nothing of the laws that permitted it. What I did know was that the scheme was vast and was intended as a total ID and tracking package, linked to and through the Home Office. Computer Science Corporation in the US appeared to be the key supplier. I found a few articles in the press, but people just didn't see the problem. I was never quoted about possible use of the system in the troubled north of the country, but tracking rebels and militants would have been very much on the mind of the military. Reluctantly, in light of the threats, I also realised I knew nothing about my rights, if indeed I had any rights.

This experience was shaping my view of global campaigning, and what was really needed to be an effective voice. That's to say, any way other than the way I was doing it. Still, some people have to learn the hard way.

I had no wish to proceed to the fourth stage of the equation: checkmate. I left for the airport at dawn the next day feeling extremely nervous, but vowing to return in more favourable circumstances, which indeed I did. Thankfully, a friend at the hotel smuggled me out the back door – for a hefty price.

A short while later I gave a plenary speech in San Francisco at the first Computers, Freedom and Privacy conference in which I outlined my concerns over US involvement in the Thai scheme. The speech, I'm delighted, was received with a level of enthusiasm that more than made up for the stress in Bangkok, and which I know resulted in a sound kicking to the Smithsonian Institute, which had been encouraging the Thai development with the awarding of a prize for "courageous use of technology".

The conference and the experience in Thailand created the motivation for a ground-breaking Privacy International report four years later on the export of surveillance technologies by the West.[180]

---

180 Big Brother Incorporated; Privacy International, 1995
   https://www.privacyinternational.org/reports/big-brother-incorporated-1995

The Philippines experiment

Unlike the Thai situation, with gentle guidance, a target may destroy itself with barely a push. As one small example, let's take the subject of the national ID card (that is to say, computerised surveillance scheme) that President Fidel Ramos of the Philippines tried futilely to introduce in 1991.[181] US tech guru John Gilmore had funded me to travel there, to campaign against it.

It was a short but surprisingly successful effort, considering that under General Ramos, the country had slid toward a military dictatorship.

And like the Thai campaign, this one too involved death threats.

So there I was, cut and bloodied after climbing over barbed wire at the head of the May Day protests. Half a million people had gathered, many in solidarity commemorating the seven Filipinos, who had been killed by army gunfire at last year's rally on the bridge we had just crossed. This annual event was the moment when the local population gathered en masse to protest against government abuses. I had been invited here by local rights groups to participate, and I had weaved my way through the chaos to the head of the rally.

Even with half a million people behind me, I have never felt so alone. As I wandered up and down the endless ranks of armed soldiers and weaved toward the rows of tanks that sprawled in front of the palace, a captain decided it was time to stick a loaded gun down my throat. Even now I can taste its acidic metal. Such are the perils of being an activist.

But rarely can campaigns – against such odds – be won solely through direct action. There is, invariably, a subtler strategic element. Following that scary event with the gun, with the help of Cecilia Jimenez-Damary and the Philippines Alliance of Human Rights Advocates (PAHRA), I met the chairman of the Senate Finance Committee, and presented him with a painstakingly researched independent cost estimate of the Philippines scheme based on the experience of other countries. In common with nearly all such legitimate estimates, it blew the government figures out of the water. He remarked, "If this is true, we will never let it pass."

---

181 Philippines national ID Card, Wikipedia
   https://en.wikipedia.org/wiki/Philippine_identity_card

The cost estimates were circulated and caused substantial budgetary infighting across government departments. It was a small contribution to the overall effort, but thanks to the efforts of my Filipino colleagues, the scheme died, and only saw the light of day again in 2018, 27 years later, when the Senate finally passed a much more cautious law.[182]

The UK idiocy card

Scroll forward almost two decades after the Australian fiasco. One early summer day in mid-2005, I listened to the Attorney General of England and Wales – Baroness Patricia Scotland – lambasting me from the floor of the UK House of Lords. It was rather depressing to hear the chief lawmaker engaging such cheap tactics.

She went on at length, impugning my reputation and deriding my university, then the London School of Economics (LSE). Her "noble" lord government colleagues, in carefully orchestrated choreography, followed suit in the debate that followed. The Opposition protested, arguing that government had embarked on a coordinated smear campaign against me.

The issue was to do with a UK national identity card – or the lack of one. This project was to be the Labour government's key platform, and I had been roundly held responsible for compromising it. The Prime Minister, Tony Blair, had attacked me the previous week on the floor of the Parliament. In the week before, the Home Secretary had taken to the airwaves on the BBC flagship programme "Today", to go on about how I was disreputable and a disgrace to my university.[183] Then followed multiple public attacks by the likes of the immigration minister and the home affairs minister. Former Home Secretary David Blunkett wrote in his book "The Blunkett Tapes: Life in the Bear Pit": "I am really sorry that the London School of Economics have allowed him (me) to even hint

---

182 Sy, M. Congress to ratify national ID bill today. The Philippine Star. - May 28, 2018
      https://www.philstar.com/headlines/2018/05/28/1819296/congress-ratify-national-id-
      bill-today
183 ID cards academic attacks Clarke, BBC online news, 5th July 2005
      http://news.bbc.co.uk/2/hi/uk_news/politics/4651299.stm

that he has any connection with them".[184] This was a rather odd observation, given that I had been teaching there for the past nine years and co-directed the LSE's Policy Engagement Network.[185]

I later learned that the Prime Minister had earlier been slamming his fist on the Great Table of Cabinet and had declared that it was open season on me.

Like all my colleagues, I didn't like the government's proposal. It was nothing short of the greatest surveillance scheme in the country's history. Everyone needs a hobby, and mine was destroying integrated national ID cards of that nature. Biometrics, real-time cross checking and perfect identity. This scheme would link all major IT systems and require everyone to be subject to a vast tracking system. Clearly it was the wet dream for all IT suppliers and consultants, who would milk it for everything they could at – ultimately – twice their initial bid estimate.

To give you an idea of just how much money was in it for these suppliers, consider just one meeting we had with the Home Office in the closing days of the campaign. PA Consulting supplied two junior people to take notes at a charge-out rate of £180 per hour. I doubt the note-takers were getting more than £10 in their pocket. Tens– hundreds – of millions of pounds filled the coffers of the consultancy companies in such ingenious ways, and that's before you even start considering the countless millions that would be channelled to technology suppliers, data outsourcers, card manufacturers, software houses, legal advisers and analytics companies. It would be nothing short of a gravy train.

Our then friend David Davis, the Shadow Home Secretary, said it best when he advised Parliament: "They are not just excessive but expensive; they are not just illiberal but impractical; they are not just unnecessary but unworkable".[186]

Still, as with the Australia Card, it was proving hard to shift public support for the plan. If authorities repeat a falsehood cleverly and often enough, many people will regard it as truth. Such was the case here.

---

184 *Blunkett, D. (15 October 2006). The Blunkett Tapes: My Life in the Bear Pit.* *Bloomsbury. p. 797. ISBN 978-0747-58821-4.*

185 Policy engagement Network https://www.lse.ac.uk/management/research/research-projects/past-projects/policy-engagement

186 David Davis, Hansard, House of Commons, 6th February 2006. Found through TheyWorkForYou.com 28th June 2005
https://www.theyworkforyou.com/debates/?id=2005-06-28b.1171.2

According to the government inspired headlines, the system would reduce illegal immigration, enable lower tax, clean out criminality, reduce welfare fraud, streamline government administration, restore social justice and – well – do almost everything other than iron your clothes. And all this for just £93 a person. It was too good to be true – and it was indeed too good to be true.

it is odd how great affairs of national policy can be determined or reversed by a single small event. In this matter, it was a phone conversation. Earlier that year, I had spontaneously called my colleague Gus Hosein at Privacy International – a call that was to trigger a domino effect of events that led to the card's demise.

I told him we probably had one shot at killing this thing, so we had to make it count. If the technical fallibility and the privacy issues did not inspire the public, then what about the cost? Cost can drive public opinion, so why don't we commission an LSE report that provides a full analysis of the system? As part of this report we could include a cost estimate. After all, this was the greatest economics university in the country, so a detailed report would carry weight.

It was a huge risk. One way or the other, the report must be made public. If the cost estimates went against us, we were doomed. But regardless, we asked twenty leading professors at the LSE to be part of an oversight committee. We then invited nearly a hundred of the world's top legal, technical and policy experts to contribute to it.

This needed to be the Mother of all Reports. It had to be weighty, serious and deeply analytical. Anything short of that would be ignored. Aside from the cost aspect, we needed to consider a focus on the many bizarre claims made by government. The report came in at over 300 pages, making it probably the fastest turn-around of any major academic report in history.[187] The workload nearly drove Hosein into an early grave, but we were fortunate to have a few volunteers on top of the hundred experts. Having said that, can you imagine the workload of managing input from a hundred experts? Getting comparable quotes from two mechanics is hard enough work.

---

187 London School of Economics (LSE). The Identity Project: An Assessment of the UK
     Identity   Cards Bill and Its Implications. June 27, 2005.
     http://eprints.lse.ac.uk/684/1/identityreport.pdf

We made a deal with the Observer, Britain's oldest and possibly most respected Sunday newspaper. Whatever the report's conclusions, they had exclusivity as long as they ran it as the front page Splash. They agreed.

Two months later the costing had been drafted and the figures were as we had hoped. At the very least, the card would cost twice the government estimates. Worst case scenario was triple.

The media went crazy over the report, but not as crazy as the government, which realised – as they say in naval terms – it had been hoist with its own petard.

The Observer led with the headline "ID Cards to cost £300 per person". Everything changed after that moment. The media swung against the government, as did the parliamentary Opposition. As media vied for the next story, they looked more closely at the LSE report. Biometrics would fail. IT systems would crash. Rights would be compromised. Government would gain immeasurably more power.[188]

The report provided fodder for ongoing media attention, building public distaste for the scheme. We could almost taste the change of mood. By way of example, later that week the debating society of University College London (UCL) put the card on the table. What would have been a relatively small gathering turned into a huge and quite energised auditorium audience. And stupidly, when the government Minister failed to show up, I volunteered to anonymously replace him as official Card spokesman, debating the leader of the Liberal Democrat Party, Nick Clegg. Following boos and loud heckling at my presentation, 99 percent of the audience voted against the Card, and I felt it necessary to leave by the back door of the hall.

When the government went into overdrive on this issue, I was the target. The full Council of the LSE convened and unanimously gave us full support and requested the university's Director Sir Howard Davies to strike back in the press. He did so quite forcefully.[189]

The writing was on the wall and when the new Conservative government was elected not long afterwards, its first act was to scrap the ID cards

188 Hencke, D and Dodd, V. Defence expert undermines Blair on safety of ID cards. 13 Feb 2006 https://www.theguardian.com/politics/2006/feb/13/idcards.immigrationpolicy
189 Academics "bullied" over ID cards; BBC online news, 2nd July 2005 http://news.bbc.co.uk/2/hi/uk_news/politics/4643467.stm

Bill.

* * * * *

Ignorant of all these future events, there I was, listening to the Attorney General ridicule me. As it happens, I was in an almost unique situation at that moment. I was actually on the floor of the House of Lords. There is only one occasion when "Commoners" such as me can be on the floor of the House of Lords in session, and that is when they are invited to sit on the tiny oak "Experts Box". Both government and opposition can do this, and it is something of a rare honour.

People in the experts' box can be approached by the Lords from either side and asked for their advice, As it happens, box persons can also call on the Lords for their advice. I certainly did that. I asked my friends the Earl of Northesk and the Countess of Marr – the grandest hereditary peers in the Lords – to advise me. What could I do about this diatribe? Surely there was some convention in 800 years that would allow a Commoner on the floor to directly respond to an attack? They had no idea, though I suspect Northesk did call the librarian. In the end, his advice was to either suck it up or stand up and demand a right of reply. I was too much of a coward to do the latter – to my unending regret.

Still, I was well defended in the Parliament. In a classically strident speech, the Earl of Northesk later remarked:

"...news also surfaced at the weekend that Simon Davies, who the Government have consistently and repeatedly vilified for his involvement with the LSE Identity Project, has written to the Prime Minister indicating his possible intention to pursue the matter in the courts should such defamation be repeated... Is the Minister prepared to take this opportunity on behalf of the Government to retract the outrageous slurs perpetrated against Mr Davies and offer an apology?"[190]

---

190 The Earl of Northesk, Hansard, House of Lords 6th February 2006. Found through TheyWorkForYou.com https://www.theyworkforyou.com/lords/?id=2006-02-06c.448.0

It was at that point all the ministers of government and all their media beasts stepped up the attack on me (though to be fair, the conservative media went nuts in my defence). We were both on the rails at that point, and when the personal attacks became too much, I decided to take a proactive strike.

I gave an interview to the Times Higher Education Supplement (THES), Britain's premier university publication. I casually mentioned that I was feeling almost suicidal, which naturally became the headline.[191] This was a few months after the highly suspicious "suicide" of UK scientific advisor David Kelly, who had been found dead after he had issued a report criticising the government's "weapons of mass destruction" claims in Iraq. The Sunday Times followed immediately with a page two lead that I was thinking of killing myself.

The Daily Express went a step further, and somehow managed to acquire a downward-looking CCTV image of me so it looked like I was hiding and running. It was a very powerful photo that took up nearly a half page of the paper.

I should add that this disclosure wasn't just fiction. I had put one of Europe's greatest universities in peril for its reputation, and I felt foreboding, despite its unequivocal backing.

10 Downing Street went onto red alert. It put me on suicide watch and called in some of my colleagues to check out my situation. "Was I likely to do this?". "Do I have a drug or drink problem?". "Would I kill myself just to spite the government?"

After the death of poor David Kelly, my suicide would have been the last thing government wanted. So, bizarrely, they placed two special agents outside the pub which is downstairs from where I live. I knew they were special agents because they were in dark suits, never talked to each other, drank lemonade and took notes whenever I moved. No-one drinks lemonade in my pub downstairs. This was the last gasp of a desperate government. Or the last belch.

The card died, though it occasionally wriggles on in various manifestations introduced by clueless backbenchers. Truth be told, it will take much more of a foundation of evidence to build any trust in a future

---

191 *"'Hounding' could lead to another David Kelly case". Times Higher Education Supplement. 10 February 2006*

scheme. The reality was that despite all those attacks on me, much glory for the defeat of the scheme rests with Phil Booth and NO2ID, which fought on and won that battle. That organization demonstrated how, with dogged persistence, it is possible to mount a vitally strategic offensive that drains the government and its corporate supporters.

India's ID scheme: the Perfect Storm of collusion

It is March 2013, and I'm in the sweltering madness of New Delhi. The stereotype is true. This is one of the most chaotic places on earth. Even the addresses are chaotic, often referring to the apartment above the block near the side-way off the lane beyond the street.

For any Westerner, getting used to this place really takes something. And that's even before you consider the challenge of understanding India's bureaucracy, which is almost impenetrable. Indeed India marvellously got back at the British imperialists by creating a bureaucracy of such opacity that even London does not compare. Try obtaining a visa from the UK, and you will quickly agree.

I'm here because I helped organise a public meeting on privacy in India. To the casual observer this project might seem a contradiction. Is there really any privacy in this crazy land of well over a billion people? Privacy International and its supporters certainly believed so, and we were funded to create projects and partnerships in India. This work was a crucially important step toward a maturing of privacy awareness in India.

But if you were to believe the representatives both from India and from US commerce at this meeting, disinterest in privacy is a national trait. Speakers made constant reference to the matter of public disclosure of personal information on trains. In response, noted commentator Vickram Crishna expressed the view that the train anecdote had no relevance and was a convenient ruse for people who for their own self-interest opposed privacy regulation. "In reality this circumstance is like Vegas," he said. "What happens on Indian trains, stays on Indian trains. People will talk about their lives because they will never see these passengers again and there is no record of the disclosures.

"What we are dealing with in the online world is a completely different matter. There is no correlation between the two environments."

So do people in India care about privacy? The answer is a resounding "yes". There's a myth that Indian people do not care about privacy, but this is far from the truth, as indeed is the case in China.

In 2012, India's largest-ever privacy survey[192] revealed a high degree of concern across the country over encroachments into private life. The survey polled the views of more than ten thousand people and concluded that Indian residents believe the threat of privacy invasion is now largely out of control.

The survey – which was conducted by the Indraprastha Institute of Information Technology, Delhi, and funded by Canada's International Development Research Centre (IDRC) – was released at a critically important moment for privacy in India. The national government was in the process of rolling out a unique identification system, and authorities were in the advanced stages of planning for data protection legislation (which is still in the pipeline as of the date of writing, only, with far greater dissent and discussion swirling around it).

Meanwhile, Europe was pressing the world's largest democracy to improve privacy protections, so that trade between the two regions could be better assured.

Awareness of online and communications privacy was high – and continues to be so. More than seventy percent of respondents expressed concern over website tracking, and a similar number were worried about surveillance of mobile phones. More than half of the participants have changed their default settings on a social network that they use, and a similar number reported that they sometimes or often cleared cookies from their computer.

One of the patterns that researchers observed across participants was that all felt very concerned about financial privacy. About 75% mentioned that they don't disclose any credit card details to 'anybody' over the phone. Most people said they use credit and debit cards but said they would avoid using online banking and money transactions, as they do not

---

192 India's first major privacy survey reveals deep concerns over privacy; the Privacy Surgeon, 23rd November 2012 http://www.privacysurgeon.org/blog/incision/indias-first-major-privacy-survey-reveals-deep-concerns-over-intrusion/

have much faith in the online process.

The Indian results parallel similar surveys in Western countries. For example the level of concern over website tracking was close to the figure revealed by 2013polling research in Europe and North America.[193]

So here we are in a nice air conditioned venue with several senior parliamentarians and bureaucrats, about to embark on this unique event. I raise the issue with one government Minister about India's plan to uniquely identify every person in India (a scheme initially named the UID, known now by its government brand of "Aadhaar", a Hindi word that loosely translates to "foundation"). I told him we had abandoned such monolithic schemes in countries such as Britain, Australia and Canada, but his response was that "everything is sorted".

The question, of course, is for whom is it sorted, in what manner is it sorted and is patronage of such a vast system motivated by nepotism and bribery (apologies; "market facilitation")?

Seriously, dealing with Indian government leaders sometimes feels like you're conversing with the stereotypical robot from 1960s sci-fi, that constantly responds "does not compute". In the first and second world wars, British troops were fond of singing a ditty that went, "We're here because we're here because we're here because we're here". The same might apply to some parts of Indian bureaucracy. In short, the government's plan was to introduce the world's largest and most comprehensive biometric-based identification scheme. It would involve all the grand claims made by every other national scheme (some of which are outlined earlier in this chapter), but of course the plan would encompass the entirety of the second most populous nation on earth.

Authorities initially said the Aadhaar Unique ID would be voluntary and would help the Indian government achieve the twin objectives of closing gaps in welfare delivery systems, through better targeting, and increasing the efficiency of welfare delivery systems, by leveraging technology.

However, over time, the use of Aadhaar has been tied to multiple services, from distribution of rations, to banking and internet services to international travel and marriage registration. Aadhaar use by private tech firms with respect to their consumer-facing digital services has also been

---

193 Global survey reveals that ad tracking is less popular than Colonel Gadaffi. The Privacy Surgeon. 12th February 2013

on the rise, and there have been reports[194] of Facebook testing new logins to its platform that would require Aadhaar, and existing implementations across a range of financial, tech and other industries[195] in India. This is a syndrome widely known as "function creep" and has been a feature of all national 'identification' systems.

The system, perhaps predictably, went into meltdown. As Vickram Crishna observed: "Tens of thousands of application forms have been found dumped in alleyways and gutters. Some of them appear not to have been processed at all, leaving hapless applicants in the dark. Real world problems with landless and migrant labourers were complicated by the deliberate rejection of an internal study that revealed fingerprinting was unreliable for vast numbers of persons engaged in physical labour, even housewives, afflicted with the impact of cooking and cleaning."[196]

The use of Aadhaar has not gone without significant controversy and challenge in India — the most critical frontier being a hefty set of constitutional challenges[197] to the Aadhaar framework in the Supreme Court of India that were filed from 2012 onwards.[198] The Supreme Court ruled in 2018 to restrict the use of Aadhaar – largely on the basis on the principle of proportionality (or lack of it)[199]. While the majority of the Supreme Court upheld the legality of the scheme, it struck down section 57 of the enabling Act, outlawing use of the scheme by the private sector.

---

194 Want to open a Facebook account? Keep your Aadhaar card by your side. Economic Times of India. https://economictimes.indiatimes.com/tech/internet/want-to-open-a-facebook-account-keep-your-aadhaar-card-by-your-side/articleshow/62267904.cms (accessed 13th October 2018).

195 How private companies are using Aadhaar to deliver better services, but there's a catch. https://scroll.in/article/823274/how-private-companies-are-using-aadhaar-to-deliver-better-services-but-theres-a-catch (accessed 13th October 2018).

196 Crishna, V. Governments take note: the world's most ambitious ID scheme is falling to pieces. The Privacy Surgeon, 7th May 2015 http://www.privacysurgeon.org/blog/incision/governments-take-note-the-worlds-most-ambitious-identity-system-is-falling-to-pieces/

197 Partial list of the lawsuits challenging the UID scheme on constitutional grounds https://cis-india.org/internet-governance/blog/the-aadhaar-case (accessed 19th November 2018)

198 Bhatia, G. The Aadhaar Judgment: a round-up. October 2018 https://indconlawphil.wordpress.com/2018/10/05/the-aadhaar-judgment-a-round-up/amp/ (accessed 6th November 2018).

199 Bhatia, G. Take me as I am – subject to the Aadhaar based biometric authentication, 26th September 2018 https://indconlawphil.wordpress.com/2018/09/26/take-me-as-i-am-subject-to-aadhaar-based-biometric-authentication-an-overview-of-the-aadhaar-judgment/ (accessed 6th November 2018)

This may result in a much slimmed-down project.[200]

A strongly worded dissenting Opinion[201] by Justice DY Chandrachud, which held the scheme to be unconstitutional, is one of the most inspiring legal analyses in the history of constitutional court cases on identity matters.

---

200 Bhandari, V. Aadhaar valid but restricted, still a problem. 26th September 2018. Deccan Herald. https://www.deccanherald.com/special-features/aadhaar-valid-restricted-and-694765.html (accessed 4th November 2018)
201 Full Text of the Supreme Court judgment on the constitutionality of UID, including Justice D. Y. Chandrachud's dissenting opinion https://www.thehindu.com/news/resources/article25048939.ece/binary/AadhaarVerdict.pdf (accessed 19th November 2018)

Chapter Eight: Starting the movement

> *In 1989 an idea emerged to create a global privacy movement. At that time, advocates in disparate parts of the world never had the chance to communicate with each other. I describe the tortuous process in a pre-Internet era of finding support to create such a movement. The task was daunting but surprisingly full of hope, drama and excitement. At one level, Privacy International became a key outcome.*

Early days

It is June 1991, and I'm seated anxiously in the private dining room of the Prime Minister of France. The place smells of rose-leaf oil, furniture polish and chip grease. With me are the distinguished government advisor Louis Joinet[202] and a couple of senators. Joinet has invited me here to discuss my effort to create an international privacy movement – and to see whether it might be possible to base it in Paris. After all, the 200th anniversary of the French Declaration of the Rights of Man and the Citizen was hovering (even though that document mainly talks about private property, reflecting the concerns of its elite authors, anxious to avoid repossession by another revolution).

Of the countless meetings I've enjoyed (or endured) over the past fifteen

---

202 Louis Joinet, Wikipedia entry https://fr.wikipedia.org/wiki/Louis_Joinet (accessed 17th October 2018).

months, this is likely to be one of the more important. I had already caused a few shock waves in Quebec – which later made a financial bid to host the movement – but France was always a tough country to crack. Its academia, bureaucracy – and even its traditional human rights institutions – can be impenetrable for the Anglophone outsider. And France has enjoyed a strong data protection regime since 1978, so it was already highly developed in terms of privacy awareness.

I am excited to learn about the new electronic surveillance law, governing wiretapping, that was about to go into force.[203] Given my past experiences fighting illegal police wiretapping in Australia, it would be interesting to find out whether there was an endemic problem in France. In turn, my colleagues seemed anxious to find out what was happening in the emerging Eastern European democracies and North America.

Before that moment, I had been on a sort of Grand Tour of Europe. Three grand tours to be precise. For me, the whole experience had been a baptism of fire. It seemed every country had a different nature and a different view of privacy back then. The Germans treated it meticulously – and had the advantage of a strong network of techies. The British, likewise, understood the concept, but had relegated it to the realm of legal experts. Northern European countries such as Sweden and Norway were comfortable with their existing protections and saw little need for change. In the South – Spain, Italy and Greece – academics were largely in control of the privacy agenda – such as it was. Privacy was thin on the ground. It took the Italian parliament twenty years to debate the data protection law, which was finally enacted in 1996 – long after some of the new democracies in central and eastern Europe.[204]

At that time, the East of Europe was boiling with revolutionary zeal. The Berlin Wall had fallen the year before I started this initiative, and it was clear that there were real opportunities for privacy development.

Or so I imagined.

---

203 Law No. 91-636 of July 10, 1991 (relating to telecommunications privacy) (Fra.).
204 Legge '31 dicembre 1996 n. 675, Tutela delle persone e di altri soggetti rispetto al trattamento dei dati personali. Amended by Legislative Decree No. 123 of 09.05.97 and 255 of 28.07.97, available at http://elj.strath.ac.uk/jilt/dp/materialiL675-eng.htm (Unofficial translation). LEGGE 31 DICEMBRE 1996, N. 676, Delega al Governo in materia di tutela delle persone e di altri soggetti rispetto al trattamento dei dati personali. www.privacy.it/legge96676.html For a list of decrees, see <http://www.privacy.it/normativ.html>

Many activists in that region told me that their Prime Directive was transparency, not privacy. It took some years before this view shifted. We kept telling them they could have both. In fact, that they "needed" both. However, the EU, in its grab to expand the union after the revolutions, ensured that data protection was a requirement.

Agreed, one shouldn't make generalisations at a national level, but a macro view is sometimes useful. If it is reasonable to argue that the Germans have adopted strong privacy protections in part because of the legacy of the Second World War, then it is equally valid to observe that Eastern Europe was suspicious of privacy, because of the secretive regimes they had endured for decades.

Ruminating on such matters and waiting for the arrival of the other guests, I start to panic. Which cutlery to use? Do the French do it differently to the English? Is the bread over here to the left – or is that the wine? I really was not accustomed to such dining environments. Looking back, I could hardly tell the difference between a *consommé* and a finger bowl – let alone whether the biblical description of "breaking bread upon the table" was literal. In my nervousness, I knocked over my water glass, so it spilled onto the immaculately prepared bread basket. I realised suddenly just how tired I was.

The travel here had been a whirlwind and, like almost all my trips, chaotic and badly planned. I just went with the recommendations of the moment and flew to wherever there's a meeting opportunity. Often this resulted in a desperate outcome.

I had flown first thing the morning before from a government meeting in Northern Ireland for a breakfast meeting with prospective UK supporters, then immediately to Amsterdam for a session with Jan Holvast from Privacy Alert (who subsequently became Privacy International's chairman). Then directly onto Paris for this meeting. Early coffee, late breakfast, lunch and dinner respectively in four countries in one day.

While that itinerary may be mildly impressive as an anecdote, the harsh reality is that, for the past year, I had been homeless and itinerant. The experience was starting to resemble my former years in a touring rock band. What I didn't know at that point was that I would be itinerant for yet another year, before deciding to ground the initiative in London. Exhausting as it was, at least travelling across borders was not the drama that it can be in the 21st century.

* * * * *

Returning to my soggy bread in the French Prime Minister's office, the travel here – like most of my travel back then – had been an utter mess. I had unknowingly arrived the evening before the Paris Air Show and had planned no accommodation. The air show – on top of two major conferences – meant there was no hotel room available in the entire city.

I ventured to Charles de Gaulle Etoile Metro, from where I wandered along the Avenue Champs-Élysées, wondering where on earth I could spend the night. I knew little of Paris, as this was my first visit here, but I recalled that grand avenue by reputation. In hindsight, I should have headed to Montmartre, but I didn't know about that area in that era. If there was a seedy hotel available anywhere back then, it would be in Montmartre.

It was a long, long night on the Avenue. A delightfully protracted overpriced dinner followed by a prolonged stay in a strange club full of androgynous New Romantics. Then an endless parade of bars and cafes, right through until eleven in the morning.

So here I am at the Prime Minister's office, desperately tired, unshaven, crumpled clothes and reeking of whisky, New Romantic perfumes and body odour. Regardless, we engaged feverishly about the new data protection landscape, the opportunities to evangelise the French respect for privacy and the possibility of government support for my effort. The other diners were delighted that here, at last, might be a real opportunity for them to engage with civil society beyond France.

Perhaps predictably, the meeting was a qualified success, and within two hours I was napping in a government limousine on its way to the CDG Airport for yet another trek to Bangkok, to meet an ambivalent government.

The founding of Privacy International

The genesis of this saga happened the year before in much less glamorous circumstances.

It was early evening on March 26th, 1990, and I was sitting in a desultory hotel bar in Luxembourg. This was my first trip to Europe and I was on edge. The beer was strong, the wine expensive, people tended not to smile, the hotel service was grudging, and the cars drive on the wrong side of the road. Plus, I had no idea how to speak the local languages. Everything felt so alien. But there I was, on the cusp of the first meeting in an effort to create an international privacy movement. I was riotously ill-equipped for the challenge.

I had raised this idea in late 1989 with Professor Graham Greenleaf in Australia. "Why don't I start a world privacy and data protection organisation?" I naïvely enquired. "We could bring in every expert and activist in every country and start communicating. We can work together".

These thoughts had sprung from my earlier work in Australia. It was only long after the 1987 ID card campaign that I learned that a similar initiative – against the Netherlands national census – had been undertaken successfully by the Amsterdam-based Stichting Waakzaamheid Persoonsregistratie (Privacy Alert), a national non-government watchdog group. There was simply no English language information available, on what was one of the world's most successful privacy campaigns. I found this information gap profoundly irritating. We might have learned so much from them. Privacy Alert had brought its country to the point of civil war, just as we had done in Australia.

Greenleaf is fondly regarded as a cynic, but he saw the urgency of such a movement, and said, "Yes, well, you just do that, Simon." It was said in a slightly patronising way, though doubtless not intentionally so. We had a very great mutual respect, but this latest brain wave of mine must have seemed a little far-fetched in the mind of any serious academic who knew me.

Starting a movement in Australia was one thing but accelerating it to the global level was exponentially more challenging. Even though there were regular government and regulatory conferences, there was no mechanism that brought everyone together – academics, government, techies and activists. The International Conference of Privacy & Data Protection Commissioners had been in existence for some years, but those events were populated by commercial organisations and legal experts. NGO's were nowhere to be found.

In my silent thoughts, I imagined how the distant future might unfurl, but I was too scared to express it to colleagues. Still, it happened as I had hoped. For example, the international commissioners conference mentioned above – back then – was an obscure talking shop amongst the regulators and a few minor company people. At its 40th annual event in Brussels in 2018 it had attracted such keynote speakers as the CEO's of Apple, Facebook and Google, the Chief Justice of India, the President of the European Court of Human Rights and the King of Spain. And some NGO advocates such as US advocate Marc Rotenberg – described later in this chapter – were on that list.

Even if Greenleaf had been intentionally cynical about this idea, he had solid grounds for being that way. I'm not saying I was exactly a laughable character back then, but I was close to it. Serious people tolerated me because of my energy and ideas, but the prospect of a high school dropout with no credentials taking on this effort must have seemed surreal. And what I knew about data protection and privacy law could probably have been written on the back of a postage stamp. A small Victorian penny postage stamp at that.

Friends described me as "feral". I had a nose for campaign tactics, networking and PR, but I was idiot when it came to the fine details of law and technology. Nothing changes. Nearly a quarter of a century later, the in-coming Deputy Director of Privacy International, Eric King, would condemn me on those very grounds. He quite rightly observed that I needed to spend time learning the precise details of all the new technologies. But by then my preoccupation was just getting campaigns on the road. And in any event, a new technology was springing up almost every day and it had become impossible to keep up. This is why privacy is now so partialized.

All these concerns were well-founded back in 1990. After all, I would need to attract exalted academics, judges, civil liberties organisations, regulators, legal experts, senior officials and technical gurus. And this in countries – particularly in Europe and the US – where privacy law had been embedded as far back as the early 1970's, and whose experts did not suffer fools gladly. But regardless of the odds, Greenleaf agreed to be deputy convener. The game was on.

* * * * *

Amidst the fake Oak and sham Royal Doulton pottery of that generic Luxembourg hotel, I watched the dozens of serious officials and academics in well-fitted suits as they filed into the bar, in preparation for a major data protection conference that would begin the next day.[205] I overheard conversations that confounded me. Terms like "informational self-determination", "interoperability" and "The Council" filled the air, which all left me baffled. It was a new language for me and – for the first time in three years as a privacy campaigner – I realised just how utterly ignorant and overwhelmed I was.

Looking down at my glass, I sensed the futility of this mission. How could I ever penetrate this vast coterie of lawmakers, analysts and legal eagles?

I tried to lift my spirits by imagining that one day there would be a global movement. That we will have hundreds – maybe thousands – of campaigners who are respected or feared by those in power. I imagined a substantial and vibrant sector that spearheads this issue and provides a foundation of reason that influences corporations and governments. I also strived to imagine that one day, I too could stand in front of these people and demand their attention, rather than being the anonymous, homesick, sad, scared figure hunched alone in a corner.

This thinking was to little avail. At that instant, I almost walked out of the bar to head back to the safe life in Australia. It was the only moment of doubt I suffered throughout the entire four-decade gestation of the privacy movement.

* * * * *

Before that disquieting event, my preoccupation had been to attract a critical mass of supporters. I can't overstate just how bad the

---

205 Conference on data privacy and security; OECD and European Commission; 27th March 1990.

communications situation was in those days. Older readers may remember. Email and Internet were only just beginning, and the task of tracking people down was arduous and costly. In January 1990, I had started the seemingly hopeless quest to find potential supporters from across the globe. Sometimes, in English speaking countries, these people were only three degrees of separation from me, so it was a matter of only an hour or two. But often it was a day-long challenge – or more.

For example, I became obsessed with securing a member from India, and it took three weeks to find P.A. Sebastian, Principal Secretary of the Indian Peoples Human Rights Commission, who after a depressingly expensive telephone call, joined the working party of the initiative. The same challenge existed for prospective members in Panama, Zambia, South Africa, Haiti, The Philippines, Thailand, Japan, Argentina, Costa Rica, Zimbabwe, Yugoslavia, Hungary, Poland, Egypt, Israel, Kenya, Hong Kong and Chile.

It says something about the dearth of privacy expertise in the 1980s that high school dropouts such as I were appointed to exalted university departments. Starting in 1987 at the University of New South Wales, and continuing across institutions in many countries, I found myself in the bizarre situation of being the least educated person in those places – even counting the students! I recount later in the book how the London School of Economics not only kept me on as the longest serving Visiting Fellow in the School's history (sixteen years), but heavily supported many of my campaigns. Universities can be a crucial resource for campaigners.

I left the University of New South Wales Law Faculty with a $650 fax bill[206] (for which doubtless they still haven't forgiven me), but my personal phone bill after six months was over ten thousand dollars. Communications was not cheap in that era. Fortunately I secured a consultancy gig with Telecom Australia – the dominant comms provider – for $9,750 to advise them on privacy developments overseas. That almost paid all my telephone bills to that same company!

I had never felt so isolated and alone. Privacy simply was not a mainstream topic back then. I would usually have to run an elevator pitch to convince people it would be critically important in the future. From memory – as addressed to the civil liberties organisations in developing countries who were struggling daily with abduction, murder, corruption and torture.

I had to keep things brief, so this was the pitch:

"The government is gaining access to vast computer systems and believe the result will be very bad for our freedoms – even worse than it is now. My thinking is if we work together over the coming year we might get in front of this issue, and maybe deal with it before it hits us."

This pitch worked to the extent that civil rights organisations from thirteen developing countries joined the working group. It was a difficult challenge to secure them, particularly as most did not understand even the basics of computing.

Sure, academics, lawyers and officials were all over the privacy landscape because of data protection law, but not so with campaigners. They were few and far between. Indeed, even after I had established – by the following year – a working party of eighty people from twenty eight countries, only seventeen could be viewed as campaigners.

I had called the United Nations in New York several times and drew a blank. They just weren't interested. "We don't do privacy," one junior official remarked. I found this odd, seeing that the UN convention on human rights specifically mentions privacy. "Please stop calling this number," the man added, before abruptly hanging up.

I also tried Amnesty International's HQ in London and received the same response, even though I pleaded that electronic surveillance would soon be the mechanism to track political dissidents. To be fair, the Deputy Secretary General did eventually call me back, but just said something along the lines of, "I'm only talking to you to be nice. I don't see how this has anything to do with us". A decade later, Professor Steve Wright convinced them otherwise and now, more than thirty years on, privacy and surveillance are core issues for Amnesty.

After all this time I still cannot comprehend the disconnect between fantasy and reality in starting an international movement. The first report of PI talked of working groups, specialist committees, interim groups and sub-committees. The reality was that we just struggled chaotically on, making decisions on the fly.

Looking back all those decades, it was disgraceful that Amnesty

---

206 Bennett, C. J. (2008). The Privacy Advocates. Cambridge. MIT Press p. 28

International was so far behind the curve. It should have sensed that surveillance was already a big issue for many countries. Mirna Anaya, General Coordinator of one of our working group members, the "Comision para la Defensa de los Derechos Humanos en CentroAmerica" (Central America Commission for Human Rights), in Costa Rica, had told us that year:

"In general, the privacy issue is one that we in Central America deal with on a constant basis. Most of the organisations in the 'popular sector throughout Central America are watched and threatened by para military and military forces. It is often the case that this surveillance and harassment, obviously an infringement of numerous rights that fall under the notion of privacy rights, is followed by illegal captures, lengthy illegal detentions with torture, and disappearance."[207]

Despite the absence of backing by those big institutions, I learned quickly that the trick to establishing any large network is to leverage degrees of separation. Or, put another way, Pyramid Selling. Australia was in the bag, so I then targeted its closest ally – New Zealand. Then onto the other English speaking countries, before taking on the infinitely tougher job of securing people in continental Europe, Africa, South America, Japan and South East Asia. As "names" joined the effort, other names felt comfortable to take part. I was ruthless in asking for contacts from each new member. Professor Alan Westin was the last of the great privacy pioneers to join. He was deeply suspicious of the endeavour.

Using this formula, I ended up with an interesting mix. People like the President of the Hungarian Constitutional Court, the President of the NSW Court of Appeal, the New Zealand Ombudsman, the Canadian Federal Privacy Commissioner, the Assistant Prime Minister of Thailand, the Vice President of Rabobank in the Netherlands, the Access to Information Commissioner of Quebec, the senior human rights commissioner of New Zealand, the executive director of the open government division of the US Department of State, the Law Reform Commission of Hong Kong and the Canadian International Development Agency. With that group – and seventy other solid members – I knew I

---

207 Privacy International interim report 1990-1991
https://web.archive.org/web/20101202201847/http://www.privacyinternational.org/artic
le.shtml?cmd[347]=x-347-145834

was onto something useful.[208]

I really was badly equipped for this task. Whenever I met influential people, that old sense of self-consciousness surfaced. I had conversations with the President of the ACLU and found myself stumbling (though the ACLU ended up joining the working group, even though the organisation back then was uncertain of its international mandate). Meetings with Presidents of national Constitutional Courts were even more shaky. During my first trip to Hungary I was introduced to the Constitutional Court President, who was having dinner with colleagues in a local restaurant. He fixed me with steely eyes, doubtless trying to figure out whether I was a serious player or a nutcase, but in the end he, too, joined the working group.

* * * * *

Before all that – back in mid-March 1990 at the birth of this idea – I was still struggling to attract even a few significant figures outside Australia. I was just a random guy with a funny accent, at the other end of a phone. It was clear that physical meetings were required.

Greenleaf advised me that the following week there would be a joint European Commission and Council of Europe conference in Luxembourg on Data Protection and Computer Crime. He was unable to attend due to lecture commitments, but I could ask the secretariat to go in his stead. Maybe it would be an opportunity to meet some of these people who had just been phone contacts up until now. I agreed to attend. I then decided that this would be the moment to formally launch the world initiative. This was, after all, the world's first major conference that connected privacy with the modern era of computers. It was a crucial gathering, that sadly, has been lost in any Internet searches.

Back then there was only a small handful of people I had been in touch with – and even fewer who would be at that conference. I recall that attendees at that first meeting were UK privacy publisher Steward

---

208 See Privacy International's Interim report, 1990-1991

Dresner, Canadian tech expert Tom Riley and the late and unsurpassable Professor Jon Bing from Norway. Their involvement at the first meeting was supported by visionaries such as Justice Michael Kirby, who had chaired the OECD privacy guidelines some years before.

I have no idea precisely what we discussed. I suspect it was along the lines of, "Look, let's just agree to do this and see what happens". They agreed, and this created the formal starting point for everything that was to follow.

The work continued. Those were strange times. Privacy was an arcane subject, one that was on very few radar screens. The Internet had barely emerged, digital telephony was in its infancy, and NSA snooping was just a conspiracy theory. We communicated largely through landline telephone and real face to face meetings that we travelled thousands of miles to attend. These days, global initiatives are started at the press of a button, but they can also disintegrate at another push of a button. It may sound retro in an age of social networking, but I still do believe that having face time and developing real relationships is the key to creating an enduring network.

The cost, however, is huge. I can't even begin to understand how I found the funds to travel half a million miles in the first three years of the movement's development. I begged and borrowed, undertook advisory work and demanded expenses for conference talks. Back then there was no philanthropic foundation forward-thinking enough to provide global funding for what I was doing.

By 1991 the initiative was getting noticed. It had been mentioned in some news outlets, including Time[209] and Scientific American, so it was the moment to find a catchy name. The "World Privacy and Data Protection Network" just wasn't going to cut it. Even the acronym WPDPN was clunky.

A couple of years earlier, I had befriended a famous management consultant called Bill (W.J.) Reddin, a man of extraordinary talents who routinely commanded ten thousand dollars a day for his services.[210] Bill had loaned me his London apartment in Mecklenburgh Square, so I didn't have to pay hotel bills. In many respects, he was a patron saint of the

---

209 Phillip Elmer-Dewitt, Peddling Big Brother. Time Magazine June 24, 1991
   https://content.time.com/time/magazine/article/0,9171,973251,00.html
210 Wikipedia entry for Bill Reddin https://en.wikipedia.org/wiki/William_James_Reddin

movement.

We were enjoying a rare evening together in the flat and I put the name problem to him. "There must be a better brand," I said. His response was Classic Reddin. The sort of Classic Reddin that set him apart from all other so-called management experts.

"What's the one word that defines what you do?" he asked

"Erm. Privacy".

"And what is your ambition – your plan?"

"Well, to be global – and inclusive".

"OK", he declared. "The name you want is Privacy International. Now open that other bottle!"

It was as simple as that. Privacy International from then on became our name – and at the time of writing, it still is.[211]

Sadly, Bill broke his hip the following year. He died several months later, probably of a broken heart, because he could no longer walk.

Taking on America

1991 was a benchmark year for the movement, but no particular date was more crucial than March 26th – precisely one year after the foundation meeting in Luxembourg.

I attended the first Computers, Freedom & Privacy (CFP) conference in San Francisco and this was my first trip to the United States. I had been in touch electronically with a couple of the people there, but this was to be our first actual meeting.

CFP was an extraordinary gathering. Every famous crypto expert, innovator, privacy advocate and policy wonk in America was there. All the pioneers of the digital age. It was the Woodstock of the privacy realm. And I was about to speak in plenary. It was a terrifying prospect. Just to

---

211 Privacy International homepage https://privacyinternational.org/

stand there at the podium in front of the entire US tech and privacy community was daunting. And here – just as in Luxembourg – I felt isolated and alone. I might have been the only foreigner there among the hundreds who attended. I was a nobody in that crowd. At best I was a sort of circus freak from down-under. The only road I could take was to be controversial.

My speech was ad-lib. I ranted and raved. I said I was proud to be an extremist, and that I detested the reasonable middle ground. I went on at length, criticising those in the hall who were silently subverting privacy, while adopting a benign face. The laughter and applause steadily grew, and then I landed a neat bombshell that gave me a much-needed free entry ticket to the US tech community.[212]

At the time, the biggest news story in America was the videotape of LA. police beating up Rodney King.[213] This event had soured the nation about the entrenched racial hatred within white-dominated police forces. I remarked, "This brings us to the position of opting-out, right? I didn't think that the opt-in, opt-out thing had reached such a controversial point here, but it has. I can't understand why opting-out has received such serious attention, because the whole basis of the American legal system is based on universalities. You know: 'Dear Los Angeles Police Department: Please don't beat me up tonight.'"

To my amazement, that speech received a two-minute standing ovation, and from that point, I was able to reach all the key US people that the movement needed. We had finally made it to America!

I made many contacts that day – and some who joined the Working Group, including Professor David Flaherty (later to become the privacy and information commissioner of British Columbia), Professor Colin Bennett, David Burnham,[214] Georgetown's Professor Mary Culnan. Robert Ellis Smith of the Privacy Journal. Evan Hendricks of Privacy Times and Jan Goldman of the ACLU. But none was more central to our development than Marc Rotenberg, then of Computer Professionals for Social Responsibility (CPSR).

---

212 CFP 1991 transcript http://cpsr.org/prevsite/conferences/cfp91/hoffman2.html/ (accessed 12th August 1998).
213 Wikipedia entry for Rodney King https://en.wikipedia.org/wiki/Rodney_King (accessed 12th August 1998).
214 Burnham, David. The Rise of the Computer State. New York: Random House, 1983.

Rotenberg is an exceptional character. Young (back then), urbane, studious, smart and articulate, he had become the respected voice of US privacy, but he wanted to take the field to new levels. He had already agreed, through the new magic of electronic mail, to be the secretary of Privacy International, and he was simultaneously contemplating a new project (one that eventually became EPIC, the Electronic Privacy Information Center. It became the most important NGO privacy initiative in US history. At the time of writing, EPIC and Privacy International are the two largest and most influential privacy organisations in the world.

A three-time Washington DC chess champion – Rotenberg brought his strategic nous to organisational development.

This was a "Crossroads" moment in the history of privacy advocacy. Rotenberg and EPIC had made a decision – based on ethics and pragmatism – from the earliest days to avoid corporate support.[215] Interestingly, at the time, it shared office space with the Center for Democracy & Technology (CDT), an influential organisation that started operations later in 1994 and which had no issue with such sponsorship. There was an immediate conflict of approach, but – more important – a question of how the US privacy movement should be positioned. Thankfully, starting with the Fund for Constitutional Government and others, privacy soon became a program stream for many philanthropic foundations.

EPIC's effort, right at the birth of US advocacy, had – even then – found many supporters. Hundreds of those supporters congregated at the CFP conferences. In many respects, the US was way ahead of the world. Campaigners in London attempted to host a UK parallel in the mid 1990's, and it maybe attracted 250 people, but it never saw the light of day after one event.

From its earliest days, EPIC became obsessed with discovering the keystone issues upon which strong privacy – or endemic intrusion – depend. That meant carefully selecting its battles. Case Law precedent was crucial, but so too was the challenge of winning the hearts and minds of the American public.

Within twenty five years, EPIC's activism had cast a very wide net and its

---

215 Rotenberg, M. Internet Freedom Advocates in Tow, New York Times. DEC. 9, 2012 ,
      https://www.nytimes.com/2012/12/10/opinion/internet-freedom-advocates-in-tow.html

mandate went beyond the traditional scope of privacy rights. For example, responding to President Trump's interference in State voter oversight, the group immediately launched a stinging series of legal actions to block the White House initiative.[216] This followed EPIC's influential intervention in the scandal over Russian interference in the 2016 US election.[217]

These were just a couple of activities in a litany of high-profile actions by the group. In 2017 alone, EPIC succeeded in forcing the transport company UBER to back off from putting its customers under surveillance.[218] It pursued the release of Trump's tax records, intervened in surveillance actions by the FBI and the DHS and created dozens of actions that have gone to the heart of government intrusion. These ranged from regular Congressional testimony, submissions, petitions and statements to FOI requests and Amicus briefs. Little wonder that even back in 2000, Britain's Daily Telegraph newspaper described the organisation as "wonderfully subversive".

We worked on numerous projects in the years that followed EPIC's founding, including an initiative to figure out how the files held by the East German Stasi should be handled, the Clipper Chip US cryptography policy[219], the Lotus Marketplace scandal [220], and the emerging EU data protection framework. One notable – and successful – campaign was the strike against Intel, which was branded "Big Brother Inside".[221] Rotenberg's creativity and scholarly thinking set a high benchmark for US privacy.

Rotenberg gave me entry to US media, and agencies such as the Federal Trade Commission. In many respects, he was the gateway that allowed

---

216 EPIC v. Electoral Commission https://www.epic.org/privacy/litigation/voter/epic-v-commission/

217 EPIC seeks special counsel reports on Russian election interference 5th November 2018 https://epic.org/2018/11/epic-seeks-special-counsel-rep.html (accessed 7th November 2018)

218 Federal Trade Commission approves settlement with UBER 29th October 2018 https://epic.org/2018/10/federal-trade-commission-appro.html (accessed 3rd November 2018)

219 Froomkin, Michael. "The Metaphor is the Key: Cryptography, the Clipper Chip and the Constitution." University of Pennsylvania Law Review 143 (1995): 709–712. www.law.miami.edu/~froomkin/articles/clipper.htm.

220 Culnan, Mary J. "The Lessons of the Lotus Marketplace: Implications for Consumer Privacy in the 1990's." 1991. www.cpsr.org/prevsite/conferences/cfp91/culnan.html.

221 Leizerov, Sagi. "Privacy Advocacy Groups' versus Intel: A Case Study of How Social Movements are Tactically Using the Internet to Fight Corporations," Social Science

Privacy International to move to the second stage.

Hugely supportive as he was, Rotenberg was deeply immersed in his own commitment to shaping US privacy. His newly acquired office at 666 Pennsylvania Avenue S.E. (where EPIC was housed for some years) was buzzing with activity. Piles of funding documents sprawled across the office, and the phones were ringing off the hook with media enquiries. Even before 1994, he had been instrumental in shaping a comprehensive network of US advocates, which in 1991 was launched as the "US Privacy Foundation". Two years later I attempted to start the UK Privacy Foundation but failed miserably because there simply were not enough activists at the time to make it work.

At the international level, I was still more or less working alone on day-to-day campaigns. It was becoming crippling. Sleepless nights working across every international time zone. When Associated Press called me from New York and asks me to speak to their Berlin correspondent in six hours for an impending story, I could hardly say no. When the Berlin correspondent then asked me to touch base for a fact check with the San Francisco correspondent six hours later, so be it.

In 1994, David Banisar emerged. Banisar worked for the newly formed EPIC and soon became deputy director of Privacy International. He was instrumental in many of our campaigns, but also co-authored with me the most important international privacy study of all time – Privacy & Human Rights. That book, published by the Global Internet Liberty Campaign and EPIC, comprised dozens of country reports and continued for several years until it became so large that, as I have mentioned elsewhere, it might best be described as ship's ballast, and was no longer economically feasible to publish.

Privacy International was still almost unique in the global context. Then in 1996, developments started to emerge that changed the equation. International initiatives started to spring up. EPIC started the Public Voice project that reached out to many developing countries.[222] The Electronic Frontier Foundation (EFF) and the American Civil Liberties Union (ACLU) also started to look globally. EPIC and the ACLU sponsored – with support from the George Soros Open Society Foundation – the aforementioned Global Internet Liberty Campaign

---

Computer Review 18, no. 7 (2000):
222 The Public Voice https://thepublicvoice.org/

(GILC).[223] The list goes on. At that point – possibly also thanks to better communications – campaigners and experts were talking freely across borders. And importantly, a new generation of journalists emerged, who were concerned with privacy aspects beyond the US border. For me, after nine years of relative isolation, this was a ground-breaking shift.

These developments were awesome, but they also served to increase the workload for Privacy International. It seemed the media interest was doubling every day, to the point where sometimes there would be forty media enquiries over any 24 hour period. It was simply unsustainable. At this point I was becoming fatigued. I needed help.

In October 1996, a guardian angel appeared in the form of a doctoral student called Gus Hosein. He came straight up to me at the university bar and announced that he would like to help.

I recall that Hosein – despite his wild hair and wide-eyed face – looked like a terribly serious man who might be able to lend support. He had a deep and reassuring voice, but not so deep and reassuring as to be cocky or over-confident, like so many people I had met in this "cool" new field. He seemed anxious to learn and to apply that learning to help grow the movement. Significantly, Gus Hosein had an eye on the global context, and was keen to take an interdisciplinary approach to privacy. This was a rare find.

Hosein not only lent support, but he ended up taking on much of the administrative and research work, of which I was pathologically incapable. Sixteen years later he took over my role as Director of Privacy International.[224] But that meeting was the single event that changed everything for me – and for the emerging movement.

It was often remarked that Gus Hosein and I were the Odd Couple. I was the crazy guy with the big mouth who would come up spontaneously with impossible ideas. Hosein was the serious guy who made those ideas happen. He sat in the background, writing reports and doing research while I was engaged in the fun bit of attacking the enemy. In some respects, in those early days it felt like I was the architect and he was the

---

223 Global Internet Liberty Campaign http://gilc.org/events/budapest/announce.html (accessed 3rd September 2018)

224 Privacy International – foundation stone of the global privacy movement – turns 25 today. The Privacy Surgeon. http://www.privacysurgeon.org/blog/incision/privacy-international-the-foundation-stone-of-the-global-privacy-movement-turns-25-today-privacyint/

engineer, plumber, surveyor, insurer and electrician. It worked brilliantly – and equally so with Banisar, who could adapt easily to most of those roles.

Chapter Nine: the combative years: 1995-2008

> *From 1995, the movement became mature, innovative and influential. These are tales of some of the initiatives, from the Big Brother Awards to constitutional reform. We learned in those early days how to take on the most powerful entities on earth – and sometimes win.*

The Big Brother Awards

It is June 29th 2003, and here I am in Tokyo, dressed unconvincingly as the Queen of the United Kingdom and the Commonwealth. I gaze from the podium of a grand theatre hall and see hundreds of bemused Japanese attendees, who wait anxiously to hear my first words. Her Majesty's appearance had been a closely guarded secret and so there is a sudden buzz of excitement at her arrival.

"My fellow citizens," I begin. "You should have been British subjects, but Douglas MacArthur and those damned Yanks interfered with our plan. If we had our way, you'd be drinking gin, not rice wine."

I spiralled into an animated presentation that involved just about every faux pas in diplomatic history. It was all uttered in that high pitched regal monotone for which the queen is famous. My translator, with wonderful humour, mimicked my every nuance.

The rather famous Japanese theatre troupe in control of this event had designed a mobile podium, so at the end of my talk three of them could race out and rapidly wheel me off-stage, as if I were an amphetamine-ridden Dalek. I crashed into the wings, regal legs v-shaped in the air, tiara spinning into the audience.

Afterwards, everyone joined in the fun, by laying down their jackets for me to walk on and bowing or curtseying to me. Even members of parliament did this.

This was the 34th Big Brother Awards event, a ceremony that recognises the villains and heroes of privacy.[225] it is an initiative I had begun on a whim five years earlier in the UK. By the time of that first Tokyo event, the awards had already spread to the US, Austria, Canada, Germany, Switzerland, France, Hungary, Denmark, the Netherlands, Finland, Spain, Belgium and Bulgaria. More countries were to follow: Australia, New Zealand, Italy, Ukraine, the Czech Republic and South Korea. They became affectionately known as "The Orwells". By 2018, there had been 160 BBA ceremonies in 36 cities, though sadly the number of participating countries is now in decline.[226] Still, it was delightful to notice that those awards sparked a whole generation of similar ceremonies – even in the private sector.

The regal appearance in Tokyo was no fluke. Our Japanese members had seen me present the US awards three months earlier in the New Yorker hotel, in the same outfit. The difference between the two events was that the Japanese had a sense of style and tried to make me look believable: lipstick, cosmetics, a good dress. In New York, I just ended up looking like the worst drag act in history, tragically wearing watercolour paints and a hotel sheet.

These events were extremely important in terms of building a new global community. They magnetised a diverse following and attracted substantial media coverage of key issues. For some countries, a BBA event was the first time all advocates, academics, lawyers and techies had a chance to get together – and to evangelise and expand their network. Having the international backing was crucial for smaller nations.

In Britain, where it had all started, the events became a milestone annual event that – uniquely – brought all shades of the political spectrum

225 Big Brother Awards, Wikipedia entry
         https://en.wikipedia.org/wiki/Big_Brother_Awards (accessed 13th August 1998).
226 Big Brother Awards International page http://www.bigbrotherawards.org/ (accessed
        12th July 1998).

together. It was the one evening when we all agreed to set aside our differences. That is, until July 2004, when it all went horribly wrong.

The judges that year had decided to give two "positive" (Winston) awards to candidates who were not of the usual hue. One was David Shayler, a former MI6 agent who became a whistleblower and was subsequently imprisoned. The other was the right wing newspaper the Daily Telegraph, which had made a courageous decision to become a champion of freedoms, in spite of its conservative reactionary readership. Assistant editor Stephen Robinson was there to receive the award. In front of him and Shayler was the biggest gathering of civil rights advocates ever assembled.

All seemed to be going well, until the room was invaded by a group of hard-core activists from the campaigning publication SchNews. They poured a pint of beer over the Telegraph editor, and violently threw a pie in Shayler's face, slightly injuring both he and his partner, the MI5 whistleblower Annie Machon, who had ungraciously slid to the floor on the residue.

Even though SchNews had been a positive award recipient back in 1998, it chose to take matters into its own hands because it simply didn't like the political complexion of the recipients. The issue divided the left, with many campaigners arguing that it was not right for anyone to "shit in their own nest". The Telegraph took it on the chin, later running an editorial that remarked, "Given the price of beer these days in London, that action demonstrates a serious commitment to the cause".

The magic was broken, and with the exception of one small ceremony a few years later, we never held the UK awards again. The rest of the world took note of that sad experience and soldiered on.

* * * * *

The idea for a Big Brother Award had sprung from a chance encounter in June 1998 at the White Hart pub in Drury Lane London, where the previous year I had met with environmental activists to plan the first major action against CCTV.

I was quietly sinking a pint of the pub's excellent IPA when a besuited man approached me. It seems he had seen me on television the other evening lambasting the data mining industry (or, at least back then, the embryo of the data mining industry).

He went on at length, informing me that he knew people at my university, and could cause me problems if I kept interfering in his start-up. He slammed his fist on the creaking table, and provided a sketchy analysis of my personal flaws, before assuring me that it was people like him who stopped this country from economically sinking into the North Sea. And, apparently, I was a son of a bitch.

I was with my former partner at the time, and we were exploring whether it might be possible to reunite, so I had no interest in this diatribe. I told him there should be a very public gong for people like him, so there would be a permanent record of just how much of a collective bastard they all were. Still, son of a bitch or not, my mind started racing with the idea of an award ceremony.

As always, I went back to Gus Hosein and Dave Banisar. They loved the concept of an awards ceremony. It was a solid idea. There were so many unsung pioneers in that fledgling movement – but there was a far greater number of data thugs who were blatantly striving to ruin the foundations of the information age. In that respect some things never change – though at least these days privacy is nearer the centre of the media radar screen. Corporations and governments in the 1990's were feasting off the veins of rich data that the digital realm had created, and few people in the mainstream of public policy could understand the complexity of those new technologies.

Organisations are well equipped to obfuscate by way of clever language and false evidence and so a blunt, uncompromising and irrevocable response was called for. A combative and photogenic award, issued in perpetuity, might be sufficient to make many governments think twice before engaging in bad surveillance. At the very least, being in a Hall of Shame might prompt an ethical debate within the nominated organisations.

What was needed back then was a fun ceremony with memorable prize categories – most invasive project, most appalling technology, most heinous government agency, worst corporate invader – and of course, a Lifetime Menace award for the utter demons of the digital age. We cooked up a powerful visual image that was to become the physical prize handed to winners: a life-size golden boot stamping on a golden head. This imagery was drawn from a line in George Orwell's '1984' (Nineteen Eighty Four): "If you want a picture of the future, imagine a boot stamping on a human face – forever". It stood to reason that they should be called the Big Brother Awards. The positive prizes were the "Winston's", though in hindsight that was a mistake, given that Winston caved in and lost. The US, more appropriately, ended up calling them the Brandeis Awards.

And so it was that the Big Brother Awards were born, backed by Privacy International and initially hosted by the London School of Economics. The first event – the following October – set a template for what was to become a global movement. To the bemusement of LSE professorial staff, it was held in the Senior Common Room, which was packed to the rafters. Never before had this exalted room witnessed so many masks, shell suits, spies, subversives and rock musicians.

The following year Austria and the US established their own awards, and were joined in 2000 by Germany, Switzerland and France. Many other countries followed. Each developed their own local award formula, though they all followed a basic set of global parameters. Dedicated activists and NGOs across the world worked on the event organisation and recruited a vast array of expert judges from all walks of life.

No ignoble privacy vandal was spared the naming and shaming – deceptive governments, greedy corporations, intrusive surveillance schemes, invasive and unjustified national security powers and idiotic laws. All were given the disinfectant of sunshine in a way that media found sexy and that recipients despised.

The award events themselves were – and still are – enormous fun. Apart from my Queen Elizabeth appearances, I was Michael Jackson and Dr Evil in San Francisco. I then became the Pope in Montreal and Chicago, where my theme song was 'Killing in the Name of' by Rage Against the Machine (I also enjoyed an all-Jewish entourage).

The Pope's favourite sermon was based on the 'Book of Eunuchs' (the pun is perhaps not that obvious, without technological context). He would parade around reminding the audience of the story of the forbidden fruit in the Garden of Eden, and then wave aloft an Apple computer. It was an opportunity to lambaste all the bad players from a holy pulpit.

Doing Michael Jackson was more of a difficult task, partly because getting into such clothes was a like squeezing a watermelon into a condom, and partly because we had just heard that day that Jackson had been charged with sexual offences. Still, the show must go on, and so I appeared on stage in the company of an armed military escort dressed in army uniforms and camping it up.

In Vienna, the awards became such a spectacle that they had to be conducted in Austria's biggest dance club with well over a thousand people in attendance. Under the leadership of Erich Moechel those awards became very gritty, involving prizes in the form of tanks of cockroaches.

And in some countries, the BBA ceremonies became the most significant annual meeting place for campaigners from all points on the political spectrum. Artists, musicians, actors, designers, technologists and writers joined privacy activists, to create spectacles that have been reported in most of the world's major news outlets.

The nature of the ceremonies varied widely. In the UK it was just a fun event with live music. In France it was a Vive le Revolution exercise that was clearly a hotbed of activism. In the Netherlands it was a serious and structured affair while in the US is was a blatant parody of everything related to power and authority.

Some of the prize winners have tried to make light of the awards by pretending to join in the fun. The UK Home Office placed two of its golden boot awards on the book shelf of the Home Secretary's ante-room. In the US, the FBI had its award publicly collected by an agent. Meanwhile in the Netherlands, prize winners often attend the award ceremonies to argue their case. Colin Bennett recalls: "At the 1999 US event, for instance, the representative from Microsoft proudly went to the stage to receive the award, adopting a 'look what I've got' attitude." [227]

Nobody was immune. In Hungary in 2004, for instance, one award was given to the Hungarian Data Protection Commissioner, Attila Péterfalvi, for remarks he had made about the necessity of certain surveillance schemes. Trying to make the best of a bad situation, Péterfalvi joined the ceremony to receive the award, but not before sending a letter to Privacy International threatening to withdraw support from the BBA process.[228]

But regardless of such PR, the awards have always been a serious matter. More important, they have become a litmus test of emerging issues. For example. In 2003, while most of the world still thought Google was cool, the US Big Brother Awards received 500 public nominations for the company to receive the 'Worst Corporate Invader' award. On that occasion, Google narrowly escaped the prize – but not for long, as the German judges subsequently gave Google the Most Invasive Company award. However, controversy over the 2003 nomination prompted Search Engine Land to publish a strident 7,000 word defence of the company.[229] From that point on, Google's halo began to slip.

The same pattern could be seen with corporations like Facebook and Apple. The Awards became an early warning system for troubles ahead.

The recipients take these awards very seriously indeed. One notable example was the occasion on which we gave the "Worst Civil Servant" award to Sir Richard Wilson, then head of the UK Civil Service, a half-million strong empire of government officials which effectively runs the country. As Permanent Secretary, he sat at the top of this vast edifice, governing not just the day-to-day running of the nation, but also steering (or in the official terminology, "advising") much of government policy.

It might be easy to imagine that a person in such a position couldn't care less what a pack of "lefties" did with an award made from an old army boot and some tin foil, but that was far from the reality.

We knew this to be true when the Constitution Unit of University College London (UCL) held its gala Christmas party a couple of months later. Wilson was the VIP guest of honour. Many of the hundreds of people who attended were anxious to catch his ear, but Wilson was having none of that. As we introduced ourselves upon his entry to the place, he exclaimed "My god! I nearly choked on my cornflakes when I read that in the Telegraph".

He then spent the next 45 minutes defending himself and arguing –just as

227 Bennett, C.J. "The Privacy Advocates". p.109
228 http://www.edri.org/edrigram/number2.23/BBA
229 Danny Sullivan, 01ˢᵗ April 2003
      http://searchenginewatch.com/article/2067677/Google-And-The-Big-Brother-
      Nomination

the CTO of Facebook had done – that "I just get into the office and there's a big pile of papers that I try to get through". We assured him that this claim revealed only a fraction of the true picture and that he was gilding the lily. It was only after the dogged persistence of the host that he finally dragged himself away to meet other guests.

As I recount elsewhere, two years later in Austria, Microsoft "reacted with horror, pain and angst" to the company's nomination for the 2001 Austrian Big Brother Awards and asked for the nomination to be withdrawn.[230]

* * * *

The question remained, how did we create this ceremony? Organising the event and the judges was the easy bit. It was building the award statues themselves that turned out to be tricky. It took us over a month of trial and error to figure it out.

To construct an award one needs fourteen components, ranging from polystyrene mannequin heads to threaded metal rods and tin foil. I recently dug up an instruction manual I wrote at the beginning of the movement and it was staggeringly complex. More than a thousand words of advice, such as 'Using a sharp knife or a hot blade, slice off the flat stand and most of the neck, leaving the skull and two or three inches of neck. Slice off the ear on the side of the head that will rest on the rim of the stand (the head must sit flat against the end of the stand)'.

I have no clue how anyone could comprehend such instructions, but apparently, they did. Or maybe not, seeing as so many ceremonies found their own award design. Advocates in many countries have invented other trophies to symbolize the repressive impact of surveillance: in Bulgaria a figure of a little cog within a big cog, in the Netherlands a statute of closing metal jaws, in Germany a symbol of a human figure spliced by a

230 Big Brother Award nomination for WPA, Passport pains MS It's not true, please take
      us off the list...
      https://www.theregister.co.uk/2001/10/25/big_brother_award_nomination/

sheet of numbers.[231]

It is notable though that most counties also bestow "positive" awards to champions of privacy. These have created a powerful motivation for many advocates. For example in 2001 Julie Brill from the Vermont Attorney General's Office received a US "Brandeis" award for her privacy work.[232] In later years, when she became a Commissioner of the Federal Trade Commission (FTC) Brill remarked to my colleagues and I that receiving that award had made a profound impact on her work and helped to drive her forward.

Scrambling for Safety

The Big Brother awards were not the only idea hatched in a pub. Within a month of meeting Hosein, we had already devised another initiative that was to change the face of Internet and crypto policy in Britain – and elsewhere. Together with a couple of other colleagues, we came up with an idea in the George IV pub in Portugal Street, London. The plan was to create a series of major one-day public conferences at the LSE around key policy issues of the day. The issue that moment was the government's plan to undermine cryptography through the hilariously coined name "Trusted Third Parties". Even fifteen years before Edward Snowden, we knew there was no such thing as "trusted" – particularly if government was involved. We called the events "Scrambling for Safety", and they continued for two decades.[233]

In testimony to how strong international ties had become, almost every leading cryptographer in the world attended, including Whit Diffie, co-inventor of public key encryption and Phil Zimmermann, developer of PGP (Pretty Good Privacy).

We held the first event in the Old Theatre of the LSE. It was a gamble, in

---

231 Bennett; C.J. "The Privacy Advocates" p.108
232 NSA and FBI big winners at the Big Brother Awards. 8th March 2001. The Register. https://www.theregister.co.uk/2001/03/08/nsa_and_fbi_big_winners/ (accessed 3rd November 2018)
233 19th May 1997 https://warwick.ac.uk/fac/soc/law/elj/jilt/1997_2/mclaughlin

that the theatre held almost five hundred people. And crypto back then was a niche issue. My thinking, based on similar attempts in the US, Australia and Canada, was that the tighter the focus, the greater the chance of attracting an entire stakeholder group of hundreds. And the closer the event was to an imminent government action, the more assurance there was of serious media coverage. This is how we played it.

We waited. On the morning of the event the queue built up. It extended down the stairs and into the street. In the end it was standing room only.

The government was speaking, as was the OECD. And media was there in droves. In one day it became clear to everyone that this was an issue to be reckoned with. In the many events that we held in subsequent years, government did not dare to decline an invitation. Scrambling for Safety (SfS) became the key event for public engagement on any serious tech issue.

That first meeting – May 19th 1997 – was also the moment when the UK tech and advocacy movements came together. I've lost count of the number of people who were inspired by that event to become tech professionals or advocates. These included Ian Brown, then a student, who became fixated on privacy and rights, and became one of the youngest professors ever to be appointed to the University of Oxford. That influence continued. Exactly seven years later, 19th May 2004, an SfS event inspired Phil Booth to get involved in – and eventually lead – the successful fight against the national ID card in the UK. Likewise, the May 1998 SfS event brought the tech and policy communities together to form the Foundation for Information Policy Research (FIPR), which had a huge impact on UK policy. And Caspar Bowden, a strategic genius, was also inspired by SfS, and went on to be Director of FIPR. By pure coincidence, each of those events happened on 19th May, which some of us imagined should become the "British Privacy Day".

Bowden also pushed for the creation of a Europe-wide membership organisation that would build a coalition of rights groups across the EU. We were sceptical because membership usually entailed massive administration, but he prevailed. By the year 2000 we met in an anonymous coffee shop near Tavistock Square London and plotted the creation of EDRi – the European Digital Rights Initiative, which soon became the most influential information rights movement in Europe. Some years later, we launched the initiative in Berlin with the appropriate numbers of beers.

9/11 and Stupid Security

Another pun session – and yet another idea. This one took shape in the aftermath of 9/11. Those events triggered a domino effect that proved a huge challenge for privacy advocates. Countries around the world – and particularly in the US and Britain – lined up a litany of intrusive policy proposals.

We were under huge pressure – perhaps more than ever. Fortunately for us, sage voices provided crucial context. In his 2001 report,[234] Marc Rotenberg said: "You may think we would be discouraged. But this is the work of democracy. We don't have the time, the luxury or the opportunity to be discouraged."

In the US it was difficult to say anything that countered the government position. Free speech was effectively eliminated on the topic, though liberal media did make an effort to publish dissenting voices, which were then subsequently branded as treasonous to the public interest.

The more thoughtful outlets did, however, champ on the bit for a reasoned response. One such publication was Communications of the ACM (the Association of Computing Machinery, which is the largest computer membership organisation in the world). Its editor had agreed to a critical piece from me on the anniversary of the attacks. Remarkably – for an academic publication – they gave me a four-week lead time for the piece, instead of the usual twelve months.[235]

The piece ran as a front page lead on the anniversary of the attacks, much to the annoyance of my more academic colleagues, who had been trying to publish in that journal for some years.

It expressed concern that the attacks had created an entire industry of band-wagon jumpers from window installers to software houses, all of

234 EPIC 1991 annual report https://epic.org/epic/annual_reports/2001.pdf
235 Davies, S. "a year after 9/11", Communications of the ACM, Volume 45 Issue 9,

which were anxious to "brand" their products with the 9/11 image (I realised only after deadline that I should have called them "brand wagon jumpers"). And that's before we even consider the vast new government security complex that had been created. It was commercial opportunism at its worst.

From that work emerged a curious idea that was to place the security threat in perspective for more than a few people. Again, this came from a brainstorming session at the Three Tuns pub, close to Christmas of 2002.

Historically, one way to destabilise hysteria is to mock it – to be satirical, yet evidence based. So why not an international award for the most ridiculous security measures? And so, the Stupid Security Awards (SSA) were born. We had enough personal experience to know that this was going to be a seam of gold in terms of public awareness. Somehow, we needed to shift the centre of gravity and get people talking about the realities of this new world of random security measures.

Early the following year, as with the BBA's, we set up a panel of well-known security experts, public policy specialists, privacy advocates and journalists. We launched the effort in February the following year, with no idea how much traction it would get. Within four weeks, the competition had attracted almost 5,000 nominations from 35 countries.

On April 3rd 2003, we announced the winners at the CFP conference in New York.[236] The material that been submitted exceeded our wildest expectations.[237]

Delta Airlines won the "Most Egregiously Stupid Security" award for requiring a mother of a four-month-old to drink a bottle of her own breast milk to demonstrate that it wasn't a threat to the staff on the plane.

The "Most Counterproductive Security" award went to a policeman who checked a pair of shoes out for explosives by slamming them down — apparently if they didn't explode, they were OK.

"Most Inexplicable Security" went to San Francisco General Hospital, which treats many homeless people. After 9/11, they started requiring ID of people entering through the front door — but all side entrances were left completely unguarded. The staff and patients started using those side entrances. The corridors filled with people desperately looking for the emergency room.

Then there's "Most Intrusive Security". A disproportionate number of security measures seem to focus on attractive young women, and many security guards take great care in carefully checking out such individuals. The Michigan State Prison demanded that any woman entering the prison (as a visitor) must wear a bra "for security". One woman who could not wear a bra due to irritation needed medical certification to be able to visit her husband.

A commercial airline pilot had contacted us to complain that after twenty years' experience he was required to undergo body searches. He added: "You know, if I wanted to take down a plane I'd just hit the co-pilot with the security axe in the cockpit and then slam down both the pedals".[238]

One commentator remarked: "the real point is not the stupidity of these examples — it's the danger in having the illusion of security and winding up with less real security, not more."[239] This is what security guru Bruce Schneier has famously called "Security Theatre".

* * * * *

Privacy International was in growth mode. It had a few additional resources, and also had many substantial wins under its belt. But post 9/11, the UK was under the leadership of Tony Blair's Labour government. Things had not been so bad for civil liberties in living memory, and we had our work cut out to fight back. Our US colleagues had an even tougher time fighting for privacy in that period.[240]

The period 2003-2008 was beautifully chaotic, made more so by our commitment to focus on Asian countries. We ran possibly a hundred campaigns over that period, some more successful than others. And

---

238 Announcing the world's most stupid security measures. The Register. 9th April 2003
    https://www.theregister.co.uk/2003/04/09/worlds_most_stupid_security_measures/
239 https://readthisblog.net/2003/04/ (accessed 24th July 2018)
240 Lyon, David. Surveillance after September 11th. Cambridge: Polity Press, 2003b.

internationally, the stakes were rising. The US was stepping up efforts to capture developing counties and avoid the passage of privacy law. And in the US itself, the emergence of the Bush administration was a dangerous moment for privacy.

We had learned how to think in military terms whenever we started a campaign. There simply weren't enough resources – or enough time – to spend months on a single issue. Our aim was to find the weak point in any opposition and exploit it quickly and decisively. This was a lesson learned from the legacy of Saul Alinsky.

The Heathrow subversion

It is March 2008, and Her Majesty Queen Elizabeth II is opening the new Terminal 5 at London's Heathrow Airport. This £4.3 billion monstrosity has taken years to build and caused a vast amount of controversy. If you haven't yet had the pleasure of passing through Terminal 5, just imagine one of those giant American retail warehouses multiplied by ten thousand.

All went well for Her Majesty, except for one missing feature of the terminal: there was no mandatory fingerprinting of passengers. I take personal pleasure in removing the obligation on the Queen to point at the machines, and the need to ask, "So do tell me about this".

We had learned the previous year that Heathrow was planning compulsory fingerprinting both in Terminal 5 and Terminal 1. Gatwick and Manchester airports also planned to follow suit. And it wasn't international travellers who were targeted: it was the four million domestic internal passengers each year. This was unprecedented.

Our views had been published in the media[241] [242], but both the British Airports Authority and British Airways were unrepentant. They claimed it was all about security. Travellers (terrorists), they argued, could swap

---

241 Cacciottolo, M, 6th December 2006 Biometric science arrives at Heathrow, BBC News
　　http://news.bbc.co.uk/2/hi/uk_news/6214592.stm
242　Heathrow Airport first to fingerprint; Daily Telegraph, 7th March 2008

boarding passes.

Be that as it may (and it is a big "may"), the real reason for the initiative goes to the heart of airport economics. The new airports wanted to expose both international and transiting domestic passengers to the vast shopping malls above the gates. The rent on those properties alone could pay off the building costs in less than a decade. It was therefore important[243] to get every traveller into the malls. For this, some form of biometric was allegedly needed, seeing as domestic passengers did not require a passport.

Because of the huge array of major surveillance initiatives being pushed by the government at the time, we weren't getting traction for a full-blown campaign. It was clear that another strategy was needed.

Here's a little-known principle of campaigning in democratic countries governed by a monarchy: the monarch cannot be associated with anything unlawful. Such was the case with Terminal 5. If we could smear the fingerprinting project with illegality, then either the airport would have to withdraw the project, or the Queen would need to feign a bad toothache that day and not show up.

It was clear that the way forward would be to convince the Information Commissioner's Office (the UK DPA) to launch an investigation – or at least, to signal an investigation. But timing was everything. If we sent in a complaint too early, the (then) notoriously ambivalent office could quickly review the scheme and give it a clean bill of health before the grand opening. If we submitted the complaint too close to the opening, the DPA could just say they hadn't had time to review it. We figured ten days was the ideal window. If there was any signal from the DPA that the scheme might be unlawful, the airport would go into meltdown.

Accordingly, we submitted an extremely detailed complaint pointing out various aspects of European case law and other judgments. We argued that under data protection law the process was prohibitive and unnecessary – a photograph would be sufficient.

Then we tipped off a number of friendly journalists in the mainstream press, who badgered the DPA until it finally conceded that there was a case for investigation. That investigation formally began a few days

---

243 https://www.telegraph.co.uk/news/uknews/1580993/Heathrow-airport-first-to-fingerprint.html

227

later.[244]

The Deputy Information Commissioner David Smith told the Mail on Sunday: "We want to know why Heathrow needs to fingerprint passengers at all. Taking photographs is less intrusive. So far we have not heard BAA's case for requesting fingerprints." [245]

"If we find there is a breach of data protection legislation, we would hope to persuade them to put things right. If that is not successful, we can issue an enforcement notice. If they don't comply, it is a criminal offence and they can be prosecuted."

As predicted, Heathrow immediately killed the biometric scheme.[246] Just occasionally, working though privacy regulators can make a difference – if done tactically.

Going for the Main Game: constitutional reform

By 2006, we were losing ground in the UK. Although there had never been such a groundswell of support for privacy – and such a powerful privacy and rights alliance – the government had become mesmerised with IT and wanted to computerise and link almost everything.

Our meagre resources were being badly depleted because of two major ongoing campaigns. One was against Google, begun in 2004 (discussed in Chapter XXX), and the other against the impending UK national ID card (outlined in detail in Chapter XXX).

But that year, a remarkable opportunity arose. The government made a commitment to introduce constitutional reform. That's to say, a new Bill of Rights. This document – in the pre-Brexit era – was to be compatible with human rights law both in the UK and Europe. The key selling point

---

244 Heathrow fingerprint plan probed; BBC News, 23rd March 2008
http://news.bbc.co.uk/2/hi/uk_news/7310158.stm
245 Computer Weekly: The cost of Biometrics at T5
https://www.computerweekly.com/blog/Identity-Privacy-and-Trust/The-cost-of-privacy-biometrics-at-London-Heathrow-T5
246 Terminal 5 fingerprinting scrapped, 26th Match 2008
https://www.theguardian.com/uk/2008/mar/26/3

was that it would be a reflection of the cultural dynamics of Britain.

No-one quite knew what those dynamics actually were. Ambivalence about politics? Well, Italy could teach Britain a thing or two about that. Italians have become even more cynical than the UK. Or was it innovation and the work ethic? The Germans had those covered. Or perhaps fairness and respect? Again, the Dutch workplace and Dutch communities prided themselves on such values.

The need for serious and inspirational change was palpable. Following the divisive, decade-long "New Labour" experiment, disenchantment with government and politics had plummeted to a dangerous level. The Scottish Nationalists were gaining ground in their struggle for independence and the Tories (Britain's centre-right Conservative party) desperately needed a unifying rallying-cry. Meanwhile, far right English nationalism and anti-Europe activism were on the ascendancy.

Simply put, Britain had yet again become a nation divided, comatose with disillusion, and bonded mainly by the occasional sporting celebration.

It was perhaps the most ambitious plan we had ever come up with, but we settled on the notion of seizing the entire constitutional reform agenda. In doing so we could embed respect for privacy deeply into the British psyche.

Perhaps this idea was more crazy than ambitious, but we decided it needed to be tried. Otherwise we'd spend the rest of our lives fighting hostile British administrations.

This was undoubtedly going to be the most delicate and intricate strategy we had ever attempted. It would require bringing all the major political parties together – and even more daunting – uniting all the experts and various existing reform groups.

Hosein and I agreed that the only way this could be achieved was to aim for a "process" for constitutional reform. Taking that path was far less controversial than figuring what words should be in the Bill of Rights. But process is everything and it would put us right at the centre.[247]

We used the LSE's Policy Engagement Network as the base for this project (Hosein and I were co-directors of that unit). That was the easy

---

247 Interview with Simon Davies on YouTube
    https://www.youtube.com/watch?v=nStdSDuuluE

bit. A much tougher challenge was finding a name. It had to be short, positive, decisive and catchy. I went through several hundred options, and we finally settled on "Future Britain".[248]
Then we figured out our game plan. Pyramid selling, yet again. First, we met with government ministers and secured their support. On the basis of that support, then on to the Shadow Attorney General in the Conservative Opposition. He nervously accepted. Then finally, we engaged the leader of the third largest party, the Liberal Democrats. He too committed to the idea.

What followed was an exhausting round of stakeholder meetings right across the spectra of academia, human rights and law. Most people we spoke to signed up to the idea, but some refused. They had their own agendas. One of the biggest stakeholders to decline was the British civil service. Senior bureaucrats bluntly told us that constitutional reform would never happen. Any readers familiar with Sir Humphrey Appleby in the TV series Yes Minister will easily imagine the sort of circuitous conversations we endured.

Still, we felt in a position to move to the next stage: a major public meeting. Again, we held it in the Old Theatre of the LSE. It was July 2007 – a good month to hold such an event because summer was at last here and people were generally happy and up-beat.

We felt we had a real chance at changing the country. And maybe, at one level or another, so did some people in government. Indeed I was invited to share the reform launch broadcast on BBC with the responsible government minister. Just he and I.

The LSE event should have been a spectacular springboard, but it wasn't. Sure, we packed the theatre. And yes, senior politicians from all parties spoke. But it was becoming clear with every passing minute that neither of the two major parties actually wanted constitutional reform – or at least, not reform that would require asking the public for ideas. The reform agenda for them was just grandstanding to make people feel their voices might be heard. It was also a cheap political trick to stop the ceaseless whining of the Euro-sceptics.

As soon as the "unity" spin at the project's launch was expended,

---

248 Future Britain https://www.lse.ac.uk/management/research/research-projects/past-projects/policy-engagement (Accessed 1st August 2018)

political leaders started to show their true colours. The Labour party made it clear to me that they had absolutely no intention of working with the Tories, despite what its leaders had said publicly. The Tory hard-liners said they didn't trust the "soft" Tories. The Nationalists feared the idea would become a tool to entrench European rights, while the pro-Europeans believed it would become a tool for the nationalists. Meanwhile, the Liberal Democrats didn't trust anyone. The Whitehall bureaucracy conspired to make the idea stillborn after only three meetings.

Having held their feet to the fire because of that meeting, the idea of a new constitution petered out within months. And to be honest, I'm not sure anything we could have done would have saved it. We tried for a while, but in the end, it felt like we were beating a dead horse with another dead horse.

Chapter Ten: Bringing the banks to heel

> *What is it like to take on the biggest banking conglomerate on earth and actually succeed? This is a detailed account on the first major privacy strike against the global finance system and how it had an impact. And also, how it ultimately failed. Nonetheless, this is a tale that underlines the importance of maintaining transparency – even in the world's biggest entities.*

The SWIFT strategy

It is the late summer of 2006, and for the past half hour my colleague Gus Hosein and I have been sitting in a sparse meeting room, suffering ridicule at the hands of one of the world's most influential banking executives.

Our antagonist is Leonard Schrank, who for the past fourteen years has been gatekeeper for the entire global interchange of money – or at least two hundred trillion dollars a year of it. He is making no secret of his hatred of everything we stand for. I've never had to sit through a tempestuous meeting with Donald Trump, but I guess the Schrank encounter is as close as I'll ever get.

At the time, Schrank was CEO of the 'Society for Worldwide Interbank Financial Telecommunications', otherwise known as SWIFT.[249] This vast, secretive corporation comprises just about every finance and banking

---

249 SWIFT home page https://www.swift.com/?AKredir=true

entity on earth. Whenever funds are transferred across borders and between banks, SWIFT executes the transaction. The equivalent of the entire annual tax revenue of the United States passes through its system every eight hours. Now, SWIFT was in deep trouble – and it was blaming us for its woes.

To the best of my knowledge, this was the first major privacy strike against the global finance system. The moment not only changed the banking sector's view of privacy, but it also magnified the potency of the world's privacy regulators.

We had wanted to target the banks for years, but the task had seemed impossible. The banks to some extent had become little more than protected criminal entities, steeped in deceptive practices and stealing billions from customer accounts in the form of excessive penalties and shoddy practices. Commitments of reform by government never materialised, court decisions in the favour of customers rarely extended beyond the individual litigant and independent scrutiny and regulation were barely in sight. These institutions privately claimed immunity from privacy laws and – back then – seldom provided their customers with the level of protection that even Walmart gives.

SWIFT is the closest you'll ever get to a James Bond scenario. Almost every bank account in the world can be linked to it through a global protocol that binds hundreds of millions of unique International Bank Account Number (IBAN) codes. You'll find your own unique IBAN bank account number somewhere in the corner of your bank statement. SWIFT also knows what it is.

The controller (Registrar) of the IBAN system happens to be SWIFT, and through those codes the organisation manages the world's money flow via two giant computer systems, the location of which until recently had been a closely guarded secret. When a request is made to transfer funds between banks, the SWIFT computers match the code with the corresponding bank transaction reference and then generate a message and an authorisation that (often instantly) permits the monetary exchange to take place. Of course, the banks hold on to the money for a few days, for the purposes of doubling their profit off the transactions.

We were here in this anonymous London office building, because SWIFT had requested the meeting in the hope that we'd call off a campaign that had caused unprecedented damage to the organisation. As it turned out, things didn't go quite the way SWIFT's advisers had hoped. Within six months the organisation was forced by regulators to relocate its operations from Belgium to Switzerland, and Schrank was out of a job.

* * * * * *

The saga had begun two months earlier.

It was the third week of June 2006, and in normal events you'd be forgiven for thinking all was well in the UK. Stunning sun, birds chirping and all that.

But while the rest of London was out enjoying its annual moment of optimism about the weather, I was sweltering over a disordered desk wondering what had driven me to lose yet another summer on what often seemed an utterly pointless fight for civil liberties. Seasoned campaigners will know these occasional pits of self-doubt.

This had been a rough year for us – and for freedoms. Bush in the White House, Tony Blair shredding British democracy and Russia falling to pieces. For my organisation, Privacy International, the pressure was relentless. Privacy was the new Big Thing, and there were a thousand reporters around the world scrambling for a thousand privacy stories. And there was one of us at the global campaigning level.

The latest media call to grace the pile was from Eric Lichtblau at the New York Times. I hadn't quite got the gist of what he was saying, so I promised to call him back. Something about the banks and a secret deal. Sounded vaguely promising. However at that precise moment I'd been preoccupied with plotting another fiendishly subversive media strike at Google, a company everyone else adored but which we feared. Back then, I never could have imagined we'd soon become the bloodiest of public enemies, until an uneasy truce in 2010.

After getting back to the Times, it turned out the call was a heads-up on a story about a covert banking giant called SWIFT, of which I knew nothing, but which apparently handled all the world's financial transfers. The organisation had cut a secret deal with the White House to silently and illegally ship to the US Treasury the personal information of people using the service throughout the world. The CIA was managing the project. It was all in the name of national security and counter-terrorism of course, like almost everything was at that time. And, in reality, still is.

The information could possibly relate to millions of people. At the time there was no legal basis for the disclosure, and no limits placed on which agencies could use the data or for what purposes. The laws of dozens of countries that protect the privacy and confidentiality of bank customers were being breached wholesale, and yet banks, customers and even governments had been kept in the dark about the deal. That is, apart from the UK, which admitted, through the Bank of England, some time later, that it knew all along, but chose to do nothing.

In short, a mass of confidential personal information was being covertly and illegally shipped to secretive US organisations, without the knowledge or consent of customers or host governments, in violation of all international and diplomatic conventions, and with the full support and encouragement of the White House. George Bush's friend Schrank had authored the deal – or at the very least, he had ghost-written it.

Inside the War Room

Within hours of receiving information about the arrangement, we had begun a global campaign to force an end to the deal. At stake was the integrity of the White House, the legal basis of global counter-terrorism arrangements, and the credibility of a big chunk of the world's financial payments system.

Whatever happened next, this was destined to be a big story. A two hundred trillion dollar a year secret banking conglomerate, grubbily brokering a dubious deal in the Oval Office with the US President, was hardly likely to go unnoticed. The Times would make certain of that.

The paper wanted a quote about the legality of the deal. To no-one's surprise, the government can get away with almost anything it wants in the States, when it comes to interfering in the affairs of aliens. Indeed it is a sport encouraged in great tradition by Washington. But the NYT wanted to know about the rest of the world. How might Europe react to the news its citizens' financial info was being secretly shipped to – inevitably – every three-letter US Agency?

I'm rarely lost for words. Twenty years in the field had filled my pores with a lot of amazing stories, but this thriller brought the lightning rods of power, deception, hypocrisy and treachery into convergence. I once again felt that old familiar surge (seasoned campaigners again will understand). That thrill you get when you feel that welling of anger and the adrenalin of the hunt.

This wasn't a case of just getting a quote in a newspaper. We live by the maxim "good strategy ensures you'll always be quoted, but a great strategy hands you the headline".[250] We had to turn it into a fight for what we stood for – and which we had to win. Our immediate thought was to engineer the most dramatic and widespread global privacy legal challenge ever mounted.

I gave him the quote anyway. I said the operation was thoroughly illegal in the EU. Bush was already on the nose in Europe and this transgression was going to cause a storm.

With us being so small, them being massive beyond belief and the issue so infinitely complex, this would be a case of bringing up that old power principle: 'strike an emperor, strike to kill'. The biggest risk would be to make a campaigning claim to the international press and then be completely ignored.

There was some information out there about SWIFT, but not much. The company was headquartered outside Brussels, in a monumental structure that Cleopatra might well have built and was run by the afore-mentioned Leonard Schrank.

Hosein and I had to move fast. The Times was running this story in less than 48 hours – that's 40 hours to deadline – and we knew if we weren't in the first wave of the story, we'd be at a campaign disadvantage. By "campaign", I don't mean just PR.

We met at the corner of our favourite pub, the Three Tuns student bar in the London School of Economics. Every organisation needs a strategy

---

250 Davies, S. Ideas for Change; Irene Publishing, 2018

room, but we had a battle bar. Back then the bar reeked of an overpowering smell of mould. The sound of a hundred shoes dislodging themselves from the heavily sticky old carpet was almost louder than the background music. Still, the place served us well. It is where the UK government lost its cursed ID card and where many of the actions were created that helped reinvent the (then) Tory party on liberties. It is where nearly all of the new generation of privacy and rights organisations were born, or at least nurtured. And it was from this spot that the Mighty Google lost most of its halo, and where a big chunk of the West Coast online industry took a battering. Now, in the way of so many British pubs, it is dead.

The plotting commenced. What resources did we have? Yes, we were broke and small and overwhelmed and stressed, but there was strength in abundance. We were feral, smart, adaptive, experienced, motivated and strategic. That at least was a start for what was then three and a half people in a virtual office. We could write well, we could talk well. We had good connections in the press, a vibrant network of colleagues, a strong working relationship with a major first class university. Oh, and no money. Though, as we were fond of saying: size doesn't matter; it's how you deploy it.

Still, the opponents were vast: a secret banking giant, the CIA and FBI and the White House. All the money, all the secrecy, all the corruption and all the power. Because of its magnitude this had to be a campaign fought on our turf. We couldn't rely on European governments to initiate action and it was clear the US Democrats would be reluctant to attack any measure that – unlawful or not – was done in the name of national security.

We vaguely knew the White House operations under Clinton, before his policies went rotten on us. We've learned now to lower our expectations when the Democrats come rolling into the Oval Office. But then, under a truly hostile administration, we could only guess at how they'd hit out.

At first, I figured we should just discount the White House as irrelevant to our plans. They were hardly likely to bother with us. And now our "friends" in government had gone, we – and our issues – weren't even on the Bush radar screen. On the other hand, I intended to get into bed with the New York Times on this, so that might trigger a response.

Having said that, I recall receiving a smack from the White House under

Clinton. I'd just done a live interview on NBC television's popular Today Show in which I'd threatened to use new legal powers in Europe to force a data trade embargo of the US, unless the government introduced parallel privacy laws (as I mentioned earlier, there's a provision in data protection that requires all countries doing business with Europe to have equivalent protections, which the US does not). I suspect the topic was insanely weighty for American breakfast television, All the same, the White House responded with hostility and annoyance. But, by then, I was already on a plane to Paris for something or other, so I missed these barbs.

Even though I believed (mistakenly, as it turned out), that the White House wouldn't get involved, we were still concerned. While we had had a nervously constructive engagement with the Department of Homeland Security and a few other agencies, there were those at the US State Department, the NSA and elsewhere who thoroughly disliked us – and for good reason. They might not be able to resist having a shot. Not that being attacked by the government was any bad thing; it would merely have been an unwelcome distraction. And a plaudit.

The Great Walk-Out

There was some very recent history which gave us certainty that we would be attacked, no matter what we did.

It was not long after my indiscreet threats on NBC about forcing a trade embargo that I was approached by the US State Department, to see if we'd attend a meeting in London of visiting US departments and the White House to discuss those emerging data trade issues.

We negotiated the terms of engagement. They wanted the meeting to be secret. We wanted it broadcast. We settled on a closed meeting.

Hosein, Ian Brown and I immediately smelled a rat. The US departments were over here for a reason, which we figured was to haggle with government and force a compromise solution to keep the trans-Atlantic data trade alive. They weren't in the least bit interested in our views.

Instead, their aim was to manipulate the fact of the meeting, so they could portray themselves to the European authorities as good guys trying to do the right thing. We figured their plan was to put out a pre-prepared statement as soon as they'd met us saying that the US had 'consulted' with us. it is a common tactic. Indeed, we've used in many times, when it worked in our favour.

There were three options open to us: call them out on the tactic, cancel the meeting, or get nasty. We decided to get nasty. There was certainly no way in hell they were there to listen to us, let alone negotiate.

So, an hour before the meeting we drafted a press release which claimed a deceptive stitch-up by the US, and that we walked out of the meeting in protest.

After the mandatory opening chit-chat about the cost of petrol in Britain and the declining quality of service by airlines, the meeting became appropriately solemn. As the US reps slowly reverted to type, things went as badly as we had predicted. They expressed frustration in a pre-rehearsed sort of way, we got angry, and on the cue of a pre-agreed signal (I recall it was a brushing of an eyebrow), we got up and stormed out. Hosein hit the send button as we left the room, and the story was published not long after.

That battle went our way, but the war was by no means over. The US departments despised us, to the point when during a conference dinner the following month, the White House advisor was yelling at me with white knuckles.

Did the US government realise it was dealing with a pack of under-resourced volunteers? Probably not. In any case, they'd seen me on NBC, so nothing else really mattered. While being on TV might not swing the hearts and minds of millions, it certainly creates vital collateral in your dealings with powerful stakeholders.

Brainstorming it, we guessed the issue would play in the media for a while, but its shelf life would be limited. it is a sort of One Trick Pony of a story, two ponies at most, after which media would move on. Then the matter might shift to the regulators, parliaments – maybe the courts. If we did our job right, the company would be forced to back down.

"Maybe we can get them to piss off out of Europe," I quipped, and we laughed. If only we'd known.

Whatever we did, it had to play big time with media. We knew the White House would wheel out the FBI, NSA, CIA, and anyone else who could say the information was needed. Then, as we'd calculated, the issue would quickly move to invisibility. A week of diminishing coverage and after that short firestorm, the company could just retreat to its bunker.

The EU privacy regulators were an obvious opportunity – such regulators are in charge of enforcing national privacy law in a way similar to the function of the US Federal Trade Commission – but there was a problem. At that time they were largely timid and passive, with many still coming to terms with the implications of the home computer 'revolution'. Not all of them were cowards, but enough were, to ensure that little might happen in response to SWIFT, and whatever did happen would be fragmented and opaque. Europe is united by its division. Still, the sheer shock value of this issue could – with the right handling – unify the regulators. If we could do that in what was now 30 hours, then SWIFT would get its kicking, and the US would raise the diplomatic traffic light to amber.

The only way we could get into the Times coverage, keep in the forefront of the issue, unite the regulators, put strike on the Bush Administration and kick SWIFT, was to launch the equivalent of a multi rocket strike on the entire landscape. That would give us a few days of exposure to line up some of the parliaments. The players were so powerful and entrenched that nothing else would work.

Working around the clock we prepared to simultaneously lodge formal detailed regulatory complaints for every EU country. Realising that Canada was becoming a diplomatic flashpoint for the White House we also prepared to lodge multiple protests in that country, specially tailored to create maximum political anxiety.

Canada's privacy commissioners were already on red alert over poor US data practices, and our hope was these complaints would tip them over the edge and inspire them to threaten suspension of financial information. A long shot maybe, but they're a maverick bunch over there.

We did as much as we could in the 30 hours to line up every conceivable strike, from national parliaments to Intergovernmental Organisations. Timing is the most important and least understood factor in campaigning, and often it is the only factor that matters. In this case we had a sixty minute launch window for the first release and then a 48 hour window to exploit the second wave of press. The press seems to have a collective instinct, for whether a story is a grower or a slower.

We'd bought a little more time by agreeing with the New York Times to delay the strike until the second edition of the story and to release the complaints in two lots. In all, we prepared actions in 38 countries, together with other national and international bodies.[251] We batched them out before the paper was published to give regulators time to form a response. To the best of our knowledge, it was the most extensive privacy action in history.

What we didn't realise at the time was that parts of the Washington administration – in an attempt to head off the scandal and take the high ground – were proposing that Bush be wheeled out that day to casually mention the affair and talk of global union. The plan never saw the light of day, and the Times led with the story.[252] Shortly afterwards, the paper ran a piece specifically on our legal action.[253] Within three days, the paper was under attack by the White House, which insisted that the Times had caused damage to national security.[254]

We were underwhelmed to say the least about the media response in the UK, and only slightly less distressed about the European coverage. For US media, anything with Bush's fingerprints on it was going to cause a storm, but we badly misjudged the extent of interest on this side of the pond.

European press did catch up after 48 hours, which is not unusual, but we at least succeeded in locking our actions into the first wave of press. The Belgian prime minister, Guy Verhofstadt, asked the Justice Ministry to investigate whether SWIFT violated Belgian law by allowing the United States government access to its data. The regulators across Europe were also already waking up to the gravity of the case. What we didn't know, until two years later, is that our complaint strategy succeeded as it had been intended, and for the first time ever regulators were forced to work

251 Pulling a SWIFT one; Privacy International blog, June 29th 2006
      https://privacyinternational.org/feature/990/pulling-swift-one-bank-transfer-
      information-sent-us-authorities
252 Bank data is sifted by US is secret to block terror; the New York Times, June 23rd 2006
      https://www.nytimes.com/2006/06/23/washington/23intel.html?pagewanted=all&_r=0
253 Group tries to block program giving data to US, the New York Times, June 27th 2006
      https://www.nytimes.com/2006/06/27/world/27cnd-secure.html
254 Damage Study Urged on Surveillance Reports, New York Times, June 28th 2006
      https://www.nytimes.com/2006/06/28/world/europe/28secure.html

together. They continue working together to this day.

The issue built a head of steam in Europe as regulators found the nerve to criticise the banking giant. Some of the company's actions were ruled in breach of law and the entire operation – ironically, given our quip at the outset – was required to move to Switzerland. Parliaments began applying pressure. That was the moment, as developments were starting to peak, that we received a call asking us to come to SWIFT's London office to meet Schrank.

It was one of those meetings we really should have walked out on. Schrank played every cheap negotiation power tactic he could muster. Our chairs were lower in height than his, there intentionally was no coffee on offer, he never once gave up the aggressive facial expression and his back was to the window, silhouetting his face. Indeed he portrayed the attitude of someone who was prepared to bite the head off a kitten. His PR adviser was whispering something in his ear along the lines of 'calm down; just be nice. Be nice, OK?'

Then he lost it completely. He ranted. He condemned data protection and flung his address book around the flawless teak board table. He told us we knew nothing about security, and that if we knew what he and George Bush knew, then we'd stop acting like children. It was like some sad 1950s film stereotype of the driven tycoon. He may as well have been yelling, "You schmuck! You ain't gonna railroad me, you sonofabitch!"

Hosein and I just sat there throwing the occasional barb, but we did try unsuccessfully to explain why secrecy really is not an acceptable way to approach this exercise. We issued a parting shot to the effect that if he didn't budge, then his enterprise would bleed like a stuck pig – which it did in abundance. As mentioned earlier, the entire operation was forced to move to Switzerland and Schrank was out of that job by year-end. Or as the organisation expressed it: "an amicable early retirement". He afterwards became head of the American Chamber of Commerce in Europe, so I'm not sure if we actually had a win there.

We were right to sound the alarm. In 2013 the European Parliament voted to recommend suspension of its Terrorist Finance Tracking Program (TFTP) agreement with the US. A key reason was that evidence had come to light that the NSA had unlawfully tapped into SWIFT's database.[255]

Within three months we weren't even in the story. It had moved on to a different level with different player., That's a crucial part of the bigger campaigning issue: knowing when to back out of the issue in order to win it.

---

255 Demanding accountability for the NSA's breach of SWIFT financial agreement; Privacy International blog, October 22nd 2013
https://privacyinternational.org/blog/1534/demanding-accountability-nsas-breach-swift-financial-agreement

Chapter Eleven: The watchers

> *Electronic visual surveillance – CCTV – has become commonplace around the world, but it can be a dangerous technology. CCTV systems are using new algorithms and apps to build a total surveillance canopy. This is the account of the first public strike in 1997 against the technology and subsequent efforts to build public awareness.*

Planning the first campaign

It's a glorious, hot summer day in the southern English seaside city of Brighton, and while thousands of tourists are revelling in the maze of quaint boutique shops called 'The Lanes' below me, I am giving a tactical briefing to a packed and sweltering room of around two hundred hard-core environmental activists. It is 1997, and we are about to undertake the world's first major direct-action strike against the explosion of a new technology called CCTV – Closed Circuit Television. The global repercussions of that action were to be more interesting than we ever imagined.

It is getting difficult to define CCTV these days. In essence, the technology is anything that connects a lens with a recording device or screen. So I guess most mobile cameras can be CCTV. However the conventional scope is the technology represented by those ugly boxes and spooky domes that you see spread across the landscape.

CCTV was a privacy threat back then – even as a quite basic technology – but it isn't merely a camera system any more. As I explain elsewhere, it swiftly moved in the late 1980s from analogue to digital, meaning that images could be quickly searched and interrogated. Then it transitioned in the 1990's to the third generation, which used software to further analyse images for behavioural and biometric aspects (biometrics relates to the physical characteristics of a person, such as face or gait). Interoperability of systems means that all these features can be combined into a national surveillance system. And now we have drones to add to this equation.

Britain is the birthplace of mass CCTV. Because the technology is unregulated it is difficult to figure out precisely how many exist, but six to ten million is the commonly agreed range. This is a thirty fold increase in just over twenty years.[256] The industry turns over many billions of pounds a year. Even back then, just about every city and town had arbitrarily decided to install these integrated surveillance systems. Entire stretches of the urban landscape were covered by the cameras. They were finding their way into almost every commercial and government building, along with toilet foyers, theatres, parks, bus shelters, railway carriages, schools and outside private homes. With the emergence of the Internet, there was only one place for this tidal wave to go. Images would inevitably be streamed live.

This, however, pales by comparison to some other countries. The newest and most dramatic manifestation of CCTV is China, where more than two hundred million cameras have been installed – a figure that is set to double by 2020. The urban environment is so saturated with the technology that – in a media demonstration – it took authorities seven minutes to identify, track and "capture" a BBC reporter, who had been at large in a major urban area.[257]

Alvin Toffler once predicted, "We will be living in the pupil of a thousand different eyes at any given moment."[258] Never has such a proclamation been so true, as it is now in China.

The genesis of the UK's infatuation with CCTV can be recounted in the

---

256 Davies, S. "Big Brother – Britain's web of surveillance and the new technological order"; Pam McMillan, London, 1986 put the estimate in the mid 1980's at 200,000, a figure that was later published by the Scientific and Technical Committee of the House of Lords.

257 China's CCTV network took just seven minutes to capture BBC reporter, BBC News Online, 10th December 2017 https://techcrunch.com/2017/12/13/china-cctv-bbc-reporter/

258 Alvin Toffler, obituary. The Daily Mail. https://www.dailymail.co.uk/news/article-3668104/Future-Shock-author-Alvin-Toffler-coined-term-information-overload-dies-sleep-Bel-Air-home-aged-87.html

CCTV development of other countries. It just requires one dramatic visual event. For the UK, it involved a murdered child.

Indeed, if an award was to be given for the most haunting video footage of the decade, it might well go to the shopping centre surveillance camera in Liverpool England that, in 1994, inadvertently recorded the last images of toddler James Bulger. The film showed the child being led out of the centre by two ten year old boys, who minutes later beat him to death on a deserted stretch of railway track. After their arrest, the footage was later used as evidence in the conviction of the murderers, though the arrest itself was not as a result of those images.[259]

The recordings had a profound impact on Britain. For millions of people who viewed the fuzzy grey pictures, the experience only confirmed what most had already suspected: video surveillance is good for crime control, and we need more of it. Within weeks a vast amount of funding was being channelled into the technology.

The UK had been slowly building its CCTV infrastructure since 1985, when – after a particularly grizzly year of football hooliganism – the Football Trust and other benefactors began constructing a surveillance network across all sports facilities. It was at that moment police learned that the technology could be useful. Even before Bulger, they were preparing to deploy cameras across the nation.

Together with civil liberties colleagues, I fought the cameras with every strategy I could muster. Conferences, news articles, complaints to the privacy (information) regulator, briefings, TV documentaries, books, papers and brochures. This activity sparked press coverage[260][261][262]but hardly made a dent in the industry. Little wonder, in view of the reality that the government was telling industry groups that it had their back covered. Still, we did surprisingly well, considering that prior to 1993, there was almost no popular media coverage about the cameras. The 1990-1991 world report by Privacy International makes no mention of CCTV.[263]

---

259 Murder of James Bulger https://en.wikipedia.org/wiki/Murder_of_James_Bulger (accessed 14th April 2018)
260 "Use of police cameras sparks rights debate in Britain; Washington Post, 8th August 1994
261 Tim Dawson, "Framing the villains" New Statesman, 28 January 1994
262 "Britons find some comfort under cameras gaze," Boston Globe, July 9, 1993
263 Privacy International, interim report for 1990-1991

I had tried to swing media around to a less benign view of the technology. I told ABC's News' 20/20 national television programme in the US back in 1995, "There is a grave risk that the CCTV industry is out of control. Fuelled by fear of crime, the systems take on a life of their own, defying quantification and quashing public debate."[264] Such messages might have created an impact on America, but they were of little value in Britain.

Back in 1997, in that stuffy war room in Brighton, we knew these details, and we also knew the problem could only become more intractable.

Three months before the Brighton action, I had convened a meeting of environmental and privacy groups to brainstorm how we might best deal with this situation. The meeting took place in the White Hart pub in Drury Lane, Covent Garden, London. It was an interesting event, in that environmental activists – notably the notorious high profile direct action group "Reclaim the Streets" – were concerned not only by the privacy aspect, but also that the cameras were spoiling the landscape. It was the first time we had formed a strategic coalition with environmental campaigners.

I was quite blunt in my views. We, as privacy advocates, had the technical and legal framework, but we lacked the human resources. Plus, most of us were cowards when it came to facing prosecution! They had the people and the activist expertise. Still, there were many issues to be resolved. We had never imagined what those might be.

We learned much from them. Slowly, we began planning the action. We knew it would be difficult because almost the entire nation was on side with the technology. Mass media were certainly supportive. Of course, the fact that authorities provided surveillance footage free of charge to media was a great economic incentive for them – other alleged social benefits aside.

I knew how high the odds were stacked against us in terms of public support. Three years earlier, I had written an op-ed piece for the UK's *Independent* newspaper which tried to warn people that if they accepted the present systems, automatic face recognition – and worse – would not be far behind. The paper received bags of hate mail.

---

https://web.archive.org/web/20101202201847/http://www.privacyinternational.org/artic le.shtml?cmd[347]=x-347-145834

264 ABC news, background to CCTV, 25th September 1995
http://wearcam.org/privacy_forum_digest_on_CCTV.html

Building the tactical framework

We decided to persist, nonetheless. We considered the option of disabling the cameras simply by slicing the connecting leads, but the tactic chosen instead was ridicule. What was required, at the very least, was a degree of satire and humour. We would climb the camera poles and place bags over them. Our hope was the operators would use the remote control function in an attempt to shake the bags off. This would produce priceless and hilarious video footage.[265]

When I say "we" would climb the camera poles, I of course mean "they". As a more rotund person, I was forced into the bunker as strategic coordinator.

This action did not just magically materialise. Many practical questions needed to be resolved. What was the tactile nature of the camera poles? What ropes should be used? Were there dangerous spiked fences underneath in the event of a free-fall escape? Would climbing those poles intrude on peoples private space? What type of bag should we use? I raised the matter of the UK crime of 'criminal damage' to the camera poles, but the activists replied, "Fuck the law. It allowed this. Fuck it".

("Criminal Damage" in UK law is a uniquely broad crime, that allows police to make an arrest even if you simply sit on a fence or interfere with any tech functionality.)

Our tactics went further than a mere "Bring Your Own Bag" party. Back then, cameras were vulnerable to lasers, so those items were used in abundance. High pressure gunge guns also provided much amusement to the many onlookers, as bright green globules smacked into the lenses.

One activist, who none of us recognised, managed to hijack a small crane, which made reaching some of the higher poles so much easier.

My favourite tactic was the Balloon Attack. In this neat action, protesters would stand under camera poles with a bunch of helium balloons on very long strings, thus impeding the view of the cameras. When police started to threaten arrest of anyone doing it, one brilliant activist came up with a brain wave. He asked his seven year old daughter to stand under a pole

---

265 Davies, Simon. "CCTV: A New Battleground for Privacy." In Surveillance, Closed Circuit Television and Social Control, edited by Clive Norris, Jade Moran, and Gary Armstrong, 243–254. Aldershot: Ashgate Publishing, 1998.

with the instruction "now just wait here, until daddy gets back". Fortunately the girl was fiercely smart and was no stranger to activism, so she got the plot immediately.

Seven years is below the age of reason, so authorities could do nothing – and they certainly couldn't arrest her. They couldn't move the child because of her father's instructions. And they could hardly take the balloons away from the girl. Soon, other children joined this delightful frolic.

These actions turned out just as we had hoped. We did, however, not anticipate the truck loads of police to descend on us. In a bizarre moment, I stood between the police commander and a small army of protesters, attempting to stop imminent mass arrests. Such is the blunt end of defending civil rights.[266]

Scroll forward six months. The German authorities got wind of my action and I was invited to a closed-door session of all the country's Attorney's General and other assorted lawmakers, which was being held in the northern coastal city of Kiel. They had heard the propaganda from UK industry and government, but they wanted to know the facts.

I gave them the best forensic presentation of which I was capable. I explained that Jason Ditton and other criminologists concluded that the crime statistics cited in evidence for the benefits of CCTV rarely, if ever, address the hypothesis that CCTV merely displaces criminal activity to areas outside the range of the cameras. In support of this, I informed them that in discussing the justification for establishing a surveillance system of 16 cameras in Manchester, Gordon Conquest, chairman of the city centre subcommittee of Manchester Council, candidly admitted, "No crackdown on crime does more than displace it, and that's the best we can do at the moment."

I then informed them that the Crime Prevention Unit of the Home Office appeared to agree. In 1993 it suppressed the findings of a survey on the crime impact of camera surveillance, on the basis that the displacement effect had been all but ignored. In other words, crime may be merely pushed from high value commercial areas, into low rent residential areas.

---

266 Holding privacy offenders accountable — an interview with Privacy International founder, Simon Davies. Express VPN blog, 2nd March 2018
https://www.expressvpn.com/blog/privacy-international-simon-davies-interview/

Perhaps the most effective piece of the presentation was my conclusion that UK police were tremendously excited by the possibilities opened up by such systems. They could covertly monitor and record vast numbers of people without risk to officers and without fear of detection. One feature of modern CCTV systems, for example, is their ability to track the movements of people. Like some bizarre computer game, the system can routinely track individuals as they walk through the city, switching cameras as the subject moves out of range. The fields of the cameras intersect, so that no-one can escape their gaze. System operators and police often follow "persons of interest" for miles, creating a comprehensive profile of all activities and contacts. All new CCTV systems have this function as a built-in facility. The cameras were powerful enough, even then, to identify individuals from three hundred metres. These days some high definition systems can recognise and automatically follow faces at more than half a mile.[267]

My parting shot was that it seemed, to me, that after decades of vilification, Big Brother was finally being paraded as a beloved member of the family. In the quest for a life that is quiet, a society which is safe and an administration which is efficient, video surveillance is seen as a real answer. Wherever there is dysfunction, threat or disorder, one authority or another will seek the introduction of video surveillance.

The Attorney General told me at the coffee session afterwards that this technology would not be allowed into Germany without arduous safeguards. He and the others in that room were true to their word. Well, for a period anyway. The Germans have at least regulated the technology and keep a close eye on its use.

Having said that, the core problem facing even the most reformist lawmakers is that visual surveillance has become a design component in countless other platforms and technologies. It has become what UK academic Stephen Graham twenty years ago called "the Fifth Utility". It is built into all urban and architectural designs. Can a computer or phone webcam be defined as CCTV, even though it has the capacity to be one? Certainly the "use" of such technology can be regulated in law, but it is a fact that almost every person now has such a device, and these items are interoperable with other platforms and devices. How to control that

---

267 Powerful CCTV cameras track faces half a mile away. The Daily Mail, 3rd October
   2012 http://www.dailymail.co.uk/news/article-2212051/Powerful-CCTV-cameras-

environment is a challenging matter for any regulator.

Later that year the then UK Home Secretary told the BBC that he didn't much care about the criminological or privacy elements. If CCTV made people "feel" safer, then the operation was justified. It was clear that no logic on the planet would shift the government's view.

So, once again, we went on the offensive. I ordered the printing of 100,000 official-looking stickers which read "Warning! You are being watched by CCTV." These were distributed to activists across the country who placed them en masse in toilet cubicles and over urinals. This caused such a commotion that a couple of the train companies had to put out press releases, denying that such monitoring was being done. I witnessed an entire train carriage boiling with rage over the sticker. The poor long-suffering rail staff tried to quell the rebellion, but it didn't help that their explanation was ambiguous.

"No! We don't put cameras in the actual toilets," they would proclaim. "Just outside them, and around the train. You know, for your protection."

Needless to say, that action sensitised the public, and brought the CCTV topic to prominence.

We continued with the fun. I had a rather subversive plan bubbling in mind that involved a small truck, a mobile CCTV system and a couple of us wearing dark suits and "Blues Brothers" style sunglasses. Finding the truck was not an easy matter, seeing that environmental activists are not inclined to have such items laying around. We finally secured one from a friendly farmer in Sussex and then equipped it with a bunch of cameras – some real and some fake. I suspect – though I can't in any way be certain – that the activists "borrowed" a couple of the cameras from government installations.

We parked outside government agencies, police stations and even MI5 and pointed the cameras directly toward exit points. Police really did not appreciate this tactic and routinely threatened to arrest us, but they didn't have any grounds to do so – and they knew it. As government was so fond of arguing that any surveillance is lawful in a public place, we were covered. And no planning permission is required for a mobile unit. We must have irritated thousands of officials and police in this way, but as they say, what's good for the goose is good for the gander.

---

track-faces-half-mile-away-breach-human-rights-laws.html

At much the same time we also decided to use the law as a weapon. The Data Protection Act gives every person the right to receive personal information that is being held on them. So, why not video images? Now that was an interesting proposition. Even though, at the time, it cost £10 ($13 USD) to lodge such a request, it would have cost the government or private body hundreds or even thousands to provide it. All faces other than that of the requesting party would need to be fuzzed-out, so only the requester's image would be visible in the disclosure files. There was no way to automate such requests.

The renowned UK human rights activist and comedian Mark Thomas gave us great support in this effort. After his TV broadcast on the matter, thousands of people made such requests, crippling the administration of many government departments. As the law stipulated that requests must be fulfilled within thirty days, it was an easy matter to cause chaos in hostile government and private sector organisations. Mark Thomas took this action a step further by organising barn dances, which made tracking and fuzzing faces even more onerous.

I was subsequently delighted to see up-and-coming music bands using this tactic. They would play on a beach-front and then demand the CCTV footage, which then became their music video. Brilliant!

Activists around the world started to militate against the cameras, using satire and ridicule. Among the most effective of these was New York's Surveillance Camera Players.[268]

Throughout that entire period, the dominant fear running through my mind was that all this technology would create a chilling effect on society. Once ubiquitous surveillance was enabled, we would become more passive, ordered and cautious. Sure, there are many who believe this might be a positive effect, but I beg to differ. My view is that free societies should resist such a panopticon at any cost. Stare at a rat for long enough and it becomes agitated and nervous.

ACLU senior policy analyst Jay Stanley explains, "We want people to not just be free, but to feel free. And that means that they don't have to worry about how an unknown, unseen audience may be interpreting or

---

268 New York Surveillance Camera Players. We Know You Are Watching. New York: Factory School, 2006.

misinterpreting their every movement and utterance."[269]:

"The concern is that people will begin to monitor themselves constantly, worrying that everything they do will be misinterpreted and bring down negative consequences on their life."

269 Artificial intelligence is going to supercharge surveillance; The Verge, 23rd January 2018 https://www.theverge.com/2018/1/23/16907238/artificial-intelligence-surveillance-cameras-security

Chapter Twelve: National insecurity

In many respects, the security services are a law unto themselves. The normal rules of accountability do not apply to them. Even after the revelations of Edward Snowden in 2013, they seem to be largely immune to change. This is a detailed account of one of my earliest campaigns to raise awareness of national security excesses, and how even the subsequent intervention of parliaments failed to have an impact on reform.

In February 2013, I was holed up with colleagues at a generic hotel bar in Victoria, on the picturesque west coast of Canada. We were meeting in advance of a major international security conference that week, and so we talked excitedly about the many triggers that are making privacy a headline news issue across North America. British Columbia has a noble tradition of privacy activism[270] but none of us had the slightest clue just how much the privacy landscape would spectacularly unfold across the world by the following summer. thanks to the revelations of Edward Snowden.

Just as I put down my glass to leave, a short, grinning man approached me with hand outstretched. I recognized him as General Michael Hayden, former Director of the CIA and the National Security Agency (NSA). He had been looking for me.

We talked tensely into the evening, both of us striving to avoid verbal violence against the other. My mind boomed with such words as rendition, torture, corruption, subversion and myriad human rights violations, hallmarks of the CIA. However, it was the issue of

---

270 Westwood, John. ''Life in the Privacy Trenches: Experiences of the British Columbia Civil Liberties Association.'' In Visions of Privacy: Policy Choices for the Digital Age, edited by C. J. Bennett and R. Grant, 231–243. Toronto: University of Toronto Press, 1999.

communications spying that we settled on, as a theme for conversation. After all, that's what the NSA does best.

The meeting in that bar was no accident. We were both about to share keynote slots at the impending conference. Hayden is a smart enough PR man to manufacture the appearance of constructive engagement. Predictably, he made exactly that claim in his speech, jovially referring to us "closing the bar" the previous night. I gave out an audible groan from the stage and put my hands over my face. He winked at me with a look that suggested "I'm going to take the first strike and screw you". Well, two can play at that game, as I discuss elsewhere in the text.

The reality of the situation is that Hayden and everyone in his position are not just operations managers; they are political players. They routinely work Congress and overseas governments, to the advantage of the spy agencies. And, of course, they claim to be straightforward and utterly transparent.

The truth could hardly be more distant. In a more formal, wide ranging, interview with Hayden the following day, I was told how he and his intelligence colleagues had reformed US law and striven to be ruthlessly open with Congress.

During the conversation, I asserted the obvious view that the NSA's interception activities were a huge fishing expedition that intruded on countless millions of people. Hayden's response was soothingly reassuring:

> *You be careful here; when it comes to intercepting calls –
> let's use that as an example – this was not a dragnet where
> we just sucked it all in and then let's sort our way through
> it. Let me repeat what I said – when we intercepted a
> communication – let's use call, that's easier for me to
> explain – when we intercepted the content of a call, we
> already had reason to believe that one or both
> communicants intended us ill, so this is not, don't think of
> this as a driftnet.*

So, there was the official line. America's spy agencies and their international partners rigorously uphold the rule of law and only target known threats – and with the strictest of due diligence. Hayden's choice of words was, however, very careful: he specified 'content' of calls, rather than the countless other elements involved in communications spying. In other words, he was obfuscating about the metadata attached to a call – who calls who, at what time and from what location.

Hayden was truthful on one aspect. He opined, "The full story of the (US) terrorist surveillance program has never been told. What's been portrayed in the press is, on a good day, incomplete." Three months later, a former NSA contractor, Edward Snowden, dramatically revealed that the NSA had – for years – conspired with corporations to create seamless surveillance of the entire planet. Computers and communications have been infected to the extent that escaping scrutiny requires an arduous – often futile – effort by individuals. It has been said countless times since then, but it is true that even the Stasi could never have imagined such powers.

As a result of Snowden's actions, it is now almost impossible to talk about privacy without discussing "surveillance". They are two sides of the same coin. And when it comes to surveillance, few issues have since then captured the public imagination more than the activities of national security agencies. Hayden was right in the middle of that issue, though – as the old saying goes – butter wouldn't melt in his mouth.

The following month I was interviewed on Britain's ITN television news together with a Home Office official. This man made the remarkable claim that "people like Snowden and Davies are always in bed together". Let it be known I have never been to bed with Edward Snowden, though we did chat once about broader strategy.

Snowden, however, was by no means the first insider to try warning the world about these covert activities. Over the decades there have been dozens of brave whistleblowers – not just functionaries – but also highly placed officials such as Bill Binney, the NSA's former Technical Director. Binney was arrested at gunpoint in his shower and prosecuted for revealing the extent of corruption within the NSA. Some of his whistleblower colleagues, including senior NSA analysts Tom Drake, Ed Loomis and Kirk Wiebe and Diane Roarke – a staffer with the US Congress – also suffered arrest and intimidation by the FBI. In a delicious irony of terminology, Binney later became Technical Director of Code Red, which was an organization of whistleblowers and activists that I established in 2014.

This is not just a case of authorities using legal mechanisms to protect their information. They also break the law. In the case of Bill Binney, the Department of Justice forged documents in an attempt to purport his guilt. Predictably, no-one was prosecuted for that offence.

The persecution of whistleblowers is routine. When Annie Machon and David Shayler – of the British security services MI5 and MI6 – revealed corruption, illegality and killings by those organizations, they were hounded across the world.[271]

As I recount later in this chapter, the act of whistleblowing in the 1970s and 1980s, was even more dangerous than today, where at least there is some hope of due process, thanks to better public awareness. Back then, it was almost impossible to interest media in the issue of mass surveillance.

Nor do governments much care about freedom of the press in such matters. In the late 1980's, investigative journalist Duncan Campbell was finishing a six-part television series on state interception, when both he and the BBC were raided by police. Tapes and computers were confiscated, and the first part of the series never went to air.[272]

Worthy of special mention in the growing list of national security activists is Lindis Percy,[273] a now-retired nurse, midwife and health visitor.

Percy lives in Harrogate, a town in the north of England. As far back as 1979 she discovered – deep in the heart of the Yorkshire moors – a secret that the British government had been trying to keep under wraps for decades.

Among those peaceful cow fields stands a stark metallic eyesore that sprawls across a square mile. The world's biggest electronic spy station – the Menwith Hill base – hosts a giant complex of computers and radomes that monitor the communications of a third of the world (a radome is a circus tent-style protective shield for radar and interception equipment).[274] Although it is located on British soil, the base is occupied

---

271 The spy who loved me. The Guardian
     https://www.theguardian.com/world/2002/nov/15/gender.uk
272 Duncan Campbell. The GCHQ and me. The Intercept.
     https://theintercept.com/2015/08/03/life-unmasking-british-eavesdroppers/
273 Wikipedia entry for Lindis Percy http://en.wikipedia.org/wiki/Lindis_Percy (Accessed
     1st June 2018)
274 http://www.raf.mod.uk/organisation/rafmenwithhill.cfm (Accessed 13th August 2018)

and controlled by American authorities – most notably the NSA.

To some people, the existence of this base in an obscenity. Protests are regularly staged outside (and sometimes – spectacularly – even inside) its gates. Percy became a dogged and persistent activist there, providing a constant public reminder that the individual can make a difference.

She decided to make a stand against the Menwith Hill base, at a time when few people had even heard of the NSA, or its now infamous global communications spy network. She stalked the base year after year, inviting prosecution.

Fifteen prison sentences and nearly five hundred arrests later, Percy became a catalyst for public awareness of the base and what it represents. With tenacious colleagues from the *Campaign for the Accountability of American Bases* (CAAB) she not only humbled the defense authorities, she also succeeded in highlighting the hypocrisy and unfairness of laws that protect powerful overseas interests at the expense of the rights of British citizens.

The emperor has no clothes

These days, the existence of global interception has become popular wisdom, but this wasn't always the case. In the past, it was almost impossible to convince anyone that the spying operations were real. What follows is the turbulent experience of one early effort to shed light on the NSA's activities.

In 1997, I began a campaign to expose the NSA's global spying operations – an activity that at the time was almost unknown to the world. The disappointing outcome of this prolonged high-profile action should be a salutary lesson to anyone who believes that the current interest in NSA spying will easily bring reform to the secret operations of governments.

The campaign's focus was the Menwith Hill base, spotlighted by the aforementioned Lindis Percy, as well as Duncan Campbell. Even back then, the place was known among researchers and some politicians to reside at the heart of a web of integrated interception systems that became collectively known as "ECHELON".

ECHELON – while not a widely used term within the security agencies – was the name sometimes used to describe the entire apparatus of automated word recognition within signals intelligence. The NSA's computers were able to pick particular key words from conversations and then transcribe the content of those calls.

The network is controlled by the United States, managed by the key English speaking countries bonded by a secret agreement called UKUSA and operates under targeting instructions from the US National Security Agency. The system uses a grid of spy bases intercepting countless communications via vast underground computer systems and satellite dishes. According to the European Parliament and other sources, almost every phone line in the world in almost every communication system can be intercepted (though presumably not all at once). The system is used not only for defence, but also for economic espionage, and to monitor the communications of Non-Governmental Organisations.

In its first decade, the base sucked data from cables and microwave links running through a nearby Post Office tower, but the communications revolutions of the Seventies and Eighties gave the base a capability that even its architects could scarcely imagine. With the creation of Intelsat and digital telecommunications, Menwith Hill and other stations developed the capability to eavesdrop on an extensive scale on fax, telex and voice messages. Then, with the development of the Internet, electronic mail and electronic commerce the listening posts were able to increase their monitoring capability to eavesdrop on an unprecedented spectrum of personal and business communications.

In the 1990's, when Privacy International first became interested in Menwith Hill, such activity was unimaginable in the public mind. Despite the enormous scale of this operation, almost nothing was reported in the press, and there was little knowledge of it in academic or political circles. The only official recognition was a consistent message from government that the Menwith area was a UK "defence facility". Even the locals in neighbouring towns and villages knew nothing, even after half a century of patronage in their pubs by visiting US operational staff who – despite homesickness and a classic inability to handle the strength of the local ales – remained loyal to their lifelong confidentiality contracts.

Nonetheless, the secrecy of the base and the entire global spy operation was about to unexpectedly unravel.

In 1997 Professor Steve Wright, a brilliant UK academic with sound credentials in the surveillance field, gave me a heads-up that he was about to submit a report to the European Parliament blowing the whistle on the system. I might, he suggested, want to prepare a media campaign.

My immediate response was scepticism. If Wright was to be believed, the UK government had been working secretly with the Americans for decades and had allowed every British phone line to be made "intercept friendly" – as indeed had most Western countries. While communications providers had been selling their services on the promise of better security, they had been part of a quiet arrangement to leave a gaping back door to governments across the world. The challenge of proving such a conspiracy would be enormous.

It was true that governments had openly forced telecommunications companies to make their networks accessible to law enforcement and security agencies, but the global operation was on a much grander scale. In 1994 the US Congress passed the Communications Assistance for Law Enforcement Act (CALEA) that – in effect – required manufacturers and providers to give agencies full access to lines and equipment. The imposition was sweetened with a $500M compensation deal.

The media vacuum

So why was nobody talking about the grandest of all global arrangements? It was mystifying that despite the fact that two extremely detailed books by James Bamford and Nicky Hager had been published on the subject – and Duncan Campbell had exposed it eight years earlier in the UK magazine New Statesman [275] – little else had emerged since. Logically, the existence of the system added up, but the silence over many years by media and governments made its existence appear

---

275 Duncan Campbell. Someone's listening. New Statesman 12th August 1988.
    http://new.duncan.gn.apc.org/menu/journalism/newstatesman/Somebody%27s_Listenin

implausible.

The matter had been raised multiple times in the UK Parliament, only to draw an aggressive denial from both species of whatever incumbent government. The official response was resolutely that such a move would run counter to the national interest. A few well informed people knew there was a secret trans-Atlantic agreement and operational cooperation between the US and the UK, but little was known beyond that point.

Campaigners such as Bob Cryer – a former Member of the UK Parliament – argued relentlessly for greater transparency and accountability over US spying. In an incident eerily similar to the controversial road death of US investigative journalist Michael Hastings seventeen years later, Cryer died in 1994 in a freak road accident – in exactly the same manner that nuclear industry whistleblower Karen Silkwood had died. I'm not alleging conspiracy to murder; I'm just stating the facts.

One of the most difficult challenges faced by any campaigner working to expose a secret global system is the lack of material evidence, and the perception that they are engaging in conspiracy theory. The bottom line – as far as most newspaper editors are concerned – is that any claim of a truly grand cover-up (or at least one that they don't already know about) is nothing but conspiracy – and anyone who peddles conspiracy is a nutcase. The fact that many great truths start out as conspiracies is immaterial (Watergate is a classic example). I decided, all the same, to make some attempt at sparking media coverage, and elevating the issue from an insular dialogue among experts to local pub conversation. The task proved almost insurmountable.

Fearful about blowing our credibility with a notoriously cynical broadsheet press, I pitched the story to the editors of a dozen smaller publications, all of whom treated me as if I were mad. As a media specialist, this failure was intensely frustrating and seemed irrational. I'd sold a thousand stories to the press, and this one seemed, to me, perfect. Even if material evidence wasn't in abundance, it was a rollicking good yarn peppered with all the elements of a great thriller. But no, not a single media outlet bit on the story. They focused instead on arguing that I needed a holiday – and perhaps some medication.

g.pdf

I started giving this failure serious thought. Why was there such reluctance to cover a huge story? it is as if it was invisible to the media eye.

The reality is that media has an ingrained denial process. If the story involves anything unknown – where there's no corroboration by a government official – smaller media will almost never risk publishing, unless the claim had been validated by a large established newspaper. Large established papers in turn rarely publish unless the claim has been referenced in another equally established paper. And big papers don't follow small ones unless there's institutional comment. A lone report written by an academic for the European Parliament didn't cut it. Thus, there was a vicious cycle.

So the reason for the continued silence about the world's biggest spy system, controlled by US security, operating outside national jurisdiction, and turning each country into a spy for the others, was purely down to the fact that it existed outside media's frame of reference – a sort of Emperor with no Clothes.

The exact opposite is true of the current NSA scandal. it is as difficult these days to find people who doubt the story, as it was in 1997 to find people who believed it. The real puzzler was whether it might be possible to change anything for the better.

Building the campaign

Understanding the stark reality that institutional involvement was required, I started working through contacts in the European Parliament, and found a political Member of the Parliament (MEP) who I thought might help. After lengthy reflection he agreed the Parliament needed to investigate, but his colleagues would require serious media coverage up front, so that the Parliament's back was covered. Put bluntly, the European Parliament wasn't going to jump first. I left with an "in principle" commitment of support for an inquiry, as long as I generated the media coverage. No easy task.

Depressingly, I continued to draw blanks across the media spectrum. One of the Guardian editors responded: "We have enough ammunition on the Special Relationship (between the US and the UK) without adding a conspiracy theory".

In a last-ditch effort, I targeted the Daily Telegraph. As the Conservative flagship it was the most unlikely place for a story that exposed US security – which was the very reason why its backing would carry weight with other media. Under the editorship of Charles Moore, the paper was slowly turning 180 degrees into a freedom fighter (which by the way is one of the great untold heroic stories of British media). I had previously been in a strategy meeting in the Board Room of the Telegraph involving several prominent media and civil society people. I sat next to Charles Moore who kept poking me in the ribs and whispering "Say something!" Even then I was reluctant, sensing risk. I was too cynical, though in the end I was right in believing that the leopard never changes its spots. Not for long anyway. The Telegraph reverted to reactionary type some years later when Charles Moore left his post to perform the task of writing Margaret Thatcher's official biography.

Armed with an informal unwritten undertaking from the MEP, I then approached a section editor there – Ben Rooney – who had published my work before. On the strength of the European Parliament going public, he agreed to commission me to write the article, adding the caveat that both our necks were on the line. For the Telegraph – steeped in loyalty to the Anglo-American alliance – this was a brave move.

On December 16th, 1997, the Telegraph published the article as a supplement cover story. Nine days before Christmas and with all parliaments closed it was the worst possible time to publish, but still, there it was – in print and in colour.

Hang around media long enough and you learn that the shelf life of a news article is usually a few days or less. However there is a rare species of story that – sometimes for completely random reasons – triggers a global wave. Despite being a poor third cousin to the fine work of Campbell, Hager and Bamford, this became one such story.

We waited. Then came the roll that all campaigners hope for. The story spread to country after country as serious newspapers covered or syndicated the Telegraph article. Excited colleagues in Germany, the US, France and on to Israel, Canada and Brazil called to express their concerns. And, predictably, people were convinced that because the story had originated in the Daily Telegraph, it was unlikely to be a hoax.

I lost count of the articles after about fifty. By February of the following year, talk of the global spying system and Echelon was common currency and few people doubted its existence. In 2001, the Guardian was routinely reporting on Menwith Hill, mentioning the base and the US involvement in no fewer than twenty articles.

In the world of the perfectly conceived strategy, there are two ideal domino cascades. The first is media; the second is political. As the parliaments resumed after the Christmas recess, questions were asked – and from across the Atlantic you could almost hear the slow roar as a surprised Congress digested the extent of the spying operation. For more than a year, representatives tried in vain to force the NSA to account for its activities and its spending, until, in 1999, the agency finally broke cover and admitted – non-specifically – what it had been up to all those years.

Steve Wright's report to the European Parliament – rather than inviting scepticism – then gave further substance and context to the growing public anxiety. The report bluntly asserted:

> *Within Europe, all email, telephone and fax communications are routinely intercepted by the United States National Security Agency, transferring all target information from the European mainland via the strategic hub of London then by Satellite to Fort Meade in Maryland via the crucial hub at Menwith Hill in the North York Moors of the UK.*

In Europe the groundswell for a Parliamentary inquiry escalated with remarkable speed. However the effort met resistance from right wing sections of Parliament, as well as security bodies, and was gutted before it even began. Finally, in 2000, the Parliament agreed to hold an inquiry. Its report was published the following year.

As if mocking the entrenched secrecy of the spy network, the first Article of the preamble to the report declared:

> *Whereas the existence of a global system for intercepting*

communications, operating by means of cooperation proportionate to their capabilities among the USA, the UK, Canada, Australia and New Zealand under the UKUSA Agreement, is no longer in doubt...[276]

The report validated the serious research that had been known all those years before. It laid out in detail the global arrangements and the technology that underpinned the secret operations. At last, ECHELON and the NSA were exposed.

What was the result of all this activity? The European inquiry, the outrage of parliaments, the acres of news coverage, the widespread public anger? Absolutely nothing. Within a year of the release of the European Parliament report, the spying operation had become normalised in the public mind. Indeed when I presented a BBC television documentary on privacy in 2000, the segment on Menwith Hill and ECHELON hardly caused a ripple. The viewing population was far more concerned about businesses selling their personal telephone and address details on CDs – and that was even before the attacks of 9/11 finally buried the EP report.

If campaigners and rights defenders want to carve reform out of the current controversy, they have a hard road ahead. Yet even so, the present healthy state of public awareness gives rise to hope that reform can be achieved.

Perhaps the true scandal at the heart of this mystery is not so much that the authorities failed to act (even where they had the power to do so), but that governments and parliaments failed to hold them to account.

Outside of the United States, where there is at least a token appreciation of security accountability, there is little or no interest in holding security agencies to account. In Britain, despite recent court decisions that ruled previous GCHQ surveillance unlawful,[277] the government has refused to demand answers from its spy agencies. In 2014 I had lodged a detailed plea to the Attorney General of England and Wales urging him to use his

---

276 Report and minority options at
http://www.europarl.europa.eu/sides/getDoc.do?pubRef=-//EP//TEXT+REPORT+A5-2001-0264+0+DOC+XML+V0//EN

277 The Unlawful UK GCHQ spying ruling may force president Obama to take action. The Privacy Surgeon. ttp://www.privacysurgeon.org/blog/incision/why-the-uk-gchq-unlawful-spying-ruling-may-force-president-obama-to-take-action/ (Accessed 2st August 2018)

powers to refer GCHQ interception to the police, only to be bluntly told by senior staff that the office had not the slightest intention of taking action.[278]

Secrecy and obfuscation have sat at the heart of British rule for centuries. After all, this is the country whose intelligence oversight commissioner repeatedly refused to appear before parliament for questioning, forcing the Home Affairs committee to issue a summons against him.[279]

Of course, spy chiefs will only respond to a firm hand by their political overlords, which in the UK and most of Europe has historically been lame. As recently as 2013, during an inquiry by the UK Parliament's Intelligence and Security Committee, GCHQ Director Sir Iain Lobban was allowed to peddle the same party line that has been trotted out to Parliament by agencies for more than twenty years. It is an eerily reminiscent line to that uttered by the likes of General Michael Hayden.

The Wayne Madsen saga

Like many of my colleagues, this intransigence by the UK and the US had become infuriating. I decided to use my blog[280] as a platform for some activism. The results turned out to be interesting.

The episode that springs immediately to mind unfurled in June 2013. Following the revelations of Edward Snowden, an old friend and former NSA contractor, Wayne Madsen, contacted me with news that the NSA's activities in Europe were far more complex and widespread than we had been led to believe. He spoke in some detail about secret NSA arrangements with Germany and other countries. This, immediately after the Germans had proclaimed horror that the UK had done such things.

---

278 The Privacy Surgeon lodges plea with Attorney General to refer GCHQ interception to the UK police March 16th 2014 http://www.privacysurgeon.org/blog/incision/attorney-general-receives-plea-to-refer-gchq-interception-to-uk-police/

279 Parliament summonses surveillance watchdog Mark Waller over Snowden. The Guardian. 27th February 2014. http://www.theguardian.com/uk-news/2014/feb/27/mps-summon-security-services-watchdog-mark-waller-snowden (Accessed 11st August 2018)

280 Www.Privacysurgeon.org (Accessed 11st August 2018)

I took this story to the Observer, one of Britain's most influential and respected newspapers and which I had worked with before on the UK ID cards story. The editors agreed that Madsen's disclosure was critically important. The paper decided to run the story as its front page splash and would give the Privacy Surgeon two hours' publication leeway, so we got onto the wires first.

For a blog site in its infancy, this deal was pure gold. Or, at least, that's what I had foolishly imagined.

True to its word, the Observer led the paper with the Madsen story. Then everything went to pieces. The US Liberal media went into overdrive. The left hated Wayne Madsen, and within an hour of the article's release, it made sure its condemnation of him – and the story – went viral.

The Editor-in-Chief of the Observer/Guardian Newspaper Group was in the US at the time, trying to sell his financially distraught publications to an American audience. Alan Rusbridger was only fresh off the plane when his phone went berserk. "This Madsen guy is a loon. He's a conspiracy nut". "He's insane – always has been".

Rusbridger called the Observer and demanded that it pulp the first edition and replace the splash. This act was unprecedented and caused the Observer to go into meltdown. Editors conveniently agreed that they had been hoodwinked by Madsen and the Privacy Surgeon.

By whatever cause, my site appeared to have been hit with a DDOS (Distributed Denial of Service) attack that night and was down for two days. It could have been the half million hits, or it might have been something more sinister, who can say.

The Observer's claim of deception was far from the truth. A week later, the respected German paper Der Spiegel ran almost exactly the same article. It turned out that the Guardian had already cut a deal with Spiegel for the rights. I got a private apology from the newspaper, but nothing public.

Messing around with national security is a murky business, but it has to be done. Angered by the Observer debacle, I then offered a $1,000 bounty for the capture of the DNA of any spy chief. There have been precedents for such actions, including a successful 2008 bounty I ran through Privacy International, for the capture of the UK Home Secretary's fingerprints.

There were repercussions. The following month, I was speaking at a conference in Berlin and was approached by a suave guy in a three-piece suit who made small talk before adding, "I would strongly advise you to remove that bounty. it is in your best interest". His parting shot was "None of us want another ID card incident," (I assume he was referring to my infamous feud with British Prime Minister Tony Blair over my campaign against the UK ID card and the subsequent media flurry over my imagined suicide because of the horrific persecution by Ministers).

No-one had a clue about this man's identity. We did learn that he was educated at Cambridge – alma mater to the spies. I never did bother to remove the blog. Nor – despite threatening phone calls – did I remove the blog which showed UK Foreign Secretary William Hague in a rubber gimp suit. Haven't these people heard of satire?

The failed US response

In the aftermath of the Snowden revelations, the Director of US National Intelligence, James Clapper, gave an interview with Eli Lake of the Daily Beast, in which he broke some superficially new ground by stating that the core problem in recent spying controversies was that the NSA should have been more open about its activities.

To a wonderfully orchestrated backdrop of fake candour, Clapper explained:

> *I probably shouldn't say this, but I will. Had we been transparent about this from the outset right after 9/11 — which is the genesis of the 215 program — and said both to the American people and to their elected representatives, we need to cover this gap, we need to make sure this never happens to us again, so here is what we are going to set up, here is how it's going to work, and why we have to do it, and here are the safeguards... we wouldn't have had the problem we had.*

To some observers, this might appear a reasonable and ethically sound view. In reality, Clapper's position masterly circumvents the profoundly important legal and ethical issues of mass surveillance. In fact, the transparency concession is constructed in part to neutralise – certainly to muddy – the privacy position. Referring to the first disclosures from Snowden, he said:

> *What did us in here, what worked against us was this shocking revelation. If the program had been publicly introduced in the wake of the 9/11 attacks, most Americans would probably have supported it.*
>
> *I don't think it would be of any greater concern to most Americans than fingerprints. Well, people kind of accept that, because they know about it. But had we been transparent about it, and say (sic), here's one more thing we have to do as citizens for the common good, just like we have to go to airports two hours early and take our shoes off, all the other things we do for the common good, this is one more thing.*

It is important to recognise that this is a well-engineered strategy, not a turning point in the consciousness of US security agencies. Companies and governments alike will almost always play the transparency card when the privacy stakes are high enough.

It is instructive to look back at my interview with General Michael Hayden the year before. See if you can spot the similarities to Clapper's utterances:

> **Davies** – *(I) wonder for example, you were in control of SIGINT at the time of 9/11 – would you behave differently, or would you have made decisions differently now, knowing what you know now than you did then?*
>
> **Hayden** – *I'll give you one, with absolute clarity, and it actually ties in with our earlier conversation, Simon. The administration opted for its most sensitive initiatives after 9/11 – to brief only the gang of eight – that's the leaders of the two Cameras and the leaders of the intelligence committees. That's a mistake. I'd have gone full monty to*

the full committees.

Davies *– But you supported it at the time?*

Hayden *– Actually, at the time I argued for as much transparency as possible. Did I say, once we'd briefed the gang of eight, did I continually tug at the sleeves of the executive branch saying, 'we've gotta tell more people'? No I didn't, but looking backward on it, because when these things become public – and they always do – the more members of Congress who know, the better you are for that one factor that you and I chatted about earlier – the political sustainability.*

And – repeating this quote for relevance – with reference to controversy over the terrorist surveillance program, Hayden added: "Again, if I had it to do over again, I'd have reached a far larger number of people on the intelligence committees... What I regret – in retrospect – is not briefing more members of Congress."

The contrition tactic over transparency is an old one, and those who care about accountability should be aware of the pitfalls that it brings. it is also important to recognise that licence through disclosure is a legal non sequitur. Rights are not so easily traded away, and certainly not merely through disclosure.

Clapper's seemingly reflective and contemporary view was also, in my view, entirely synthetic. Otherwise, why would Clapper not have taken on board Hayden's alleged advice much earlier in the NSA scandal?

The illusion of privacy protection

In terms of national security, if transparency before parliaments is not functioning, what might work? In theory, our privacy is protected by three mechanisms: technology, law and a web of oversight officers spread throughout government and industry. It is instructive to take a quick look at the failure of the latter.

The US government still has a lot of explaining to do about the role of its oversight privacy officers in the NSA affair. In short, these watchdogs appear to have done nothing and yet have entirely escaped media and political scrutiny.

Privacy oversight over NSA-related matters rested with the Chief Privacy Officers (CPO's) of the Department of Defense (DoD), and the Office of the Director of National Intelligence (ODNI), but it is as if those roles never existed. Not a word has been heard from either of them.

Perhaps the true scandal at the heart of the mass surveillance issue is, not so much that the spy agencies failed to act (even where they had the power to do so) but, that governments and parliaments have miserably failed to hold them to account.

Outside of the United States and Germany, where there is at least a token (though usually false) appreciation of accountability, there is little or no interest elsewhere in holding security agencies to account.

Politicians will often emphasize the vital role of Congress and parliaments, pushing the line that there is accountability and process. This rarely takes place. Usually there are agendas that run deep and swift beneath such mechanisms.

In 2013, for example, EU Justice Commissioner Viviane Reding gave a commitment that Europe was winning concessions from the US over NSA snooping. However, subsequent developments showed that the US simply cannot be trusted to honour any commitment to reform the arenas of privacy or security.

If the negotiation process was to be left to the likes of Reding, there may have been a slim chance to twist a few arms in Washington. But unfortunately Europe – at least until Brexit – had a viper in its nest. And that viper is the UK.

The UK's special relationship with the US means that the Brits have a seat at almost every table in the negotiations. The Americans insist on it. As James Bamford noted, in his ground-breaking analysis of the NSA, "The Puzzle Palace", US and UK operatives in the security field work so closely together, that their roles become indistinguishable from each other.

Even though Reding carved out some media space for her own views, the back-room machinations appear to always involve UK representatives who will ensure that there will never be European unity against US spying. Without unity, the US can portray the opposition to the US agencies as fragmented and unstable.

Of course, the UK never needed help from America to corrode privacy. It has been at the forefront of almost every devastation of privacy since the 1980's, from data retention and air passenger surveillance to the General Data Protection Regulation. With Britain institutionally engrained in the negotiation process, it would have been impossible for the Commission or member states to achieve traction.

Even without Britain's assistance, Europe is at a fatal disadvantage in claiming the moral high ground. Under the international signals intelligence agreement (known as UK-USA or Quadripartite), several EU states including Norway, Denmark, Germany, Italy, Greece and Austria have cooperated for decades as "third parties" with the US on spying activities (the US is "first party", the UK is described as "second party", while third party countries are less trusted).

Setting aside for a moment the mass of often one-sided bilateral and multilateral mutual assistance agreements that Europe allowed the US to bully its way into existence, the nature of US commitments is at best shaky, and at worst a downright deception. For example, US commitments to reform the Safe Harbour agreement, the NSA (1999), SWIFT (2006), Guantanamo, extradition, Patriot Act reform, restriction of warrantless wiretaps, cryptography policy, LGBT rights and strengthening the right to US privacy have almost all failed to materialise.

I have documented elsewhere in this book the history of past scandals, involving the NSA's ECHELON interception system and the SWIFT financial data interception arrangement, both of which attracted commitments to reform by the US, and both of which resulted in almost no beneficial result. The unlawful interception and disclosure by SWIFT continued with cover from the White House, while the NSA's role in the ECHELON scandal was institutionalised through greater Congressional scrutiny, but with no significant limitation on the powers of the agency.

None of the US administrations, from Clinton onward, have delivered on commitments to reform the arenas of privacy and surveillance. Safe Harbor, for example, was a device used to ensure that the data trade could continue between Europe and the US after the 1995 EU Data Protection Directive was passed. It was a minimalist solution that was supposed to evolve into something stronger, but it transpired that the US never intended to follow through on commitments to strengthen it. Europe – cheered on by the UK – sat by complacently and allowed it to continue as a transparent sham.

Europe can bluff and bluster all it wants about the evils of US surveillance, but the reality is that the EU is neck-deep in the surveillance game, and it can't easily extricate itself from the mire that it helped create. Campaigners need to understand that this particular river runs very deep, and so their strategies need to be merciless and ingenious. Even back in 2004, Europe was on the cusp of passing a law that would require mandatory fingerprinting of all EU citizens. The plan was thwarted thanks to some astute lobbying by rights campaigners.[281]

---

281 Open letter to the European Parliament on biometric registration of all EU citizens and residents, 28th November 2004 https://privacyinternational.org/blog/1359/open-letter-european-parliament-biometric-registration-all-eu-citizens-and-residents (Accessed 1st July 2018)

Chapter Thirteen: Taking on the silicon merchants

> *This is a peek into the machinations of some of the world's most powerful tech companies. These organizations proclaim to have an interest in privacy, but their business models are often antagonistic to privacy. Here are accounts of several major campaigns that sought to sensitize public awareness on privacy issues and the big household brands in search and social media.*

It is February 2013, and I'm standing at the podium in front of hundreds of very angry Google staff and contractors. The occasion was the company's annual Global Communications Forum, and anyone who was anyone in Google's massive PR effort is here. They had clearly been waiting a very long time to take a shot at me.

Hosein and I are in the Googleplex HQ in Mountainview, California, in the nest of one of my archenemies. The road here has been long and arduous. It had taken nine years to get here, ever since our first strike against the company. Still, I was adamant about finding that dart board in one of the engineering rooms that allegedly has a picture of my face on it.

The Googleplex is an odd sort of place. It sprawls across the outer reaches of the comfortable Silicon Valley city of Mountainview, oozing prosperity and glamour. Architecturally, the place looks like a larger version of a tin can that someone just stomped on, but inside there are untold treasure troves of games corners, highly advanced coffee machines, relaxation balls, stuffed toys and brightly-coloured ergonomic chairs that go "squeak". And some very good restaurants where you can eat what you want, when you want, at the company's expense. Every visitor gets a full briefing on the restaurants. It distracts them, whenever they futilely ask to see the coding rooms.

The journey began several months earlier when, Peter Barron – Google's PR chief for EMEA (Europe, Middle East and Africa) – and I were together yet again at some unseemly early hour at the studios of BBC breakfast television. I wondered then, "Who the hell can stomach breakfast at this hour?"

We were about to debate Google's latest scandal – the unlawful collection of the Wi-Fi details of millions of people[282] (I talk about this case at some length in chapter XXX). We had already sparked an investigation by Scotland Yard,[283] and caused hell for the company in other countries over this issue.

The notorious feud between Google and I had reached back to 2004, at which time the company wasn't just the "Next Big Thing" – it was also the coolest thing on the planet. We thought differently, and realised Google would eventually control much of the planet's information, using a platform of advertising revenue. This would not end well, no matter how charitably you view it. Their business model was simply dangerous. We struck at the company time and time again, attracting the venom of the tech community and deep hostility from the company. By 2009 the Guardian newspaper in Britain was describing the relationship between us as an "increasingly ferocious battle"[284] Matters became much much worse in the years that followed.

Our fears weren't just about the vast privacy threats – almost all of which we figured out a few years in advance. It was also that holding the world's online information hostage to fortune to an advertising company would inevitably cripple access to almost everything. Yes, in the early days Google did provide a better search than the earlier engines like Alta Vista and Ask Jeeves (rebranded as Ask.com), but as the amount of data increased, so it became almost impossible for anyone but serious researchers to find anything pertinent. The issue at hand was Pluralism: the process by which we receive a full spectrum of information – and the way by which Google subverts it.

It is probably useful to examine this point in more detail.

---

282 The Wi-Fi database that shamed Google 30th April 2010
     https://www.newscientist.com/article/dn18844-innovation-the-wi-fi-database-that-shamed-google/
283 Google under investigation by Met Police, BBC News, 23rd June 2010
     https://www.bbc.co.uk/news/10391096 (Accessed 12st August 2018)
284 Jemima Kiss; Google and Privacy International at war over claims of dirty PR tricks
     and Microsoft bias; The Guardian Digital Content Blog, 25th March 2009

Giving you the news that matters

I advised, back in 2012, that across Europe, the protection of media pluralism has been a high priority following the totalitarian regimes of WWII, which used and developed control of the media for propaganda purposes. The goal of pluralism is broadly to ensure that citizens may access a diverse range of information and opinions, free from undue interference by private parties or governments. Pluralism is essential both to the fundamental rights of the individual and to the proper functioning of democratic society, which relies on a constant and vibrant exchange of ideas and opinions among citizens, stakeholders, and government.

The advent of the internet and the digital era has created an opportunity to facilitate media pluralism, by enabling people to easily access a broader spectrum of content and views. But this new era also raises significant new threats, as we increasingly obtain information from the internet via gateways – foremost among them, Google search – that have the effective power to limit the information citizens can access. It is imperative to update the media pluralism regimes, to address this modern threat to plurality.

True, pluralism in Europe is regulated at national level, in the constitutions and laws of many Member States. These national laws often include measures to ensure that dominant public broadcasters present a diversity of opinions; parallel rules seek to restrain media concentration, by limiting the ability of any single individual or entity to hold significant control over the private media. While the European Union does not have competence to legislate rules relating to media pluralism, the goal of "freedom and pluralism of media" is included in the EU's Charter of Fundamental Rights.

Importantly, national laws have typically focused on ensuring pluralism in *traditional* media (TV, radio, printed press). While some Member States are now considering updating their rules, digital developments have not yet been widely reflected in Europe's media pluralism frameworks. The Internet is open season, in the same technique that citizens' use of drone technology is being systematically undermined by state authorities.

The internet and modern telecommunications revolution has radically changed the delivery, distribution, and consumption of information. A

March 2013 study which surveyed over 32,000 individuals found that "more media time is spent online than offline in 23 out of the 31 major [media] markets."[285] Further studies indicate that as Western populations age, the media consumption habits of today's youth will become the majority's habits. For example, studies in the UK concluded that almost 30% of youths aged 18 to 24 had not read a printed newspaper in the last year,[286] and over half of those aged under 35 said their primary source of news was the web.[287] Advertising spending at the time further reflects this trend and is increasingly shifting from traditional media to the internet.[288]

This transition to consumption online should enhance pluralism, allowing citizens to publish and access vast amounts of information. But instead, new threats to pluralism have emerged, necessitating an update of the existing regulations.

For example, European citizens increasingly access information through though a single "gateway" to the internet: Google. Google's search engine was used by more unique searchers in Europe than the next five largest search engines combined. Further, Google's website properties received more daily visitors on average than the next two largest web properties combined, and viewers in Germany, France, Italy, Spain, and the UK watched more videos on Google's video platform, YouTube, than on the next two largest video sites in those countries combined.[289]

This dominance presents significant threats to pluralism in Europe,

---

285 See GlobalwebIndex, "Global Media Consumption: The Digital Reality," March 2013, available at: http://blog.globalwebindex.net/online-time-now-exceeds-offline-media-consumption-globally/. (Accessed 1st June 2018)
286 See YouGov & the Guardian, "Changing Media Summit 2013: Optimising Media in a Changing World," available at: http://cdn.yougov.com/cumulus_uploads/document/jrlh273vq2/YG-G-Changing-Media-Summit-Report-PARTI.pdf. (Accessed 1st August 2018)
287 See Reuters Institute, "Reuters Institute Digital Report 2013," available at: http://cdn.yougov.com/cumulus_uploads/document/jrlh273vq2/YG-G-Changing-Media-Summit-Report-PARTI.pdf. (Accessed 13st August 2018)
288 In 2013, the Interactive Advertising Bureau found that, in Europe, online advertising overtook print advertising by volume in 2012, and noted that online advertising continues to post double-digit percentage gains every year; it will overtake TV advertising as the largest medium for advertising in Europe in the near future. See IAB, "IAB Adex Benchmark 2012," Interact Barcelona 2013, available at: http://www.iabeurope.eu/files/8813/7363/8652/Interact_2013_ADEX_Presentation_FINAL.pdf.
289 See comScore, "Europe Digital Future in Focus 2013: Key Insights from 2012 and What They Mean for the Coming Year," March 2013, available at: http://www.ris.org/uploadi/editor/13646247392013_europe_digital_future_in_focus.pdf
       .

among them is that Google is not a neutral arbiter of information. Instead, Google routinely shapes – and distorts – the results that it surfaces in response to queries on its search engine, exercising granular controls over what information users see. Manipulation of this sort poses tremendous concern. According to one study, involving a double-blinded experiment in which users were presented with different sets of manipulated search results, voting preferences were demonstrably affected, and over two thirds of users showed no signs of awareness that the results were manipulated.[290]

Even without any misuse, Google's dominance hinders the true potential of the internet to facilitate pluralism, as citizens all generally view the same few websites at the top of the Google search results. Over time, page rankings based on popularity algorithms result in "echo chambers," where most receive the same news from the same news sources, inherently suppressing plurality. Further, Google's business model – where 90+ percent of the company's revenue is based on the sale of targeted advertising – necessitates a high degree of personalized filtering, where citizens do not see diverse viewpoints, and instead only receive information in line with their own perspective.

Google holds significant quantities of information on the online search histories of many people – information that it can and does combine with many other pieces of data about its users. These broad and deep user profiles – and Google's overall lax approach to privacy – may make users think twice about accessing alternative points of view, for fear of these searches later being discovered and used against them.

A push to analyze and address the new threats to pluralism in the digital era has already begun in Europe: In October 2012 the UK communications regulator, OfCom, recommended that online players should fall within its regulation of pluralism, and urged Parliament to pay particular attention to "gatekeepers" – i.e. online entities that can "control" access to Internet content.

In Germany, the recent coalition government agreement includes a provision to modernize media plurality regulation to take account of

---

290 See Robert Epstein, "Democracy at Risk: Manipulating Search Rankings Can Shift Voters' Preferences Substantially Without Their Awareness," May 2013, available at: http://aibrt.org/downloads/EPSTEIN_and_Robertson_2013-Democracy_at_Risk-APS-summary-5-13.pdf (Accessed 16st August 2018)

media convergence in the digital age, and to regulate online content to protect principles of neutrality and non-discrimination. Prominent politicians from both coalition partners have confirmed that these issues are high on their agenda. The French media regulator, the Conseil Supérieur de l'Audiovisuel (CSA), in 2013 announced its support for the reform of media plurality laws to cover digital content providers. Two bills were introduced in the French Parliament in the first half of 2014 that collectively should have promoted media plurality online. Additionally, the French Council for Digital (Conseil National du Numérique) was recently asked by the French Government to work on requirements that would ensure "platform neutrality," primarily in relation to search engines.

Finally, in 2013, a report from a European Commission-backed panel noted the threat posed to democracy by the risk of arbitrary action by search engines, and the long-term consequences of a "filter bubble", where extreme personalization results in users getting access only to news that reinforces their existing opinions. The panel recommended that search engines should be included in the market assessment of the media landscape under competition policy both at national and EU level.

It was inevitable that Google – and later Facebook – would create a debilitating effect on the visibility of information. One such example was published in 2014, when an international NGO analysed the way Facebook displays Pages posts from advocacy organisations.[291] Less than five percent of Pages followers were able to see any particular post on that Page – a figure that dropped 75 percent below the preceding two years. The result is that announcements, articles and commentary routinely slip through cracks in the platform. Or put another way, they simply disappear.

As for Google, the reality that was emerging even a decade ago was that the service isn't so much a gateway to the world's data – it is a peep hole. And a very small peep hole at that.[292]

Perhaps the most substantial and challenging problem relates to language. Understandably, commercial search engines are designed to offer results

---

291 Facebook is throttling nonprofits and activists. Gawker. http://valleywag.gawker.com/facebook-is-throttling-nonprofits-and-activists-1569877170 (Accessed 7st August 2018)
292 In 2013, Simon Davies founded an initiative called the Freedom Index to help resolve many of these search problems www.freedomindex.org

primarily in the searcher's own language (and ideally for them, from the local region), and thus intentionally exclude other languages. One result is that anyone publishing online is increasingly required to present data either in the English language, or in one of the half dozen other dominant languages, resulting in what has been described as "digital language death".[293] Try searching, say, for information on an Argentinian worker's rights campaign in 2012, and the odds against success are overwhelmingly huge.

Conscious of all these threats, we engaged a series of media, research and legal strikes over the following six years.[294] This was often interpreted by media as open warfare with the company. The analogy was not far from the truth. We kept the pressure on, never relenting even for a week.[295] [296]The pain that we, as a small organisation, caused Google is noteworthy. Astute campaign strategy can outwit even the most well-resourced opponent, resulting in a series of consequences that negatively shifted public perception of the web giant. Indeed, Evgeny Morozov observed, in the New Republic: "You would think that Privacy International (full-time staff: three) is a terrifying behemoth next to Google (lobbying expenses in 2010: $5.2 million)."[297] [298] That lobbying budget trebled in the following five years.

* * * * *

So, here we are in London's BBC Television Centre. Google's Peter

---

293 http://journals.plos.org/plosone/article?id=10.1371/journal.pone.0077056
294 Call to shut down Street View; BBC online news 24th March 2009
   http://news.bbc.co.uk/2/hi/technology/7959362.stm
295 Google 'trying to smear Street View critic', The Belfast Telegraph, 28th March 2009
   https://www.belfasttelegraph.co.uk/business/technology/google-trying-to-smear-street-view-critic-28473625.html
296 Simon Davies; Google is watching you; The Guardian 1st March 2012
   https://www.theguardian.com/commentisfree/2012/mar/01/google-watching-you-privacy-policy
297 Morozov, E. The New Republic, 12th October 2011
   https://newrepublic.com/article/96116/the-internet-intellectual (Accessed 17st August 2018)
298 This figure rose in 2017 to $18M Time, 24th January 2018
   http://time.com/5116226/google-lobbying-2017/

Barron and I sit opposite each other, bleary eyed, over some badly cut cheese sandwiches and sad coffee in the Green Room. We vocalise what we each are thinking: this has to stop. Of course the motivation for each of us is starkly different. Our team at Privacy International had a vast array of campaigns and reforms to undertake, and this battle with the web giant was draining our thin resources. South America, Asia and Africa were squarely on our radar then. Besides, the halo had already slipped from Google, and there were now many other NGO's in that space.

A couple of months later – to our unending surprise – Hosein and I ended up sitting down with Erich Schmidt, Google's Executive Chairman. Even after all this time, I can never talk with a billionaire without getting distracted by the cut of his clothes. An odd obsession, I know, but you wonder what these people choose in terms of suits and t-shirts. Schmidt chose to wear a sad, slightly checked light brown tan coat. Very disappointing.

"Are we going to call off this war?" asked Schmidt nonchalantly, pretending to be disinterested. We informed him things weren't so simple, but maybe there was room for dialogue instead of constant conflict. As I foreshadowed in the first chapter, I won't disclose the precise details of our discussion, but suffice to say that within three months, mainly due to the efforts of Peter Barron and Anthony House, here we are in the HQ of the new evil empire.

We had just given a Google Tech Talk,[299] which is a regular open meeting for any of Google's eighty-five thousand staff. Given the relations between us, this was a huge gamble by the company. They had agreed to webcast the event (apart from the question and answer session), but we could have blurted out anything we chose. We decided instead to focus on technology transfer, and the risk of hostile government surveillance for developing countries. That topic, at least, wasn't so controversial for the company.

---

299 Avoiding the privacy apocalypse October 18, 2010. Full recording at
https://www.youtube.com/watch?v=SSYXw87BWXo (Accessed 1st July 2018)

* * * * *

But right now at the Global Communications Forum, controversy was the flavour of the moment. Earlier that year, in the white heat of the Google Wi-Fi scandal, I had randomly suggested during a BBC interview that Google was guilty of "criminal intent".[300] That comment had sent the company into meltdown. Now, here we are, bearding the lion in its den.

The hostility was hot in the air. I throw petrol on the flames by reminding them that there was only one of two possible scenarios. Either Google was lying that the Wi-Fi grab was the work of one rogue engineer, or the company was lying when it claimed that all its products were subject to rigorous internal audit. Either way, they were liars.

Diplomacy or not, sometimes you have to call a spade a spade.

To its credit, the company gave us unrestricted access to all its senior executives, including the heads of technology, search and Street View. Those conversations were entertaining in that all of us strived to be civilised. The Senior Vice President for technology spent most of the discussion seeing if we could help him locate the best undiscovered brains on the planet.

This was a refreshing advance in our relations, but you can't easily cover a damp wall with paint.

A brief chronology of the battles with Google

In the 2013 spy spoof film "Kingsman: the Secret Service", Colin Firth and Samuel L Jackson play characters that might be eerily familiar to almost anyone who has been privacy-aware over the past couple of decades.

One of the film's main figures is Richmond Valentine, an Internet billionaire who owns the Valentine Corporation. Valentine's ambition is

---

300 Google accused of "criminal intent" over Wi-Fi data; BBC News, 9th June 2010
     https://www.bbc.co.uk/news/10278068 (Accessed 12st August 2018)

to capture the world's population for nefarious intent. To achieve this, he offers a SIM card that gives free Internet and free calls in perpetuity. Most of the planet sign up, despite warnings that there's no such thing as a free gift of that magnitude.

Nearly a decade earlier, Google had done a Valentine. In 2004 the company offered a gigabyte of free email. No strings attached... or so the story went. It was just a gesture of good will by the entity. The entire online community – well, almost all of it – embraced this wonderful gift.

Back then, one gigabyte was an insane amount of space. Moore's Law states that computational power doubles every year. Well, more precisely, Moore's law is the observation that the number of transistors in dense integrated circuits doubles about every two years. This rule applies equally to space. In those days we were thinking in megs rather than gigs – unlike now when buying a terabyte of space is something that most people can factor into their beer budget.

That offer by Google sparked one of the biggest wars in its early history.

The birth of Cloud: outsourcing the planet

It is worth spending a moment to think about this astonishing shift in computing capacity. I'll take you back in time to 1996, a period when computer power was enabling the entire field of data outsourcing – the parent of cloud computing (back then the industry was labelled "facilities management").

The biggest outsourcer of them all was the secretive US corporation EDS – Electronic Data Systems.[301] At that time I had gone onto red alert over this operation. As far as I was concerned, the implications of EDS' popularity were far reaching and serious. Privacy, security, sovereignty and accountability could be substantially affected.

Even in those early days, EDS controlled and processed the data not just

---

301 Wikipedia entry for EDS https://en.wikipedia.org/wiki/Electronic_Data_Systems (Accessed 14st August 2018)

of the Bank of America, France Telecom, General Motors, Sony, Philips, the US Immigration Service and the government of South Australia – but also the entire British tax system. Some of those contracts turned into utter fiascos. If you wonder what went wrong with so many aspects of cloud computing (from a privacy perspective) this glimpse at the antecedents is possibly instructive.

Developments in the field back then were way too arcane to spark a public campaign – unless possibly it was on the basis of xenophobia. These days, knowledge about Cloud is remarkably advanced. "Facilities Management" has given way to "Cloud-based Enterprise Solutions", and many advocates are aware of the implications. Even as late as 2013, Norway and Sweden had restricted access to Google cloud, because of breaches of privacy law.

I was drawing a blank at finding campaign supporters. So I decided to write an investigative article to pave the way. After some research, I ended up choosing Wired Magazine, which that year had just launched a UK edition. That seemed the logical place to publish – and it would give me space for the five or six thousand words I needed to adequately lay out the complex issues.[302]

EDS – to the best of my knowledge – had never allowed any writer even close to its operations (and certainly not one who was also a controversial privacy campaigner). Almost nothing was known about the company or what it did. Still, its executives were aware that at some point the bubble would burst and they would be forced into more transparency. They agreed to give me unrestricted access to all areas of the company. I suspect they came to regret that decision.

As I later learned, the corporate view was that I was a safer bet than giving the story to the well informed experts at the Washington Post or Scientific American. I was just a silly Brit that could be managed.

So here I am, in the midst of EDS, beneath a bland building in West London. This is one of the two international hubs of the biggest information management organisation on earth. Banks, airlines, oil companies and myriad multinationals depend on EDS to move, sort and make sense of their data. And so, as previously mentioned, do governments. Most of its operations are located in bomb proof quarters

---

302 The article was published in Wired (UK), October 1996.

underground (one executive told me those facilities were also resistant to nuclear attack, though I still don't know whether this claim was just a PR stunt. It probably was a stunt – or more precisely, a lie).

Deception or not, EDS was in a position to create anything it wanted. The global employee count was approaching 140,000, with revenue well over 22 billion a year.

So, I'm standing in a dimly lit passageway deep inside this uncharted facility, accompanied by its Supreme Commander. We've successfully negotiated two security points, including one of those annoying bullet-proof glass turnstiles. Now we can go no further. Even the boss can't get to the next level because the passcode changes every hour. He's growing impatient waiting for help. For something to talk about, he sweeps his hand in the direction of a neon studded metal map of the world.

"We manage this." He reminds me strangely of P. T. Barnum.

In time we file into an observation gallery. Stretching into the distance is a scene that vaguely resembles something out of Battlestar Galactica. Rows of workers are dwarfed by vast screens displaying unintelligible flow charts and maps. Behind a wall-size window – just a grenade's throw away – is one of the grandest computer rooms I had ever laid eyes on: 70 terabytes (70,000 gigabytes) at the last count – enough to give god himself a momentary headache. The organism grows constantly. At the moment of that article, it boasted 50,000 MIPS processing power (millions of instructions per second) and services 400,000 terminals around the world.

Many advanced home computers can now reach that power. For example, in 2016, the Intel core i7 processor achieved just shy of 50,000 MIPS, while the 2017 version reached nearly 66,000 MIPS.[303] Meanwhile, the future can be glimpsed in the AMD Ryzen 7 chip, that streaks past the EDS system capability milestone by a factor of six. In 2018, that processor was for sale for around two hundred dollars.

At the time, it looked like enough crunching power to run governments. Which is fortunate, because of course that's exactly what it did.

To put this computing storage in perspective, nearly twenty years later, police raided the home of Austrian IT administrator William Weber, and

---

303 https://en.wikipedia.org/wiki/Instructions_per_second

confiscated 20 computers and electronic devices, together with some 100 terabytes of storage. The action was taken after police had allegedly detected illegal traffic passing through Weber's network, Tor, which is a popular provider of online anonymisation. In other words, Weber had EDS in his bedroom.

In the UK, this was quickly turning into the biggest privatisation exercise in history – or as the government was fond of saying, it was a "public-private-partnership". At that moment, EDS was handling at least some of the data needs of the Child Support Agency, the Driver and Vehicle Licensing Agency, the National Health Service, the Department of Social Security, and the Inland Revenue, among others. Its contracts with the British government were worth billions. And it is not just a matter of money. EDS was part of a fundamental change in the nature of government services and government accountability.

In some respects, the outsourcing boom was nothing new. In the eighties, many people with uniforms or gardening shorts, found themselves on the front page of a private sector employment contract. In this first phase of outsourcing, government agencies were divided into core functions (collecting tax, paying welfare benefits), and peripheral or support functions (mowing lawns maintaining building security). The core functions were maintained.

In the 1990s, the equation took another step. Agencies evolved a more complex division: Executive functions (manufacturing and issuing passports, issuing ID cards, processing data), and Judgmental functions (issuing documents of identity in transit, granting asylum). In this second phase of outsourcing, the judgmental functions were maintained by government.

This distinction is a line drawn in sand. Like cloud computing today, there is no policy – only what is often described as "Developing Practice". I explored these issues in more detail with senior EDS staff.

John Bateman was Managing Director for Europe, the Middle East and Africa. Part Australian, part South African, part British, the gravel voiced supremo came across as a bluff mixture of pragmatism and ruthlessness. The EDS vision, he told me, is not merely national. It is global. It transcends boundaries of time, context and geography. Bateman believed that the localised way of doing business is disappearing. The way people work is transcending culture.

In this truly multinational world, John Bateman believed data protection law is pointless. Everything is rising above the national consideration. Countries that try to protect data within the confines of their own borders are trying to legislate against the sea.

In some ways, I have to agree. I've seen his world. I've seen the gleaming new buildings set into the solid traffic of Bangkok. One gun-toting security guard per satellite dish. Container loads of sensitive personal information – health records, police files, insurance data, credit card accounts and government records – are despatched from all over the world for processing here. EDS, needless to say, is a player. Investment is concentrated on American health and insurance industry, but the clients for data outsourcing come from all sectors and all countries – particularly Britain. Conventional borders disappear before our eyes, and where our most intimate personal details are shunted around the globe behind our back. It is cheaper for companies and governments. It is more efficient.

Bateman, like everyone else in EDS, believed that efficient, market based information management is the only solution for a troubled economy. Governments are steeped in obsolescence. The civil service is an oxymoron. All things are possible through the application of logic, common sense, innovation, partnership and passion. In EDS, such ideas were not discussion points: they were axiomatic truths. Without so much as a blush of reserve, people there would tell you EDS is creating templates for the world's future.

Finally, I ask the BBC Newsnight "killer" question that rocks the company. I asked Bateman if he saw any role for government in the future.

"The role of government may well be associated with..." he begins, but then pauses for reflection. "To be honest I really struggle to come up with a clear definition of ultimately what role government has."

Astonishingly, he laughs.

The EDS Board went into meltdown. A good result!

So it seems that Orwell was wrong. Big Brother doesn't have a party apparatus, and he doesn't wear a uniform (except perhaps for the obligatory tie). He doesn't care what you believe. He just sits in West London piling up the data and trying to make an honest buck. Just a conscientious partner in the great global enterprise. You could almost get to like him.

* * * * *

So here we are, eight years on in 2004. The world has changed, but its trajectory has been consistent. If Google could reach a billion people with its new Gmail offering – each of whom uses a gigabyte – that would be a storage requirement 1,300 times greater than that of EDS. But in 2004, Google could work that outlay into its margins. The cost of a gigabyte in 1996 was $1,000. By 2004, it had dropped to ten cents.[304] Google monetises the advertising value of each of its customers at around thirty dollars a year.

At the very moment that we were contemplating the potential risks of the Google offering – unbeknown to us – a new start-up called Facebook had just appeared. We could never have imagined the fallout from that initiative.

We had to think strategically. Here was a company that was universally loved by the techies, our supposed allies. Any hint of an attack on Google was rebuffed with vigour – often aggressive vigour. "You're just a bunch of Luddite idiots," was a classic attack. So in early April we helped organise a petition of 31 civil liberties organisations aimed at raising awareness on the Gmail issue.[305] Then later that month, we launched our missile.

Privacy International filed detailed (4,000 word) complaints asking the privacy and data protection commissioners of many of the EU countries to investigate the serious privacy problems that Google's Gmail service posed. The complaint was sent to France, Germany, the Netherlands, Greece, Italy, Spain, Czech Republic, Belgium, Denmark, Sweden, Ireland, Portugal, Poland, Austria, Australia and Canada along with the European Commission and the EU Commissioners' internal Article 29 Data Protection Working Group.[306]

---

304 http://www.mkomo.com/cost-per-gigabyte (Accessed 1st August 2018)
305 www.privacyrights.org/ar/GmailLetter.htm
306 Privacy International press release, 17th April 2004
      https://privacyintyqcroe.onion/press-release/1370/pi-files-complaints-sixteen-countries-
      against-google-mail (Accessed 1st July 2018)

This was perhaps the first time such a strategy had been undertaken, and it certainly galvanised the press – and the company. Still, in classic arrogance, Google founder Sergei Brin never bothered to return my calls.

We hit the company with allegations of breaches of just about every data protection principle on the books. The fact that Google was scanning and analysing all emails was the foundation. The process was unfair, deceptive and was occurring outside any reasonable concept of informed consent.

Recently, we had lodged a test complaint with the UK Information Commissioner. The Commissioner – in the sad tradition of most British regulators – decided to delay taking action on the complaint after assurances from Google that the company would "consult" with officials before it offered the service in the UK. This approach, as I angrily told ITV News, was a "complete crock of shit."

We took the decision to take global action against Google, after it became clear that a similar assurance to meet US privacy advocates was not honoured.

I warned Google that it should tread with great caution: "Google is showing its true colours. The company pays lip service to privacy but in this case has demonstrated no real commitment to it. I am beginning to suspect that Google looks at privacy in the same way that a worm looks at a fishhook."[307]

I challenged Google to "come out from its bunker and meet the advocates", but it did not rise to that challenge, until much later, nearly a decade later. Instead, Google unleashed its tech wolves, with the intention of ripping us apart and dividing the tech and policy communities. That strategy worked for around four years, but then fell apart with breath-taking speed.

---

307 ibid

A race to the bottom

The Gmail complaints weren't getting us anywhere. Most regulators ignored our correspondence. Some said we had no standing. Most were perplexed. At that time, the commissioners generally had one IT guy who may or may not have had a tech diploma, but he probably had a PC in his bedroom. Germany and France were among the exceptions.

We brainstormed on this. Google had already started moving to a dominant market position and it was clear to us it would soon have a global monopoly. So we decided to go to the heart of the matter by creating a report that gave a privacy ranking to all the major comms and social networking platforms. If our suspicion was correct, Google would come out at the bottom.[308] Indeed it did. We had theatrically designed the ranking in a colour scheme, with black at the worst. Google was the only company that came out in black, though none of the other nineteen contenders achieved the Green status. Most ended up in the "red or amber" mode; in need of serious correction to their practices. Like our identity card costings the report was a gamble in that we had no way of predicting the outcome, but we had our suspicions.

I should add that we had enjoyed some good success with the ranking formulae.[309] The previous year we had ranked all the major countries for privacy compliance. I believe the report attracted a million downloads, partly because Britain achieved the lowest rating in the developed world.[310]

Based on this successful formula, we released the Internet rankings in June 2007,[311] and it created a global media storm. We had given the story at first to Associated Press, and it ended up being published on over seven hundred news outlets including all the major US papers. Reuters and UPI followed almost immediately. Almost every newspaper in the world carried the story.

---

308 A Race to the Bottom. Privacy International, June 2007,
     https://privacyintyqcroe.onion/sites/default/files/2017-12/A_Race_Bottom.pdf
309 UK singled out for criticism over protection of privacy 5th September 2002. The
     Guardian. https://www.theguardian.com/technology/2002/sep/05/security.humanrights
310 PI international surveillance map
     https://web.archive.org/web/20120110142304/https://www.privacyinternational.org/sur
     vey/phr2005/phrtable.pdf
311 Danny Sullivan. Google Bad On Privacy? Maybe It's Privacy International's Report
     That Sucks. June 10, 2007. Search Engine Land. https://searchengineland.com/google-

On that day, Google's share price blipped downward for the first time since it had gone public. My analyst friend in the New York Stock Exchange told me that these matters were not predictable, but he did conclude that the only variable that day was our report. This fact was not lost on Google's shareholders.

This had been an interesting and crucial period for Google. Eight years earlier, Google's founders Brin and Page had attempted to sell Google for $750,000 to Excite's CEO George Bell. He rejected the offer, in the manner that record labels had rejected The Beatles 34 years before (Bell subsequently became known in Britain as "Bell End", which is slang for penis). Then the duo entered into a twenty year deal with Erich Schmidt, and everything changed. When the company went public three years before our attack, it had a market capitalisation of 23 billion dollars[312].

There were concerns that all this wealth would change Google's stated Prime Directive of "Do No Evil" (a claim which by 2018 had disappeared from the company's published vision).[313] In response, the company appointed a Chief Culture Officer.[314] It was just a cheap sop to the investors. In all our encounters we never met this person or had any dealings with the office.

Regardless of this outcome, much of the tech press continued to give benefit of the doubt to Google. Old habits die hard. Even Wendy Grossman, one of the most astute and sensitive commentators in Britain, wrote in the Guardian[315] "...as far as anyone knows, Google has yet to do anything bad with those masses of data. And shouldn't the company actually commit the crime before we punish it?"

The impact, nonetheless, was poignant. In the Gmail offensive of 2004, we received thousands of hate emails. In 2007, with the Internet rankings,

---

bad-on-privacy-maybe-its-privacy-internationals-report-that-sucks-11428
312 Wikipedia entry for Google. https://en.wikipedia.org/wiki/Google
313 *"Quirky Google Culture Endangered?". Wired. Associated Press. April 28, 2004. Archived from the original on August 14, 2010. Retrieved November 27, 2010.* https://web.archive.org/web/20100814174333/http://www.wired.com/techbiz/media/ne ws/2004/04/63241
314 *Olsen, Stefanie; Kawamoto, Dawn (April 30, 2004). "Google IPO at $2.7 billion". CNET. CBS Interactive. Retrieved November 27, 2010.* http://news.cnet.com/2100-1024-5201978.html
315 Wendy Grossman; How big a threat to privacy is Google, really. The Guardian 26th July 2007 https://www.theguardian.com/technology/2007/jul/26/guardianweeklytechnologysectio n.google

we got maybe five hundred. When we went on the attack over the Wi-Spy conspiracy, this dropped to a couple of dozen. Slowly, people are becoming educated.

Microsoft: the most nervous company in the world?

It is February 2012 – and I'm here in a sterile meeting room at Microsoft's headquarters. They call this area a "campus", and for good reason. Dozens of buildings sprawl across a wide area, separated by trees and parking lots. Unlike the monolithic design of the Googleplex, this place gives out an aura of serious research.

Not much praise, however, can be given to the nearby mistake of Redmond, one of Seattle's less glamorous satellite towns. Microsoft staff sometimes refer to it as Deadmond.

The long, laminated board table is packed with some of the company's top legal experts. And opposite me are two men with piercing eyes. They had been introduced as former agents of undisclosed security agencies. I later came to the conclusion that one was from the FBI, and the other had been seconded from the NSA. Or, maybe more precisely, the NSA simply invited itself here.

I am here to learn about how the company manages the tens of thousands of demands it receives from agencies for customer information, and these two men are the front-line gatekeepers – and the technical enablers. As a rule, such people are invisible, but I had pleaded for this meeting.

This is a unique experience for all of us. Activists never get this sort of deep exposure. Microsoft, understandably, was nervous. How does it tell a maverick campaigner how the company goes about satisfying requests from police, the CIA or the Chinese government?

There wasn't even an NDA (Non-Disclosure Agreement) in place. There should have been one – and everyone thought there was one – but somehow the matter had been overlooked. At Google, you digitally sign an NDA the minute you walk through the door. You have no choice.

Still, I'll treat the present event in a spirit of trust – not that I learned much there that Edward Snowden didn't reveal three months later.

Microsoft and I had not always enjoyed the warmest of relations. Even years later, some staff still despised me for presenting a Big Brother (Orwell) Award to the company in Washington DC in 1999 (which I mention elsewhere). That really did sting the company. We had given them the "People's Choice" award because of online tracking software that had been built into Microsoft's products.

It could have been worse for the company. For at least two years before then – and in the months that followed[316] – Microsoft had been dogged by accusations of enabling backdoor access in its products and that its security was vulnerable. The latter claim alone would have been justification enough for an award (as a side-note, security matters at Microsoft have measurably improved in many respects since those days).[317]

Nearly two decades on, I'm prepared to give Microsoft some benefit of the doubt on a number of scandals that it has faced, but I can't speak on behalf of the judges for the various national awards. I'm not a crypto or security expert, but those panels were packed with the world's leading figures in those fields. My job as Founder was to put on a silly costume and present the awards. Microsoft – like other companies – has historically claimed that the awards were unfair and factually unsound. What I can say is even though at the time – as now – few of us trusted anyone in government or the private sector, the judging process was always robust and technically sound. Yes, we were all openly cynical, but our cynicism was often justified.

As I mention elsewhere, the representative from Microsoft proudly went to the stage to receive the award, adopting a "look what I've got" attitude."[318] I learned later that the company went into palpitations over the award.

Such a response is not unusual for that company. In 2001 the Big Brother Awards in Austria nominated Microsoft for its Passport authentication

---

316 Microsoft has denied such claims https://www.wired.com/1999/09/ms-denies-windows-spy-key/

317 See http://www.stat.rice.edu/~dobelman/kstorm.txt for a summary of press reporting at the time.

318 Bennett, C.J. "The Privacy Advocates". p.108

scheme, which was widely viewed in the advocacy community as a dangerous centralisation of identity. One news outlet from the time remarked: "Microsoft Austria has reacted with horror, pain and angst to the company's nomination for this year's Austrian Big Brother Awards and has asked for the nomination to be withdrawn. But the begging email it sent to the organisers merely seems to have drawn more attention to the nomination."[319]

Unlike Facebook and Google, Microsoft is hyper sensitive to criticism. We attacked the company in 2000 over the aforementioned Passport project. The plan was scrapped, and instead the company started developing innovative products that would allow for multiple identities. That technology – like so many good products the company creates – never saw the light of day.[320]

The company was anxious for me to understand the complexities of law enforcement requests. Microsoft has physical offices in a hundred countries and it has a duty of care to the safety of its staff as well as to the privacy of its customers. On that point, I agreed. It seems a delay on one such government request recently resulted in a raid on Microsoft's building in Hong Kong, with the outcome that servers and PC's were seized. I understand on that occasion the data was not compromised, but avoiding such situations is a rather sound idea.

Microsoft, like most other large companies, receives many thousands of requests from governments for customer information. In 2017 it received more than 60,000 such requests[321], a figure that – all circumstances considered – is comparable to other major companies in the field.[322]

There must have been more staff in the disclosure unit other than those two seated in front of me. Foolishly, that's one question I didn't ask. If it were just the two of them, they would need to process a request every three minutes of the working day. Possible I suppose, but that leaves no time for any sort of challenge to bad requests. In reality, there were

---

319 Big Brother Awards nomination for WPA, Passport pains MS. The Register. 25th October 2001.
https://www.theregister.co.uk/2001/10/25/big_brother_award_nomination/
320 Thoughts on Google's policy changes, 2012,
https://privacyintyqcroe.onion/blog/1342/thoughts-googles-policy-changes
321 https://blogs.microsoft.com/on-the-issues/2017/04/13/microsoft-releases-biannual-transparency-reports/ (Accessed 1st July 2018)
322 The figures for Google are available at https://transparencyreport.google.com/user-data/overview?hl=en

probably around thirty to forty people in the disclosure unit. Even back in 2012, Facebook had twenty five people working full time just managing the handover of customer information.[323]

I listened carefully to the company's story. It seemed convincing that they had due process in place to deal with this mass of requests, but something was missing: context. it is one thing to publish a bunch of figures, as the company had done for a few years, but quite another to create a context, so the public could get a more rounded picture. Microsoft didn't say it was "in bed" with government, but even an infant could have joined the dots.

The reality is that Microsoft – like almost all older companies – is a complex organism. There are liberals and there a hard-line supporters of government collusion. At one meeting I had in Microsoft's EU HQ in Brussels in 2013, one executive told me the company had a duty of care to work with government, while another told me it had a duty of care to protect customer privacy at any cost. The reality was that decisions within the company are made by consensus, and even the slightest dissent usually results in a veto on any potentially risky issue.

I mentioned elsewhere that more than a decade ago Microsoft created a substantial foundation called Trustworthy Computing and has sought to build on that foundation to improve its internal compass. It appears however that the corporation is dependent on an internal committee system, that precludes brave choices. Trustworthy Computing bit the dust.

This internal formula can, however, sometimes work to the advantage of customers. For example, Microsoft has an extraordinarily strong network of privacy "champions" within the company that has become embedded into the corporate culture. Facebook could learn a lesson here. That mechanism helps protect privacy and cannot easily be subverted. However the company has a deep respect for hierarchy and – in reality – whatever is decided by the General Counsel is accepted without question.

There are key distinctions between the attitude of Microsoft compared to, say, Facebook and Google. I have written a hundred blogs that criticise the latter two companies and the collective response from them has

---

323 Interview with Chris Soghoian, American Civil Liberties Union in the 2012 film "Terms & Conditions May Apply".

generally been "pfffft... who cares". Microsoft however reacts differently. When I wrote a blog post condemning the company over its amalgamated privacy policy (a legal mechanism over which it had always criticised Google), the company went into meltdown and sent me innumerable explanations and briefings. This distinction arises in part because Microsoft believes it can massage its way out of any PR dilemma, whereas the younger companies still have religion over what they do and don't give a damn. I often felt that Microsoft's people lived in fear of being challenged within the company, while Google's people lived in fear of not being challenged. That's why Microsoft has devised a complex decision process, whereas Google's process tends to be more organic.

This approach leaves much to be desired. Legal challenges brought by Microsoft have been left twisting in the wind because of internal disputes. For example, the company's high profile action to contest the release of customer information to the US government ended abruptly.[324]And, some years earlier, Microsoft's court challenge in the UK against Google's unlawful subversion of cookie preferences ended with an out of court settlement by Google. Microsoft never bothered to continue the case.

Of course the reality is that many people hate Microsoft because of its proprietary business model. Microsoft makes no excuses for this, arguing that its model has enabled interconnectivity between systems.

That's not to say that Microsoft doesn't care about its customers' privacy or public interest. It apparently does, to at least some extent. The first Microsoft executive I had positive dealings with was Peter Cullen, who served as Microsoft's chief privacy strategist from 2003 to 2014.

In an interview,[325] Cullen remembers writing to me and another leader at Privacy International to say, "Hey I'm kind of new around here, I'm coming to London, want to have dinner?" And we did: "We had a great meal," Cullen recalls, "And a glass, or glasses, of wine."

That led to an "extremely advantageous relationship" where Microsoft could "...get the consumer perspective from an advocacy standpoint. In terms of not just how we built a product, but how we marketed and talked

---

324 For background on the case see
https://en.wikipedia.org/wiki/Microsoft_Corp._v._United_States and
http://www.privacysurgeon.org/blog/incision/uk-landmark-ruling-has-dealt-a-double-blow-to-google-while-boosting-consumer-privacy-rights/
325 Eliza Krigman; Privacy Activism: Turning threat into opportunity. Data Privacy

about it." He continues, "Simon and others have actually had a greater influence on the way the company builds markets, promotes its products and services."

But this is a world removed from the reality of key corporate decision making. A case in point. After the Redmond meeting, I called over a couple of legal executives and said the company needs to create a narrative. It needs to walk people through the entire process of information disclosure, including risk areas. "You realise the shit will hit the fan one day?" I advised.

Microsoft considered this idea at quite a senior level for some time, but by April it decided that the narrative was risky and unnecessary. Three months later, the biggest story on the planet was Edward Snowden's revelations about corporate collusion with the spy agencies. Had Microsoft heeded my words, it might not have endured quite so much bad PR fallout. Still, I learned that all older major corporations are driven by a sliver of risk, rather than an archway of opportunity.

There are some amusing differences between the three major West Coast ICT companies – Google, Facebook and Microsoft, and I observed some of them first hand, on my visits to their HQ's. The meeting agendas are indicative. At Google, the agenda was firm but flexible. At Facebook, the meeting schedules were random and often spontaneous. We would just drop in to the executives. Facebook, which I'll discuss later, was in a constant state of flux and chaos, so a strict agenda might not even have been feasible. At Microsoft, in contrast, there was barely a minute of unscheduled time. I later discovered that not only did I need pre-briefings, but other participants also scheduled separate pre-briefings. Then there were post-meeting briefings based on the pre-briefings that eventually were circulated to senior staff under the truncated title of "briefings". Interestingly, those three degrees of schedule management reflected precisely the age of the respective company.

Here at Microsoft, the planning is entirely different to that of Google and Facebook. I was there for a couple of days and was handed a three-page schedule, which allowed for ten minutes between meetings. The days were micro-managed to such an extent that breakfast sessions and post-dinner drinks were also included. In some respects, that sort of management is helpful, but it also indicates a corporate environment that

---

Leadership Council. 2016

has become hyper-sensitive. If that means the company takes fewer risks, the question is how that approach stacks up with its more aggressive competitors. Maybe Microsoft realised this conundrum when, in 2015, it called off the war with Google. The company was never going to win with such a combative approach.

Frolics at Facebook

Hmmm... suspicious. This is the second time I've been escorted to Mark Zuckerberg's private office, and the second time – straddled on his swivel chair – that he turned his back to me. Possibly a coincidence? Who can say, indeed?

When I say "private" office, I should add that in the first few years Zuckerberg's room was surrounded entirely by walls of glass. That should have been a hint of things to come, regarding privacy.

Privacy International had publicly engaged Facebook, ever since it became clear that it was following Google's lead by running on an advertising platform. But back in earlier days, the company had some sort of discernible privacy ethos. That's to say, a privacy ethos that permeated most of the senior teams and engineering, rather than just a specialist legal unit in some corner.

I should mention that we were well aware of Zuckerberg's attitude to privacy. One famous IM exchange back in the formative days in the dormitory room with his colleague went:

> **Zuckerberg**: *Yeah, so if you need any information about anyone in Harvard. Just ask. I have over 4,000 emails, pictures, addresses, SSN. People just submit it. They 'trust' me... Dumb fucks.*[326]

In the mid 2000's, we got to know Chris Kelly, Facebook's Chief Privacy Officer and Number 25 employee (the company now has around 30,000

---

326 Recounted in "Terms and Conditions Apply"

staff). Chris was anxious that the company worked toward a strong privacy framework, and that all its activities were ahead of the curve in terms of customer protection. In those early days, when the user population was merely in the hundreds of millions, he made an impact on the company. That impact appeared to lessen as the company grew, and he left some years later to pursue other interests. For some considerable time after his departure, Facebook never bothered to replace him, and was sailing rudderless. But in the meantime, in the middle years, he was very keen for us to get involved at the core of the company.

Our first visit to Facebook had followed a media storm over various risks that were emerging in the company. Its growth had been exponential, and it was clear that – with an IPO in the wings – executives would make billions, if they cleverly leveraged the advertising business model.

We agreed with Chris that the key focus should be to train and evangelise the engineers. They were – well – the engine room. Accordingly, we visited the company's HQ two or three times to conduct training and engagement.

In those days, the company was based in the Silicon Valley city of Palo Alto. This elite area (well, elite in parts) is located on the train route that traverses every major tech company from Apple to eBay. Of course, very few employees ever bother using the rail system. Most of the corporations have their own fleet of Wi-Fi enabled transit vans to escort their workers wherever they need to go.

It would be a misnomer to describe the Palo Alto HQ as a "campus". More accurately, it was a crazy collection of buildings, that randomly grew as the company's fortunes soared. Any time that Palo Alto commercial real estate went on the market, Facebook was head of the bidding queue. In those days the buildings looked quite bohemian: bicycles stacked chaotically in lobbies and corridors; walls adorned with the work of local artists; pyramids of tech piled on the floors. We did our lectures in a converted dining area, which was chaotically confused, with sandwich ordering and piles of orange juice cartons.

Working with the engineers was always a constructive experience. Their questions were pertinent and probing. They were seeking solutions to practical issues that they faced on a daily basis. It would be fair to say in those days, there was a mood in engineering – and in most parts of management – that reflected the European ideal of "Privacy by Design", in which privacy is embedded throughout a product's conception and development rather than merely being bolted on as an afterthought.

My theory is that this outcome was due in part to the work spaces. Staff from all parts of the company freely mixed and socialised. Well, they had no choice, given the urban layout. Nonetheless, this was a company in high growth and it was getting too big for central Palo Alto. Plans were drawn up for Facebook to move one train stop down the line to Menlo Park.

You can tell much about the attitude of a company by its building architecture. As opposed to the Palo Alto layout, Zuckerberg signed off on a monolithic design. The shiny, vast new HQ was built roughly in two hemispheres: one for advertising and management and the other for engineering. The two populations were physically divided. The place looked like a souped-up version of an anonymous accounting company in an industrial estate.

On our last visit to Facebook, we were entertained in this complex. It seemed a universe away from what we had known before, and it wasn't entirely clear whether people enjoyed the experience. The place was sterile and lacked character. We got the impression that everyone was just getting on with the grind, rather than being excited about the enterprise.

This was the mid part of Facebook's high growth. And while its building architecture might have attempted to portray an image of order, the place was in as much chaos as it had always been. We had two briefing sessions with legal teams, neither of which seemed to have a clue what was going on. Then we met the CTO (Chief Technology Officer), who candidly told us, "Look, I just get here, and there's a pile of papers that I try to get through before end of day". This man, responsible for the company's tech, seemed to have no head space to ruminate on how Facebook should grow. Such decisions seemed to be made by the board and the revenue teams.

When we raised the issue of privacy and how that challenge was being addressed, we were told, "We have suggestion boxes... privacy stuff sort of just organically happens". Given the vast number of privacy scandals that hit Facebook in the subsequent years, it seems no-one was tasked to open those boxes.

It should come as no surprise that Facebook became the US (and other governments) greatest surveillance ally. Indeed Christopher Sartinsky, Deputy Director of the CIA, told US Congress:

"After years of secretly monitoring the public we were astounded that so many people would willingly publicise where they live, their religious and political views, and an advertised list of all their friends, personal email addresses, phone numbers, hundreds of photos of themselves and even status updates of what they were doing moment to moment. It was truly a dream come true for the CIA."[327]

This activity goes to the heart of a process called the "Third Party Doctrine", which anyone using digital or other media should know. We instinctively think that government is required to jump through many legal hoops to obtain our information. Not so. In the legal environment of many countries – including the US – anything we publish online can be easily accessed by government. This includes banks and retailers. The companies we have a "trusted" relationship with are, in effect, agents of the government.

The uncomfortable truth about Facebook's revenue model

In 2013, faced with constant media condemnation over its impossibly difficult privacy settings, Facebook started to plan a "streamlined" control panel. This initiative was to be the company's shop-front with the aim of demonstrating just how deeply it cared about privacy. Desperate for a good news story about Facebook, media then went into hyperdrive over these changes to the site's new privacy settings. I mean, gosh, they were now so easy to use.

"Facebook caves in to privacy pressures,", declared the stately Financial Times.[328] "Facebook's privacy evolution crawls another step out of the ooze", crooned ReadWriteSocial.[329]

---

327 Recounted in "Terms and Conditions apply".
328 http://www.ft.com/cms/s/0/4eb2fc2c-43f4-11e2-844c-
00144feabdc0.html#axzz2Esv2cWNJ
329 Facebook moves toward transparency and away from creepiness. 12th December 2012.
Readwrite.com http://readwrite.com/2012/12/12/facebook-moves-toward-transparency-

Did any serious privacy supporter really believe Facebook was just being random with the timing of its privacy changes? Certainly not anyone who took the trouble to look at the fine print and join the dots from that period. Facebook had blocked everyone from opting out of search, and said it intended moving into search in a big way. Yahoo and Facebook were in discussions about a search partnership to take on Google. Instagram pics were being merged in Facebook search while Yahoo had already said it is gunning to buy Flickr. Facebook bought Face.com that year and then owned the most powerful face recognition software in the world. Put it all together and you have the most mind blowing search technology on earth.

What many media outlets had overlooked was that the overall privacy of all Facebook users had now been pushed into an abyss. Journalists were mesmerised by the glamour of a new privacy portal that turned out to be just a distraction from the main game.

There's no doubt that the new privacy settings were an improvement. The problem is that users have less privacy to set than they had the day before. It became impossible to hide yourself from user searches. The company was also fusing images with Instagram, meaning that users would be exposed to searches beyond the social network itself.

Having said that, you can now more easily block users, though you can't prospectively block users from searching you. Of course if they ever found you – and if you could find out that they had found you – then you can block them from finding you again... except by then they'll already know how to locate you.

Anyway, saying the new privacy settings were an improvement was giving too much credit to a company that was advised, eight years before, to build settings that didn't require a doctorate in engineering to use. After all, the betting is that in 2008 Mark Zuckerberg – himself no fan of privacy – became exasperated by the constant criticism over privacy, slammed his fist on the desk and screamed, "If they want privacy controls, we'll give them so many that the bastards drown in them". Or words to that effect.

Go on Facebook... I dare you to tell me that didn't happen. I was there.

To create a fanfare about the simplification of already burdensome privacy controls is like praising Delta Airways for improving its customer

---

and-away-from-creepiness-with-privacy-control-revamp (Accessed 16st August 2018) service: it shouldn't have been that abysmal in the first place. I had already passionately argued to various teams in the company that they should consider a "privacy slider", which could be fun to use, and which would also inform people more effectively about the exposure of their information. That idea was probably just kicked into the nearest suggestion box.

There had been some celebration that, when posting an item to Facebook, users will be reminded that even if they hide something from their timeline, for instance, that item could still show up on other places around Facebook. Some observers said this is a helpful reminder, because the leakage currently isn't always clear. [330] Predictably perhaps, I'd say that's like putting a health and safety warning in an execution chamber.

The voting fiasco

It was April 2009 in London, and I had been up all night on the telephone, in a heated and prolonged exchange with Facebook HQ. It is the eve of the company announcing that it intended raising the threshold for its user voting system. It was the last time I had any sort of constructive engagement with the company on a core issue.

At that time, if Facebook wanted to alter its terms and conditions, the members had a right to vote on the proposal. The vote of the members – however the result turned out – was binding on the company.

But let's look at the facts. The membership vote was a confidence trick. It was a confidence trick when it was proposed earlier in 2009, and it turned from a confidence trick to a swindle three months later when its guts were removed. Ever since then, the scheme mutated into a sad illusion held aloft by symbolic democracy.

The user vote was, in theory, a great idea – and particularly so for a privately owned start-up. The move resonated well with a Californian process called "Citizen's Initiated Referenda", where ordinary people get

---

330 http://gigaom.com/2012/12/12/facebook-changes-privacy-policy-public-search-app-permissions-affected/

to propose measures that – if supported by the majority – are binding on government. The blindingly obvious difference, of course, is that Facebook users didn't get to initiate anything: only respond to an official proposal.

But the voting system was never supposed to actually work. Anyone who runs a social networking site knows motivating users to take part in democracy usually falls flat on its face. Facebook knew it too, but just to be on the safe side it changed the rules, so not even the intervention of god would work in the users' favour. The company had originally said that if 25 per cent of users voted in favour of a change in its terms and conditions the result would be binding. Within two months that threshold rose to 30 per cent.

argued that they'd never attract more than half one percent of the active user population. I was way off the mark. It turns out 360,000 people – only one thirtieth of one percent of active users – took part in a vote on changes to the T&Cs ("active" is defined as a user who logs on at least once a month).

Why the company even bothered irritating people with this change is beyond me. It was a pointless amendment because the vote was never going to reach anywhere near the threshold. All that being said, the figures were still a lightning rod for negative coverage, and that risk did not sit well with the company.

Think of it like a government that knows it will be outvoted in a public consultation, so it changes the process to an "outreach" and removes any requirement to publish responses. Or an agency which knows it will lose in a public opinion poll, and so shifts to a "focus group" model. And so on.

With voting out of the way, Facebook was free to do whatever it pleases, and further penetration into search does seem the logical path.

What's the difference in terms of search potential between Google and Facebook? Answer: Google gets to know you intimately because of your searches. Facebook however already knows you intimately before you even start searching.[331] It has a natural advantage in the advertising market. Right now Facebook sells to advertisers on the basis that it can

---

331 http://www.insidefacebook.com/2012/09/18/what-facebook-search-can-answer/ (Accessed 1st August 2018)

categorise you, based on your profile content. Imagine how that targeting precision would shift if the company could also marry content profiling with conventional search profiling.

Some media organisations are already on the case. A Los Angeles Times article headlined "Facebook adds search feature; the 1st step in taking on Google?" postulated that Facebook was positioning itself to take on the search market by slowly introducing features that acclimatised users to the idea.[332]

I don't believe in conspiracy theory, as such, but that hypothesis sounds to me like a conventionally phased business plan, rather than some dark secret hatched up in someone's cellar.

Facebook sinks to an all-time low

It is 2012, and I'm in Islamabad, in the studio of the most watched morning television programme on Pakistan television. I am being grilled about free speech and the right to privacy.

This is not a safe situation. The government had been implicated in the deaths of many freedom fighters. I'm critically aware that my words will be noted by people in power who do not like my sort. But it had to be done. Over the past few years the authorities had commenced a clampdown on free expression and had changed all the rules, regardless of the national constitution. I knew things were going to get worse.

As I mentioned in the interview, if evidence was ever needed about the impact of Facebook's influence on the world, you could do no better than to look at its effect on Pakistan. A senior Pakistan government official told the High Court of Lahore later, in 2014, that the company had entered into a covert working relationship with national authorities to censor online content[333].

---

332 http://articles.latimes.com/2012/sep/21/business/la-fi-tn-is-google-facebook-search-feature-20120921

333 Pakistan government reveals secret censorship arrangement with Facebook The Privacy Surgeon. 18th July 2013.

To put this matter in perspective, Pakistan – a nation of two hundred million people – is a country in constant conflict over rights. The government continually attacks activists, sometimes resulting in assassination. The nation is on a knife edge over the right of free expression. It is easy to characterise Pakistan – as with so many countries – as an Islamic nation opposed to rights, but the reality is many leagues far from that.

True, there is a strong religious element. Although the national constitution provides for privacy and free expression, there is a powerful religious counter influence. I had submitted expert evidence to the High Court of Lahore arguing that the Holy Book demanded the right of free expression, but this position was not agreed by the court. I never expected it would be accepted.

The government admission was made in 2014, during a hearing of public interest claims brought by Bytes for All Pakistan (B4A), against the government's policy of widespread online censorship. The government policy had already resulted in an outright ban on YouTube.

The claim, made by an official of the Pakistan Telecommunications Authority (PTA), established that Facebook has agreed to a secret working relationship, in which its staff work directly with government officials to swiftly remove content that transgresses official policy.

Waseem Tauqir, Director General of the PTA revealed that the government of Pakistan had an existing "arrangement" with Facebook, which allows them to directly remove "undesirable" content.

Indeed if the government's claim was correct, it is likely Facebook had taken a commercial decision to barter its commitment to online freedoms, in return for an assurance that the government would not push for another outright ban on the social networking site.

While the evidence was not given under oath, in Pakistan any misleading or untruthful statement in court could result in contempt charges being brought. It is therefore widely assumed that the government's testimony is correct.

In a strongly worded open letter published later, B4A warned that such a

---

http://www.privacysurgeon.org/blog/incision/pakistan-government-admits-secret-censorship-arrangement-with-facebook/

practice represented a "betrayal by the company towards the users of Facebook in Pakistan."

The campaign body demanded a response to the admission, saying that the arrangement "breaches the trust of its users, vehemently opposes what Facebook publicly proclaims in its principles and is in stark contrast to the social network's commitment to freedom of expression, peaceful assembly and association as a member of Global Network Initiative (GNI)." [The GNI is an industry-led initiative to promote democratic values, particularly in the online realm. It is supported by numerous large IT companies].

"What makes this extraordinary turn of events even more disturbing is the fact that several important Facebook pages focusing on alternate discourse have recently become inaccessible, blocked or removed from Facebook in Pakistan."

The Pakistan government's admission was a grave embarrassment for Facebook, and tested the integrity of the GNI principles, that claim to provide assurances that essential freedoms will be protected in repressive environments such as Pakistan.

In a stinging rebuke to GNI, the Pakistan campaigners noted, "While we are not yet aware of the scale of this banning and filtering exercise agreement between Facebook and Pakistani Government authorities, we feel that some of the known blocked pages are essential for the promotion of peace, harmony and alternate narratives in the country. We reaffirm the fact that unhindered accessibility of such pages on the Internet is very much in tune with the ideals of freedom of speech, opinion, expression and assembly that the Internet represents and GNI promotes through its charter and principles, to which Facebook must have signed before becoming a member."

Facebook's penetration in Pakistan is extremely high, with the social network now being the most visited site in the country. The B4A case in the High Court was a crucial test of the viability of the government's censorship policy.

The open letter noted that the entire process was secret. "We strongly protest against such incidents of censorship and Internet filtering and note that this has been done without any legal process or notice to the content owners. The nature of the technology used to block these pages, and the reasons behind their removal, has also not been made available to the citizens."

This is an important issue for online freedoms not only in Pakistan, but potentially for freedoms throughout the Islamic world. It is therefore important that we hear the facts, and soon.

I asked Facebook, on the day of publication in the Privacy Surgeon (July 18th), to provide a precise explanation of its relationship with the Pakistan government. Facebook responded that day with the message that as soon as it heard back from its people in Pakistan, Facebook would issue a statement.

Nothing more emerged. Since then the Bytes 4 All campaigners were subjected to a vicious smear campaign in the press and have been harassed by officers of the Special Branch.

What has Facebook been doing all this time? From what I can gather it had been negotiating with GNI to save its skin. While campaigners in Pakistan have put their lives and liberty on the line to protect freedoms, Facebook was apparently figuring a way to massage its way around a claim that it should be booted out of GNI.

How else can we explain this delay? If the relationship with the Pakistan government was an "ordinary" Notice and Takedown process, Facebook's membership in GNI would be secure (every online organisation does it). Importantly, if that relationship was so simple, the Pakistan government's integrity in this case would be damaged.

GNI is supposed to exist to provide some degree of assurance that online companies will protect online freedoms. At the moment, it is giving every appearance of being just another PR stunt.

And as for Facebook, the company should consider being ashamed to have left these vulnerable campaigners twisting in the wind.

While international civil society support for Pakistan rights groups is extremely strong (for example through active involvement by the Association for Progressive Communication and Article 19), news coverage of the nation's struggles is thin. According to both Nexis and Google News, mainstream news coverage of the Turkish ban of Twitter outstripped coverage of the Pakistan ban on YouTube by more than thirty-fold.

Indeed the BBC news site, which proclaims balanced coverage of international affairs, has just over three days published more stories on the Turkish Twitter ban, than it has on the entirety of Pakistan's communications censorship since 2012.

In some respects, this disparity of reporting isn't surprising. Turkey's geographic location on Europe's border provides a point of reference. Pakistan, in contrast, is frequently seen as isolated – and is thus both out of context and irrelevant.

Pakistan, however, is anything but irrelevant. Its legal and policy shifts are crucial to developments in the Islamic world, but neither media nor many philanthropic bodies have embraced this reality.

It is often argued that the West has institutionally ignored Pakistan's development. Evidence of this situation can be seen merely by searching through the databases of grant-making bodies. For example, the world's wealthiest philanthropic body, the Ford Foundation, rarely even includes Pakistan among its listed regions.

According to the foundation's grants list in 2013, only three Pakistan-related projects have received support since 2010 (two of these being filmmakers). Even accounting for population difference, this is a tiny sliver of the funding, for example, to Indian grantees. Other bodies such as the MacArthur Foundation exhibit the same dynamics.

This is not to say there isn't support for Pakistan or its struggle for freedom and development. Of course there is. The inescapable reality however is that the disparity is glaring, and – unlike growing institutional support for civil society in Arab Spring nations – appears not to be improving.

A renewed support for freedom in Pakistan should not come at the price of reduced support for other regions, but it is certain that unless the international community shows a greater interest in this critically important nation of 200 million people, the implications for freedom in the rest of the Islamic world will be severe.

Such issues are not confined to Pakistan – nor is the sometimes dangerous influence of Facebook's policies. In October 2018, television presenter John Oliver ('The Week Last Night') broadcast an in-depth report on the impact of unregulated Facebook activity on Myanmar, contributing to the massacre and eviction of hundreds of thousands of Rohingya, people from the North West of the country, into India and Bangladesh. The scandal around the tragedy has even tarnished Nobel laureate Aung San Suu Kyi, who is a media figure in the UK, where she lived for many years in exile, and is the present head of the country.

Chapter Fourteen: The rise of consumer activism

> *Respect for corporations and government is declining. People simply do not trust them. But who or what can fix this problem? There are some tech solutions, but few companies will adopt those, because they have the potential to actually work. Perhaps the answer is to demand transparency and honesty in the way organisations deal with us, and in the way they promote their products.*

All that having been said, consumers are responding in a way that all entities should fear and respect. Each day, one person in seven on the planet uses WhatsApp, a secure end-to-end messaging system. True, this is doubtlessly driven by the creation of free calls, but most people do – regardless – take action to protect their privacy. Following a privacy issue at WhatsApp, there was a substantial migration to Telegram.[334]

People take the time to adjust their disclosure settings, and they get angry when organisations do the wrong thing. This shift in the public psyche is worrying to many organisations. Microsoft, once very much the Evil Empire of privacy, has now become almost paranoid about disclosing the personal information of its users.

It is heartening to witness a new generation of astute and dedicated activists and experts, who bring truth to an arena noted for its deception. The challenge for these people is that they work under enormous stress, engaging fields that expand and mutate with breath-taking speed and complexity.

These developments are essential to building trust in such a critical moment for information. For example, the global online advertising industry is currently being allowed to control the privacy agenda, by

---

334 Telegram becomes the new cool of messaging as millions of customers abandon WhatsApp over privacy concerns; The Privacy Surgeon, 9th March 2014 http://www.privacysurgeon.org/blog/incision/telegram-becomes-the-new-cool-of-messaging-as-millions-of-users-abandon-whatsapp-over-privacy-concerns/

arguing that it has a natural right to track customer activities without their explicit consent. The industry's hilarious claim to be the Internet's engine room is peddled to justify an opt-out tracking regime.

The industry argues that its revenue fuels the development of the Internet. Not only is this one of the most brazen deceptions of recent times, but it is also completely irrelevant. Even if it were true that advertising fuelled the Internet economy, the onus should be on industry to find ways of conducting its business within a framework of safeguards and rights. That's how most other industries have learned to function. Try running an airline with reduced on-board safety facilities, and you'd be grounded in an instant.

Elected representatives who promote the argument that economic development and profit need protection at the expense of rights should be ashamed. it is intellectually dangerous to compare, say, environmental sustainability, with a contrived notion of privacy sustainability. Information industries have never even been required to seek privacy solutions that will nurture current growth. Indeed in the view of many analysts, there's ample evidence that an overall improvement across industry in privacy would increase consumer trust, and therefore would expand and enrich the information economy. Why, otherwise, would WhatsApp and Telegram be so successful?

The business models of major corporations are forcing a re-conceptualisation of data rights in ways that are perilous to privacy. Defining consumers as online publishers – and thus dumping corporate liability onto them – is a dangerous notion. Creating privacy policies that stress what will be done to compromise consumer data – rather than what will be done to protect it – is a pernicious trend.

And as James Rule observes, Information privacy policies may produce a fairer and more efficient use and management of personal data, but they cannot control the voracious and inherent appetite of modern organizations for more and more increasingly refined personal information.[335]

Rather than recognising that rapidly emerging facets of the information age require a rigorous and far-reaching framework of rules, many

---

335 Rule, James, Douglas McAdam, Linda Stearns, and David Uglow. The Politics of Privacy: Planning for Personal Data Systems as Powerful Technologies. New York: Elsevier, 1980.

business lobbies and governments are working to re-set the clock. Consumers – now defendants – are constantly reassured that our rights are respected, while in the background powerful interests stitch up the odds in their favour. Those standing up in defence of rights are belittled as naive and uninformed – or are said to be extremists with no awareness about how the world 'needs' to work.

In the privacy realm we have become accustomed to the machinations of greedy governments and data-hungry industry. We wearily accept the manipulative language and deceptive claims that characterise the constant battle against meaningful consumer protections.

It has not always been this way. Eighty years ago the manufacturing industry's bogus justification for avoiding health and safety measures was ripped apart by forward-looking legislators. In the 1960's, thanks to the activism of people like Ralph Nader, the deceptive safety claims of the automobile industry became totally unacceptable. Forty years ago the fake accountability of the nuclear power industry was shredded by outraged public sentiment. In each case, informed people realised that rigorous rules were needed to nurture trust, growth and public safety.

History teaches us that unless strict and unequivocal standards – and honest language – are put into place early in the development of new industries, then people and communities will suffer. Entire regions are denied decent public transport; nations devastate priceless historical precincts in favour of investment; the environment is irrevocably damaged because of short term economic convenience. Such case studies are depressingly familiar.

In the case of the information and communications sectors, laws that unequivocally put people – rather than entities – at the centre of the ecosystem need to be put in place without delay. We need to enshrine these rights now, before the information economy reaches a level of complexity that we can yet barely comprehend.

The intersection of mobile and Internet was merely the first stage of a seamless fusion between humans and technology. In less than the time span that was historically required to deploy a single technology, we now face the challenge of managing a rapidly evolving global matrix of platforms upon which are deployed apps of almost infinite variety created by millions of (largely) unknown and unregulated developers. This situation requires immediate and sharply focused public attention.

313

Instead, many mobile and social networking platforms fiercely compete for new apps by making the entry barrier on privacy as minimal as possible.

Future generations may view such tactics as an utter disgrace. Some powerful and wealthy household brands are lobbying to remove almost every foundation stone of data rights. In their view, consent should be implied – not explicit. In their view, our information should be aggregated into vast data lakes that can be harvested for profit, rather than contained in ways that allow people to exercise full control over it.

The unswerving universal rights we imagined the 21st century would bring are thus being downgraded to discretionary values. We "share" our lives with huge entities that convince us they are our partners.

We – as advocates – live in hope that this will not always be the case. Industry polluters once argued that environmental protections would bankrupt the global economy. Slave traders once argued that white people enjoyed intellectual superiority. And opponents of universal suffrage pushed the view that women were incapable of understanding politics. These lies eventually lay twisting in the wind.

Privacy campaigners often become despondent about the odds that confront them, but it is easy to forget the above reforms that changed much of our life for the better – and changed them in spite of the vast resources devoted to maintaining the status quo.

The importance of honesty

The US industry magnate Harvey Firestone observed: "fundamental honesty is the keystone to business." A century on, the new information and communication industries could do well to heed his words. There is a crisis of public trust brewing, that only a dose of honesty will cure.

Since 2012 opinion polls have suggested that there has been an overall decline in trust and respect for big business, but in recent times ICT companies have suffered disproportionately. In traditional markets, product satisfaction is more easily measured, and trust can readily be linked to merchandise or service delivery. Organisations in the online world are dependent on a much more robust foundation of trust, that can withstand the legal and technical turbulence of virtual space.

In the post-Firestone world, honesty is often wrongly interpreted as "brand integrity". And as far as most organisations are concerned, the trick to ensuring brand integrity is never to get caught out being dishonest. This is a cynical and disingenuous position that flies in the face of public expectation.

In 2013, the Privacy Surgeon and the London School of Economics published a report on the emerging trends in privacy.[336] The clear outcome was that transparency and accountability will become important factors in the public consciousness. This means people will increasingly expect companies to be straight with them.

The key condition is "fundamental". Fundamental honesty isn't the same as "not lying". Firestone wasn't talking about "not lying"; he was referring to something greater. Fundamental honesty is a quality, not a statement, and it is what business needs to build within its core environment, as well as with the customer. All solid personal relationships depend on an intrinsic honesty, rather than a contrived set of communication filters. Business should behave no differently.

A company can be dishonest without lying. Indeed many are institutionally dishonest. They deceive by telling half-truths, massaging language or creating imagery, rather than nurturing a solid foundation of evidence and reason. Most of the successful consumer campaigns against corporations are based on this circumstance.

There are countless examples of such dishonesty sparking a fatal crisis of trust. When, for example, the UK government attempted to introduce a national identity card a few years ago, the entire scheme failed because the sponsoring department was opaque and deceptive. The doubt and debate happening within government was silenced – smoothed over with a fake accord. The public meantime was left to ponder concerns that the government refused to acknowledge.

In the Firestone view, honesty is the path that navigates between

---

336 Predictions for Privacy: A report on the issues and trends that will dominate the privacy landscape in 2013. Available at www.privacysurgeon.org (Accessed 1ˢᵗ August 2018)

deception and ambiguity. Honesty has the characteristics of clarity, truth and introspection. The organisation that exhibits those qualities will engender public trust, although being so honest can be internally painful for an organisation.

Trust is one consequence of honesty and privacy advocates have a key role to play in affirming that trust. They do this because customer expectations have shifted, and leading companies often recognise that their role must shift too. Most large enterprises have plenty of lawyers to help focus on data protection compliance, but "trust is a big issue" and activists can help with that agenda, Microsoft's chief privacy officer, Brendon Lynch, said in an interview. "People will not use technology they do not trust."

Advocacy organisations "have direct connections with the media," Lynch said, "and they can really set the tone for how your privacy practices are going to be received." [337]

All the same, being frank and open with the public is alien to the nature of large organisations. Within corporations there is rarely such thing as a "definitive view". Many major decisions are resolved organically through a complex process of doubt and challenge – just as they are in all human relationships. With friendships and partnerships, a discussion of doubt is often more important than a contest of definite views. Disclosure is usually more nurturing than secrecy. People display their vulnerability, openness and uncertainty to help strengthen trust, whereas corporations believe such a display would raise the stigma of weakness and risk.

Governments are much the same. They enforce "cabinet solidarity" with the threat of dismissal for dissident views. Corporations enforce corporate solidarity with the threat of sacking or excommunication from the core. Either way, this strategy is pointless. Anyone in media knows that enforced solidarity under pressure leaks like a ripped sieve.

Corporations, generally speaking, are terrified of appearing uncertain or transitional. However the prevailing policy of smothering public discussion of internal debate is increasingly unsustainable in a world where the building of trust is critically important to success.

Compare this ideal with what the public is presently forced to deal. Large

337   Eliza Krigman; Privacy Activism: Turning threat into opportunity. Data Privacy Leadership Council. 2016

corporations manage their relationship with the public through the triangulation of three mighty dynamics. The first is risk, which is managed by their lawyers and spin doctors. The second is profit, which is steered by the relevant business model. The third is corporate culture, which determines how a company establishes a process (or – more often – a lack of process). Corporate culture is often theoretically measured through indices, such as a Corporate Social Responsibility framework.

The problem in the new ICT age is that few organisations have been able to create a corporate consciousness that can build enduring trust. In the past – on issues such as the environment, employee care or global responsibility – some corporations managed to embed a belief system within the corporate culture. This permeated all elements of company decision making and thus created a resilient bedrock of trust.

Most ICT corporations haven't yet been able to enshrine such a process. They swerve chaotically between the dynamics of risk mitigation, profit and a constantly shifting ethical compass. They speak through PR agencies, who are paid by the column inch to make the companies look good. They ratchet the risk sensitivity so high, that every public utterance is a compromise that never quite tells the whole truth.

Let's explore for a minute the dynamics of trust. Going back to what Firestone observed, there is a powerful bond between trust and honesty. In the world of real human relationships trust is built through a narrative of thought – not a set of assertions.

But where is the narrative in the modern corporation? Well, it does vaguely exist in the form of plausible deniability. Different departments are often free to commission pieces of conflicting research, though in reality only those pieces that are in harmony with company policy will ever see the light of day. This is only natural. Organisations do not want to inspire an image of conflict.

What if we were to turn the conventional wisdom on its head? What if – instead of seeing a variance of views as a threat – corporations publicly exposed the entire process of decision making within the context of a reasoned framework? That would create the ultimate level of honesty and accountability, and possibly the highest ever level of public trust.

To provide benchmarks, let's look for a moment at two major industry players, Google and Microsoft.

At a superficial level, Google is an honest organisation. It is thoroughly transparent about the fact that it has little intention of respecting privacy regulation. Its corporate compass proclaims a higher ethic of unrestricted data without control. In this context the company has little interest in abiding by restrictive legal conditions, but it is endearingly blatant in its rebellion against legal control.

While this ethic has instinctive appeal to some, I doubt it is sustainable. The company's problem is that it continues to mask its internal narrative. There is little or no knowledge of Google's processes – if indeed there are any processes – at an ethical, intellectual or an engineering and management level. The high ideal is reduced to dogma. Thus when the company is caught with its pants down over such issues as the Wi-Fi scandal or the Safari circumvention, the company goes into PR meltdown in a way that corrodes public trust even further. The fact that the ethical compass is linked to advertising revenue has created widespread cynicism about the positions the company has taken with regard to legal compliance.

Microsoft on the other hand – perhaps as an older and more war-torn organisation – has a more evolved intellectual and ethical framework but the company is often too risk averse to promote its full potential.

More than a decade ago Microsoft created a substantial foundation called Trustworthy Computing and has sought to build on that foundation to improve its internal compass. It appears however that the corporation is dependent on an internal committee system, that precludes brave choices. Trustworthy Computing was a way to ensure that the entire company was in tune with a set of standards that would nurture public trust. Given the company's parlous state pre-2002, this was an essential move. However the quest to create internal harmony has resulted in nervousness about alienation of any part of the corporation. The aphorism 'Error will slip through a crack, while truth will stick in a doorway' might well be the in-house motto of many of the world's major IT companies.

If management can't fix the trust issue, can engineers do so?

On 10th June 2000, amidst great ceremony, Her Majesty Queen Elizabeth cut the tape to open the first new Thames river crossing in more than a century. The Millennium Bridge had won acclaim for its sleek shape and elegant design – and London was buzzing with excitement about its new landmark.

Then… unexpected drama. The bridge lasted less than 48 hours before a fatal design flaw caused it to be closed for over two years.

The problem came down to people's refusal to respect the engineering limitations of the structure. As soon as the bridge was traversed by pedestrians it started to sway unnervingly. Everyone was at a complete loss to explain why such a beautiful and efficient design went haywire. Authorities however showed no hesitation in shutting it down.

It turned out that the newly named "Wobbly Bridge" was the victim of a positive feedback phenomenon known as synchronous lateral excitation. The natural sway motion of people walking caused small sideways oscillations in the bridge, which in turn caused people on the bridge to sway in step, increasing the amplitude of the bridge oscillations, thus continually magnifying the effect.[338]

This resonance had been known to engineers for decades, but the Millennium Bridge had been conceived for submission to a prestigious design competition, so elegance was the primary driver. The interface between human behaviour and engineering was never addressed.

The same phenomenon is all too common in the world of information and communication technologies. Those who design the machines that enable the invasion of privacy are often oblivious to such outcomes, while privacy advocates and data protection regulators are often a million miles from understanding the dynamics and priorities of engineers.

While 'Human-Computer Interaction' and 'Security Usability' are taught in many security and information systems courses, the reality is that the interface between users and machines is still a niche interest. Engineers will design the most ingenious systems, but it is usually only in the latter stages of development that someone may ask the difficult question, "How

---

338 Wikipedia entry for Millennium Bridge
      http://en.wikipedia.org/wiki/Millennium_Bridge,_London

will people interact with this device?"

How people behave is of course crucial to privacy. Will users generate vast amounts of sensitive data that machines will unlawfully process? Will they understand the risks associated with information technologies? Will the design attract privacy-crunching apps that are allowed to exploit personal information?

These are of course critically important considerations for concepts such as Privacy by Design (PbD), which seek to embed privacy protection at every level from conception to deployment.

PbD is one of the main pillars of future privacy protection, but it currently exists mostly in the theoretical realm. As a concept PbD was known to the architecture and building sectors from as early as the 1960s, however, within the information arena at least, the expression "Privacy by Design" appears to have emerged only in the late 1990s, and not before another phrase – "Surveillance by Design"[339] – was coined during the debates over the US Communications Assistance for Law Enforcement Act" (CALEA) in 1994. This, and related legislation globally, was intended to ensure that surveillance capability was embedded into communications design, by mandating that systems were constructed in such a way that law enforcement agencies were able to access whatever data they wanted.

In an effort to counter this trend, researchers and regulators started to develop countermeasures that might provide a higher standard of privacy protection, built from the core rather than as bolt-on measures. PbD is amongst the most important of these. This emerging approach is intended to ensure that privacy is maximised by embedding protection seamlessly across every strand of design and deployment of a product or service. As one prominent contributor to the field, Ann Cavoukian, observed:

> *How we get there is through Privacy by Design. Where PETs [Privacy Enhancing Technologies] focused us on the positive potential of technology, Privacy by Design prescribes that we build privacy directly into the design and operation, not only of technology, but also of operational systems, work processes, management*

---

339 Samarajiva, R. (1996) 'Surveillance by Design: Public Networks and the Control of Consumption', in R. Mansell and R. Silverstone (eds) *Communication by Design: The Politics of Information and Communication Technologies,* Oxford: Oxford University Press, 129-56.

structures, physical spaces and networked infrastructure. In this sense, Privacy by Design is the next step in the evolution of the privacy dialogue.[340]

Some organisations now appear to be more open to the argument that data minimisation is a sensible approach to risk mitigation and that giving users a degree of data autonomy is central to nurturing trust. In both respects, the use of PbD can be an invaluable benefit to seeking practical alternative approaches, but is the world of engineering ready for it yet? Yes, there are celebrated examples of privacy awareness in the world of engineering, but the key question is whether this awareness has permeated the mainstream of IT development.

The answer appears to be a resounding "no".

The reality check for me occurred a few years ago. I was visiting a city that has a very good university with a large and strong Computer Science department – one of the top rated in Britain.

I had been in touch with the department to let them know I planned to visit the area, and to ask whether a small gathering over coffee could be organised to discussed emerging data protection and privacy issues. Amazingly, there appeared to be no interest in privacy in this department. The meeting never took place.

This got me to thinking that there may be a real disconnect in the academic world between engineering and data protection. The interface between human behaviour, personal data and privacy rules seems to exist mainly in the theoretical realm (Information Systems is the closest we get, but even that field is largely theoretical).

Is it that pure engineering, design and coding is still a world removed from the discussions my colleagues have about legal rights? This is a lost opportunity. People might not trust management, but it could be that mathematics and engineering could provide some certainty of protection.

Some of the experts in my alma mater Privacy International seem to believe this is the case. One experienced IT professional observed: "There is generally some ethical red tape associated with new projects, but once that fence is cleared, then anything goes. In my experience, legal

---

340 Privacy by design: the definitive workshop. A foreword by Ann Cavoukian
     http://www.springerlink.com/content/d318xq4780lh4801/fulltext.html

issues are obstacles to be overcome after a novel IT solution has been built, and it is to be rolled out."

Some exciting tools are being adopted that might assist a more dependable PbD formula across organisations. The notion of *Differential Privacy* in which a mathematical approach is taken to determining the privacy value of data may in time create a common standard which might form the basis of agreement on the common foundation of PbD techniques. The Differential Privacy approach itself is currently little understood in the general business community as it dramatically challenges in a complex way more traditional legal and political approaches to privacy protection by instituting a hard ceiling at a mathematical and engineering level on the storage and exploitation of data.[341]

Falling victim to fashion

One of the most striking features of Privacy by Design is the contrast between the popularity of the concept and the actual number of systems and infrastructures that use the technique. PbB has become a fashionable idea, and in the wake of fashion came the pretenders that falsely claim their organisations or products have a genuine commitment to the PbD process.

Many PbD efforts are false, selectively assessing a particular strand of the organisation to lower the risk of criticism or creating a modular approach that selectively fits the organisation's structure. There are some notable exceptions, but the overriding challenge is to identify instances where a PbD effort has been undertaken with the full consent of all stakeholders within an organisation.

PbD appears to be increasingly adopted at the level of principle by large companies and sectors. The mobile phone network provider organisation GSMA for example announced that it is attempting the development of a

---

341 See the work of Cynthia Dwork and others at
   http://en.wikipedia.org/wiki/Differential_privacy for a general background to

set of global privacy principles for mobile based on a PbD process. The need for collaboration to be established with handset manufacturers and apps stores is central to a PbD approach in this instance, but such seismic positioning is fraught with logistical problems that would confront any sector attempting an integrated approach to privacy protection.

However the key messages embraced by PbD have not been lost on regulators. In Europe for example the RFID industry is required by the European Commission to establish a PbD process that will bind the industry to a set of privacy conditions that should provide assurance that privacy is embedded seamlessly throughout the design and deployment aspects of the technology.[342] An industry-led first draft of these principles has been rejected by the Article 29 Working Party of privacy commissioners.[343]

The European Data Protection Supervisor has also signalled a possible embedding of PbD into the basis of data protection law, which might ultimately create a general requirement:

> *It would be important to include the principle of "Privacy by Design" among the basic principles of data protection, and to extend its scope to other relevant parties, such as producers and developers of ICT products and services. This would be innovative and require some further thinking, but it would be appropriate and only draw the logical consequences of a promising concept.[344]*

The key messages embraced by PbD have not been lost on regulators. In Europe for example the RFID industry is required by the European Commission to establish a PbD process that will bind the industry to a set of privacy conditions that should provide assurance that privacy is embedded seamlessly throughout the design and deployment aspects of the technology.[345] An industry-led first draft of these principles had been

---

Differential Privacy.
342 COMMISSION RECOMMENDATION of 12.5.2009 on the implementation of privacy and data protection principles in applications supported by radio-frequency identification http://www.rfidjournal.com/article/view/4890
343 Opinion 5/2010 on the Industry Proposal for a Privacy and Data Protection Impact Assessment Framework for RFID Applications Report
     http://ec.europa.eu/justice/policies/privacy/workinggroup/wpdocs/2010_en.htm
344 http://www.springerlink.com/content/8258q1566232h0u4/fulltext.html
345 COMMISSION RECOMMENDATION of 12.5.2009 on the implementation of

rejected by the Article 29 Working Party of privacy commissioners.[346]

There is a vast gulf to traverse. In a paper titled "What IT Professionals Think About Surveillance" noted privacy expert Ivan Szekely observed: "It can be concluded that the attitudes of the IT professionals only marginally influence their actual behaviour... Those who care more about privacy do not appear to be using more PETs {Privacy Enhancing Technologies – the forebear of Pbd] in their own online activities or in the products they have helped develop."

This parlous situation needs urgent attention. The challenges are, however, not insurmountable. The theory and practice behind PbD is commonplace, and thus should not be seen as controversial. The concept of embedded protection on the basis of sensitive seamless design has been embraced over the years in numerous environments. In the field of forensics, investigators have for many decades known that the forensic chain of events (collection of material, recording, processing, analysis, reporting etc) is only as reliable as its weakest link, and that a "total design" approach should be taken across the entire chain to reduce the risk of failure.

According to this rationale, the "spaces" between events and processes are seen as posing as much of a risk of failure as the component parts themselves. With this threat model in mind, a system or infrastructure can be designed from ground up, to ensure a seamless approach to risk reduction.

The same approach has been pursued to a varying extent for environmental protection, workplace safety, urban planning, product quality assurance, child protection, national security, health planning, infection control and information security.

This approach is rooted in a belief that reliable protection in a complex ecosystem can only be achieved through an integrated design approach. It is reasoned that unless a system is developed from "ground up" with protection at its core, failure will emerge through unexpected weaknesses.

The three key perspectives in PbD – regulatory, engineering and

---

privacy and data protection principles in applications supported by radio-frequency identification http://www.rfidjournal.com/article/view/4890

346 Opinion 5/2010 on the Industry Proposal for a Privacy and Data Protection Impact Assessment Framework for RFID Applications Report http://ec.europa.eu/justice/policies/privacy/workinggroup/wpdocs/2010_en.hm

managerial – involve significant intersection. However, while the PbD concept continues to run along divergent paths, there is a substantial risk that the technique will be characterised by difference rather than convergence. More interaction and dialogue are required involving regulators, business managers and engineers.

Currently, the evolution of PbD is being conducted sporadically. This dynamic is true for the early development of all such techniques. If proponents of PbD are arguing for an integrated and seamless adoption of systems, then they must argue with equal vigour for an integrated approach to developing PbD as a practical framework. Without such an approach, investors will remain uneducated and unmotivated, and the PbD concept will remain a largely theoretical concept, adopted by a small number of the "good" privacy actors.

The big question – not just for the Googles and Facebooks of this world but also for startups and governments – is whether they are prepared to adopt an engineering approach as a means of garnering greater public trust. As the public become more sensitive and educated on the privacy issue over coming years, such an approach may well become the defining element of trust.

PHOTOS,

THROUGH THE YEARS

The campaigning corner of the
Three Tuns pub. London, 1996.

Negotiating with police at the first CCTV
action. Brighton, 1997.

The Big Brother Award statues.
London, 2004.

The OECD conference on data protection
where Privacy International was born.
Luxembourg, 1990.

View from the podium before addressing the European Parliament
for the crucial debate on the General Data Protection Regulation.
Brussels, 2015.

The Pope rocks the 75th Big Brother
Awards. Montreal, 2007.

Some of the faces at the very first Big Brother
Awards. London, 1997.

Raising a toast at the foundation meeting of EDRi.
Berlin, 2002

Her Majesty' spectacular
appearance at the Big
Brother Awards.
New York, 2003.

Looking after the privacy of UN refugees.
Ethiopia, 2008.

Simon Davies, David Flaherty, Marc Rotenberg, and Robert Ellis Smith.
Establishment of the U.S. Privacy Council.
Washington, 1991.

Simon Davies.
Launch of EPIC Observing Surveillance campaign.
Washington, 2002.

Bibliography

Agre, Philip E., and Marc Rotenberg. Technology and Privacy: The New Landscape. Cambridge, Mass.: MIT Press, 1997.

Albrecht, Katherine, and Liz McIntyre. Spychips: How Major Corporations and Government Plan to Track Your Every Move with RFID. (2005). Nashville: Nelson Current.

Alinsky, S. (1971) Rules for Radicals, New York. Random House.

Australian Privacy Charter. (1994). published by the Australian Privacy Charter Group, Law School, University of New South Wales.

Banisar, D and Davies S. (1999). Privacy and Human Rights. Washington DC. Electronic Privacy Information Center,

Bennett, C. J. (2008). The Privacy Advocates. Cambridge. MIT Press

Bloustein, E. (1964) Privacy as an Aspect of Human Dignity, 39 New York U. L.R. 962 at 971

Blunkett, D. (2006). The Blunkett Tapes: My Life in the Bear Pit. Bloomsbury.

Burnham, David. The Rise of the Computer State. New York: Random House, 1983.

Culnan, Mary J. "The Lessons of the Lotus Marketplace: Implications for Consumer Privacy in the 1990's." 1991.

Davies, S. (1994). Big Brother: Britain's Web of Surveillance, London. Pan McMillan.

Davies, S. (1992). Big Brother: Australia's web of surveillance and the new technological order; Simon & Schuster, Sydney.

Davies, S. "CCTV: A New Battleground for Privacy." In Surveillance, Closed Circuit Television and Social Control, edited by Clive Norris, Jade Moran, and Gary Armstrong, 243–254. Aldershot: Ashgate Publishing, 1998.

Davies, S. A year after 9/11. Communications of the ACM, Volume 45 Issue 9. September 2002.

Davies, S. Ideas for Change. (2018). Irene Publishing.

Davies, S. "Spanners in the Works: How the Privacy Movement is Adapting to the Challenge of Big Brother." In Visions of Privacy: Policy Choices for the Digital Age, edited by Colin J. Bennett and Rebecca Grant, 244–261. Toronto: University of Toronto Press, 1999.

Davies, S. (1997). Re-engineering the right to privacy : how privacy has been transformed from a right to a commodity, in Agre and Rotenberg (ed) "Technology and Privacy : the new landscape". MIT Press.

Davies, S. (2004). The Loose Cannon: An overview of campaigns of opposition to National Identity Card proposals, Published by Roger Clarke.

Davies, S and Hosein, I. (1998). Liberty on the Line in Liberating Cyberspace, Pluto Press, London.

Davies, S and Hosein, I. (2009). Privacy Impact Assessment for the United Nations High Commission for Refugees: a late stage PIA for UNHCR's trial of an automated fingerprint identification system;

Flaherty, D. (1989). Protecting Privacy in surveillance societies, University of North Carolina Press.

Froomkin, Michael. "The Metaphor is the Key: Cryptography, the Clipper Chip and the Constitution." University of Pennsylvania Law Review 143 (1995): 709–712.

Gavison, R. Privacy and the Limits of Law, [1980] 89 Yale L.J. 421, at 428.

Greenleaf, Graham. "Quacking Like a Duck: The National ID Card Proposal (2006) Compared with the Australia Card (1986–87)." 2007.

Hansson, Sven Ole, and Elin Palm, eds. The Ethics of Workplace Privacy. Brussels: Peter Lang, 2005.

Hixson, R. Privacy in a Public Society: Human Rights in Conflict 3 (1987). See Barrington Moore, Privacy: Studies in Social and Cultural History (1984).

House of Commons, Canada, (2003). Report: A national ID Card for Canada.

Keck, Margaret, E., and Kathryn Sikkink. Activists Beyond Borders: Advocacy Networks in International Politics. Ithaca: Cornell University Press, 1998.

Leizerov, Sagi. "Privacy Advocacy Groups' versus Intel: A Case Study of How Social Movements are Tactically Using the Internet to Fight Corporations," Social Science Computer Review 18, no. 7 (2000):

The Identity Project: An Assessment of the UK Identity Cards Bill and Its Implications. The London School of Economics (LSE). June 27, 2005.

Lyon, David. Surveillance after September 11th. Cambridge: Polity Press, 2003.

Marx, Gary. "A Tack in the Shoe: Resisting and Neutralizing the New Surveillance." Journal of Social Issues 59, no. 2 (2003)

Mill, J.S. (1859) On Liberty.

New York Surveillance Camera Players. We Know You Are Watching. New York: Factory School, 2006

Packard, V. The Hidden Persuaders. (2007) New York. D. McKay Co.

(first published April1957)

Privacy International (2018). The Keys to Data Protection.

Smith, Robert E. War Stories: Anecdotes of Persons Victimized by Invasions of Privacy. Providence, R.I.: Privacy Journal, 1993.

Volio, F. Legal personality, privacy and the family in Henkin (ed) The International Bill of Rights, New York : Columbia University Press, 1981.

Warren, S and Brandeis, L. "The right to privacy", Harvard Law Review 4, 1890 pp 193- 220.

Westin, A. (1967). Privacy and Freedom. New York. Atheneum.

Westwood, John. "Life in the Privacy Trenches: Experiences of the British Columbia Civil Liberties Association." In Visions of Privacy: Policy Choices for the Digital Age, edited by C. J. Bennett and R. Grant, 231–243. Toronto: University of Toronto Press, 1999.

Wright, S.T. (1997). Assessing the Technologies of Political Control. Published by Science and Technology Options Assessment (STOA). Ref: project no. IV/STOA/RSCH/LP/politicon.1

About the author

Simon Davies has spent his life fighting institutional barbarism. From his teenage years campaigning on such issues as historical sites preservation, housing reform and drug law reform he shifted his primary focus in the 1980's to the fledgling world of privacy. He became one of the pioneers of the international privacy arena and was the first person to campaign at a global level. He is now widely acknowledged as having been one of the most influential privacy advocates in the world.

Simon is the Founder, and for 22 years, the Director-General of the influential watchdog group Privacy International, which has been at the forefront of almost every major sphere of privacy. Over the years he has helped expose the secret machinations of governments, police authorities, corporations and spy agencies. In this role he has organised hundreds of campaigns and actions.

He is also an academic, consultant, journalist and author. He has been a Visiting Fellow in Law at both the University of Greenwich and the University of Essex, a Distinguished Visiting Scholar at George Washington University, a Fellow of the University of Amsterdam, and for fifteen years until 2012, was appointed to the London School of Economics, where he taught the ground-breaking MSc Masters course in "Privacy & Data Protection". He is also co-director of the LSE's Policy Engagement Network.

In addition, Simon has also advised a wide range of corporate, government and professional bodies, and has worked on technology, privacy and identity issues in more than fifty countries. He has been an Expert Advisor to the United Nations High Commissioner for Refugees.

Simon has founded many initiatives and organisations including the Big Brother Awards which recognises the heroes and villains of privacy. Since 1998 there have been 160 award ceremonies in twenty countries. He is also currently on the advisory boards of numerous organisations.

In April 1999, he received the Electronic Frontier Foundation's "Pioneer" award for his contribution to the development of Internet freedom. In 2004, and again in 2005, Silicon.com voted him as one of the world's fifty most influential people in technology policy. In 2007, he was made a Fellow of the British Computer Society.

Made in the USA
Middletown, DE
10 January 2019